Wine Style

Other Books by Mary Ewing-Mulligan and Ed McCarthy

Wine For Dummies

Red Wine For Dummies

White Wine For Dummies

French Wine For Dummies

Italian Wine For Dummies

Champagne For Dummies

Wine-Buying Companion For Dummies

WINE
STYLE

Using Your Senses

to Explore and Enjoy Wine

Mary Ewing-Mulligan, MW

Ed McCarthy

WILEY

JOHN WILEY & SONS, INC.

Published by John Wiley & Sons, Inc., Hoboken, New Jersey

Published simultaneously in Canada

Limit of Liability/Disclaimer of Warranty: While the publisher and the author have used their best efforts in preparing this book, they make no representations or warranties with respect to the accuracy or completeness of the contents of this book and specifically disclaim any implied warranties of merchantability or fitness for a particular purpose. No warranty may be created or extended by sales representatives or written sales materials. The advice and strategies contained herein may not be suitable for your situation. You should consult with a professional where appropriate. Neither the publisher nor the author shall be liable for any loss of profit or any other commercial damages, including but not limited to special, incidental, consequential, or other damages.

For general information about our other products and services, please contact our Customer Care Department within the United States at (800) 762-2974, outside the United States at (317) 572-3993 or fax (317) 572-4002.

Wiley also publishes its books in a variety of electronic formats. Some content that appears in print may not be available in electronic books. For more information about Wiley products, visit our web site at www.wiley.com.

LIBRARY OF CONGRESS CATALOGING-IN-PUBLICATION DATA:

Ewing-Mulligan, Mary.
  Wine style : using your senses to explore and enjoy wine / Mary Ewing-Mulligan, Ed McCarthy.
    p. cm.
  Includes index.
  ISBN-13 978-0-7645-4453-8
  ISBN-10 0-7645-4453-5 (hardcover : alk. paper)
  1. Wine and wine making. 2. Wine--Flavor and odor. I. McCarthy, Ed. II. Title.
  TP548.E984 2005
  641.2'2--dc22
                                    2005012601

Book design by Richard Oriolo

Printed in the United States of America

10 9 8 7 6 5 4 3 2 1

Contents

Acknowledgments

After writing three editions of *Wine For Dummies* and six other wine books in the *For Dummies* series, we found particular pleasure in the challenge of creating a book that offers a new approach to understanding the fascinating topic of wine.

Many people at John Wiley & Sons helped us. But our biggest cheerleader has been Wiley's Senior Culinary Editor, and our friend, Linda Ingroia. We are extremely grateful for her support and encouragement, and the hours upon hours that she devoted to this book.

We were also fortunate to have one of the finest project editors that we have ever worked with, Caroline Schleifer, overseeing the editing. Ever cognizant of the needs of the reader, she contributed a valuable perspective that helped bring the book alive.

Thanks, also, to Publisher Natalie Chapman, Production Editor Mike Olivo, Art Directors Jeffrey Faust and Fritz Metsch, Todd Fries and Michael Friedberg in marketing, and Gypsy Lovett and Jaime Harder in publicity. Special thanks to our agent, Steve Ettlinger.

Mary acknowledges the staff of International Wine Center, whose hard work and dependability gave her the time and the freedom of mind to devote herself to this book. And of course we thank our family for their support and affection.

Introduction

*H*ave you ever longed for an easier way to deal with wine? Have you ever wished that you could feel confident choosing wine without having to memorize the names of European wine regions and remember which grape varieties grow in each one? That you didn't have to know the names of half a dozen different varietal wines in order to bring a little diversity to your wine choices?

Wine is a complex field of ever-changing information. It's rich and exciting territory for people who want to make wine their hobby or profession. But for wine drinkers who just want to select a wine they'll enjoy, wine can be a jungle.

The structures that exist for dealing with wine either are too technical for most people or have built-in limitations. Categorizing wine according to its region of production—the classic approach— requires you to accumulate far more information than you probably really want to bother with. Categorizing wine according to grape variety—the preferred approach for many people today— limits your choices to wines from the relatively few grape varieties that make it to market as varietal wines. And choosing wines according to ratings from critics means that you end up drinking what somebody else likes, not necessarily what you might want to drink yourself (but you tell yourself that you should like it).

This set of approaches has resulted in just a few varietal wines—such as Chardonnay, Merlot, and Cabernet Sauvignon— dominating the U.S. market today. It has concentrated enormous influence in the hands of a few wine critics, whose tastes define how winemakers all over the world are making their wines. It promises to lead to the extinction of certain styles of wine that are no longer popular today.

We've written seven wine books in the *For Dummies* series, and they're all structured according to wine regions and grape varieties—because that's how it's done. That's how you talk about wine and teach wine. But when it comes to buying wine, we believe it's time for all that to change.

It's time for wine drinkers to be able to choose a wine according to what the wine tastes like—something that can be done even by wine drinkers who aren't armed with an arsenal of traditional wine information or the special vocabulary of wine tasting. And it's time that wine drinkers have access to the whole range of wine tastes, not just the best-selling flavors of the day.

Wine Style is our answer to wine drinkers' dilemma in choosing what wine to buy. By grouping the wines of the world into taste categories, or styles, we provide a structure that enables you to choose wines according to how they taste. When you know the fundamental taste categories, you can ask for a wine according to the taste profile you prefer at the moment. Communicating with sommeliers and wine retailers becomes easier and more effective. You'll enjoy a whole world of wines without having to know detailed information about any particular region or grape variety.

But choosing wines according to how they taste does require something of you. You have to pay attention to what you drink, and decide what you like and what you don't. You have to decide which style of wine you prefer for a particular occasion or with a particular meal.

People are always teasing us about what hard work (wink wink) the wine business must be. The homework that the stylistic approach to wine requires of you is similar. You have to pause now and then to think about what you're tasting. That's because taste is extremely personal. Only you can decide what you really like. We couldn't agree more with the statement made to wine drinkers by the late, great wine professor Emile Peynaud in his book *The Taste of Wine*: "The wine you drink is the wine you deserve."

We believe that attentive wine drinkers are the best wine drinkers. You might not have much experience in wine, and you might not know much of the traditional information, but if you taste carefully and learn what you like in a wine, you will be able to get it.

The wine industry is not necessarily in your corner. Wine producers want to convince you that their wine is delicious, whether you agree or not. (If you've ever thought, "Maybe there's something wrong with me" when you failed to like a wine, you're not alone.) They also want to convince you that their wine is higher in quality than the next brand—even though, frankly, quality is only a secondary consideration in choosing a wine, as we explain in the first chapter. That's the sales and marketing game. But by deciding what you really like, you get the last laugh.

In this book, we present four styles each of white and red wine, plus two styles of rosé wine and two styles of bubbly. For each style, we describe the taste of the wines and name the types of wine that generally fall into that category. We discuss what foods are appropriate for the wines, and at what occasions they tend to be drunk. We also explain how to judge the quality of wines based on their styles.

Because this book is all about how wines taste, it will help you become a better wine taster. We've included a section on wine tasting—not just the rudimentary "look-smell-taste" procedure (although that's here, too) but a discussion of aspects such as texture, weight, and flavor intensity that will bring a whole new dimension to your appreciation of wine's taste.

We intend this book to be useful and clear to regular wine drinkers. But its purpose is not to be a comprehensive wine primer. We already wrote that, in *Wine For Dummies*—and we encourage you to refer to that book when something we mention falls outside your experience or knowledge, or when you want to know more about a place, grape variety, or anything else we mention here.

We are not the first people ever to group wines according to their taste characteristics. Your retail shop might do it (although most adhere to the regional and grape variety systems), and some restaurants are doing it on their wine lists. Other books have been written on the topic in other countries. It's a movement that has gradually been gathering steam. (One of the terrific things about it is that it's a grassroots movement, because it serves only those who drink wine, not those who make and market wine.)

At home, we use this approach constantly in choosing which sort of wine to pull from our cellar for dinner. We have written this book because we believe that the stylistic approach to wine deserves more consideration. We sincerely hope that this book will make choosing wines by style so accessible that wine drinkers everywhere can benefit from this approach.

By delineating eight styles of white and red wine, we are not trying to be dogmatic. We believe that writing about wine styles is a means to several important ends.

- We want to encourage wine drinkers to think about what they're drinking.

- We want to help them find wines that they genuinely enjoy, whether those wines are popular, best-selling types or not.

- We want to put the power in wine marketing where it belongs, in the pockets of wine drinkers.

- And we hope that in the process, the diversity of wine styles that exists today will manage not to disappear and wine tastes not drift to universal sameness.

Think about it: nothing about a wine—not its quality, its price, its region of production, or its grape variety—matters as much as how that wine tastes to you and whether you'll like it. This book puts the emphasis right where it belongs, on you and your tastes. May it empower you to find a lifetime of pleasure in wine!

For more information, check out our website: winestylebook.com.

Mary and Ed

What Is Wine Style—
and Why Does It Matter?

Categorizing wines by taste, and

where quality enters the picture

One rainy Saturday afternoon many years ago, when we were in the throes of a tight writing deadline, the walls of confusion suddenly closed in on us. We began to question the meaning of basic words that we use all the time, and we felt the need to differentiate terms that most people use interchangeably. Even though our topic was just wine—nothing critical to the world's survival, after all—we realized how much confusion imprecise language can cause. We took a legal pad and scribbled notes that went something like this:

- Wine—the liquid
- Wines—variations of the liquid
- A wine—a specific individual instance
- Category of wine—a subset based on official distinctions, such as table wine or sparkling wine

- Type of wine—a subset that has come into existence through commercial usage, such as Bordeaux, Burgundy, Merlot, or Chardonnay
- Style of wine—a subset based on sensory characteristics

Types of wine are what you read about and talk about. A wine is what gets a high point score from a critic, and what you order in a restaurant. But the style of a wine—how the wine tastes—is what you respond to when you drink that wine.

A wine's style is the set of characteristics through which that wine manifests itself—the composite personality of the wine. Whether a particular wine is white, red, dry, sweet, flavorful, subtle, youthful, or aged is all part of its style. You taste the composite, and you like it or you don't.

TODAY'S WAY OF DIFFERENTIATING WINES

Wine style, in short, is how a wine tastes. In wine circles, *tasting* actually refers to the whole sensory experience of a wine, from looking at it and smelling it to experiencing it in your mouth. A wine's style is therefore the whole package of how a wine looks, smells, and tastes.

Every single wine is unique. But many wines share similar styles—that is, they have similar taste characteristics, even though they don't taste identical. Grouping wines into styles provides a manageable way of approaching the huge variety of wines that exists, and choosing those you personally prefer.

Experts have always classified wines into groups for the purpose of discussing or selling wine. Traditionally, wines were classified according to the region where the grapes grew—Burgundy, Bordeaux, or the Rhône Valley in France, for example, or the Rheingau or the Mosel in Germany. In recent decades, classifying wines according to their main grape variety—such as Chardonnay or Cabernet Sauvignon—has become fashionable.

Both systems are valid, but in practical terms they have their downsides for wine drinkers. You have to know an awful lot about the wine regions of the world in order to decide whether you would enjoy a Châteauneuf-du-Pape more than an inexpensive Bordeaux, for example. And grape variety is a dead-end street for adventuresome wine lovers because it limits them mainly to wines from a few internationally famous grapes, at the expense of blended wines or wines from interesting but obscure grape varieties (wines that, incidentally, often cost less than those from the major grapes).

Because of these limitations to regional and varietal classifications, some wine professionals have begun grouping wines in their wine shops or on their wine lists according to style. What could possibly be more meaningful to you as a wine drinker than a simple description of how a wine tastes? This type of classification doesn't require you to know anything about the world's wine regions, and it doesn't exclude wines made from unusual grape varieties. In fact, it opens the door for exploration. When you know that you like a certain style of wine, you can feel free to try wines of that style that you've never heard of before.

DEFINING A WINE'S STYLE

What's a style of wine and what isn't? You could say that red wine is a style, and white wine is a style. But each of those styles is so large that it encompasses wines that taste vastly different (even if most whites taste more similar to each other than they do to red wines). When you walk into a wine shop and tell the salesperson that you want a white wine, that's just the starting point of the discussion; from there, you'll narrow down the possibilities by remarking that you like dry whites, for example, and that the flavor shouldn't be too strong because you're serving a delicate fish dish. You've now defined a style of wine that's more specific and pragmatic than "white wine" alone.

Grape varieties are not styles. We remember a retailer friend telling us how he had recommended a Chablis—a white wine from the Burgundy region of France that's made entirely from the Chardonnay grape—to a customer who asked for a Chardonnay. Big mistake: the subtle Chablis had none of the intense, ripe, tropical fruit flavor that the customer expected when he asked for Chardonnay. A grape variety is a helpful starting point for choosing a wine, but it is not a reliable predictor of how the wine tastes. As you browse through our chapters discussing specific styles of white wine and red wine, in fact, you'll see wines from certain grape varieties falling into two, three, or even four different styles.

A wine region is not a style, but the wines of classic European wine regions do tend to be somewhat consistent in style within each region. Even if one winemaker makes his or her wine differently than a neighbor does, the variables that could cause the wine to have a vastly different style are few, because regulations dictate that wines bearing a regional name be grown in certain ways, using a specific grape or blend of grapes.

Every wine has a style because every wine has its own taste characteristics. You could describe a wine's style any way you like, using metaphors based on people (an "Arnold" wine or a "Gwyneth" wine, for example), music, or any other descriptive language that comes to mind. Wine style is a fluid concept, not a rigid rule, and you can have lots of fun with it if you like.

But fitting a wine into a fixed stylistic framework, such as the one that we offer, makes for more effective communication with people in restaurants and wine shops, who help you select the wines you will drink. Starting with the chapter "Fresh, Unoaked White Wines," we describe eight basic styles of white and red, and a couple more styles for rosé and sparkling wines. These are real-world taste categories that apply to most wines today.

QUALITY VERSUS STYLE

If you've ever browsed the aisles of a wine shop, chances are that you've seen cards and stickers proclaiming that a wine scored 90 points from a wine critic, or that another wine won a gold medal in

NAMING TASTE

*W*e've always been fascinated by two particular aspects of wine: how wines taste, and the language that people use to describe that taste. Both are challenging issues. Wine's taste itself is not straightforward, because each of us experiences the taste of a wine personally and privately, in our own mouths. Describing taste is even more complicated, because wine professionals use various words that don't necessarily have the same meaning for everyone. (How can they, when the experience of them is so personal?) Then wine drinkers who hear these terms place their own connotations on the words. It's a gustatory and linguistic free-for-all!

But food and drink products can't exist in the commercial world without language that describes them. Starbucks divides its coffees into taste categories and names them "mild," "smooth," and "bold." (One of us enjoys decaf espresso roast, a "smooth" coffee that tastes sort of "bold" to us.) Best Cellars, a pioneering wine retailer that groups its wines according to taste, categorizes white wines, for example, as either "fresh," "soft," or "luscious." Phillips Newman, a British retail chain that has recently adopted a stylistic approach for its wine selections, names its white wines as "bright," "smooth," or "rounded." These terms are all efforts to communicate what beverages taste like, using snappy, proprietary descriptors. But these descriptors don't mean the same thing to everyone—not to all wine drinkers, and not to all wine professionals.

Guess what? Our own style categories face the same pitfalls. But we trust that by explaining each of our styles in detail, we communicate clearly what the wines in that style taste like (at least what they taste like to us). And by using fairly straightforward terms to name the styles, we hope to have created taste categories that have real-world meaning for you, your wine merchant, or the wine captain in your favorite restaurant.

some wine competition, or maybe that a magazine named a wine one of the Top 100 wines of the year.

Some people choose their wines according to these scores or awards because they want to buy only high-quality wines—and who can blame them? We all want to buy the highest-quality merchandise that we can afford. In fact, quality ratings are so popular that they are an extremely powerful marketing tool in the wine business; wines that receive high scores from critics sell very well—as if quality were the single most important feature of a wine. In some wine shops, the buyers won't stock a wine unless it has been reviewed favorably by a top critic. An adage in the wine trade is that if a wine scores less than 90 points, you can't sell it, and if it scores 90 or above, you can't keep it in stock.

But choosing your wines according to quality ratings is impractical unless your main goal is to impress your friends and gain status in their eyes. For one thing, wines that achieve high scores are often very expensive or hard to find. Even more importantly, a quality rating tells you absolutely nothing about what the wine tastes like and whether it will go well with your roast chicken and butternut squash.

The fact of the matter is that for wine (as for food), quality matters only within the context of style. If the style of a particular wine is not your liking, or if it doesn't suit the occasion or the food you're serving, what difference does it make how good that wine is?

WHAT IS QUALITY IN WINE, ANYWAY?

What's ironic about the wine market's obsession with quality is that no fixed definition of wine quality exists. The quality rating of any wine is a judgment by a critic (or a group of critics) who brings into play the beliefs about wine quality that he or she holds, and applies them to evidence gathered subjectively in the tasting of the wine. The system is far from scientific.

Individual wine experts have various beliefs about what constitutes quality that are based on personal experience. Some people

WINE HAS A MIND OF ITS OWN

*T*he experience of a wine is not only subjective but also extremely variable. First of all, wine is a living, changing liquid that's affected by storage conditions and even its packaging. One bottle of a wine can differ from another bottle of the same wine if the two bottles were stored at different temperatures or if one of them had a slightly looser cork. Just like theater, every bottle of wine is a live performance.

Even if a wine were always exactly the same from bottle to bottle, your experience of it wouldn't be. A wine can taste better or worse to you during different seasons, at different altitudes, with different foods, or according to your mood. Even the same bottle of wine on the same day in the same circumstances can taste different: just change the glass the wine is in, and you change the taste of the wine—sometimes subtly and sometimes dramatically. And as the wine sits in the glass over the course of your meal, it changes with exposure to air. As you eat different foods with it, you perceive the wine differently.

When a critic rates a wine, what he or she is really doing is rating the *experience* of that wine. Your experience will almost certainly be different.

believe that a wine must express the flavor of its grape variety in order to be high in quality, for example. The winemaker from a small, family-owned winery in Europe might believe that a high-quality wine must express the essence of the vineyard where its grapes grew. Scientific sorts such as enologists (people who hold a degree in winemaking science) generally believe that a wine must be correct from a technical aspect—microbiologically stable, and free of flaws—in order to be a quality wine. Wine collectors who have had the opportunity to experience legendary Bordeaux wines that are fifty or even a hundred years old often believe that a wine cannot be great unless it has the potential to develop with aging.

Not only does the concept of wine quality differ from person to person, but also the activity of judging that quality is totally subjective. When you think about it, how could it not be? We experience wine in the privacy of our own mouths and process the experience through our individual brains. Our personal wine and food history—the kinds of wines we have tasted in the past, what we have read about wine, and the kinds of food we eat—filters the experience of every new wine. Whatever conclusion a wine critic draws about the quality of a wine, it is necessarily subjective.

Which is not to say that determining wine quality is akin to chaos theory. Experts often end up agreeing more or less on the quality level of a particular wine because a set of quality standards does exist—it's just that the standards are not rigid, and each critic applies them differently. We discuss quality criteria for wine in the next chapter.

STYLE TRUMPS QUALITY

We once saw a customer present a Top 100 list of wines to a salesperson in a wine shop. Did they have the number one wine? he asked. No? Well, did they have number two, or number three? He settled for wine number five, which the shop had in stock. "By the way," he asked just before handing over his credit card, "is that a white or a red?"

The moral of the story is that quality alone is a silly reason for buying a wine. A wine's style—what it tastes like—is more critical to your enjoyment of it than its quality is. A wine's style determines what foods it goes well with, whether it's appropriate to the occasion at hand, and whether the wine is to your taste. Go ahead and pay attention to the point scores and gold medals and stars, but only in comparing wines that share a style that you know you like.

Tasting Wine for

Quality and Style

What constitutes a wine's taste and its quality

ine style—the taste of a wine—is a bit like the sound of the proverbial tree that falls in the forest when no one is listening: it becomes meaningful only when you, the drinker, perceive it. Wine quality is the same: even if some aspects of quality can be calibrated in a lab, the determination of any wine's quality requires a human being to experience the wine.

Because it's your taste that determines what style of wine you enjoy, you'll improve your odds of finding wines that you like when you taste wine thoughtfully and figure out what it is that you like or dislike about any particular wine. While you're at it, you can build the experience that enables you to recognize quality. In this chapter, we explain what gives a wine its style and quality, to help you become a more skilled and thoughtful taster.

THE ELEMENTS OF WINE STYLE

Each wine owes its color, aroma, and taste—its style—to the particular combination of hundreds of substances within that wine. These substances either came from the grapes the wine was made from or formed in the wine as a result of fermentation (when yeasts convert the sugar in grape juice into alcohol) or aging.

Some of these substances determine the wine's aromas and flavors. These are *aromatic compounds*—aromatics for short. Other substances in wine dictate a wine's color, its apparent weight in your mouth, its texture, its relative sweetness, and the impression of energy the wine give you as it moves across your tongue. These are *structural components*—structure for short. The particular aromatic compounds a wine has plus its particular structural components together account for everything we see, smell, and taste in that wine, and determine the wine's stylistic category.

A wine's aromatics are volatile molecules that you smell as the wine's aroma and also perceive your mouth as the wine's flavors. Aromas and flavors of fruits, flowers, spices, vegetables, earth, and even chemicals are all aromatic characteristics.

A wine's structure is just about everything else that goes into the wine's style. Structure encompasses the wine's body (the impression of weight that the wine gives you in your mouth), its texture (smoothness or roughness, for example), its sweetness or dryness, and its balance (more on balance later in this chapter). It derives from what are called the four "components" of wine—alcohol, sugar, acid, and tannin. Actually, water is by far the main component of wine, because most wines are about 85 percent water. But it's the other components that make the difference between one wine and the next.

AROMATICS

Most discussions of individual wines tend to revolve around the wines' aromatics. Descriptions on the back labels of wine bottles invariably mention whether the wine has notes of fresh berry or mint, for example, even if they fail to mention that the wine is dry or full-bodied. Friends at dinner are more likely to comment on the fruit flavors they detect in a wine than to note that the wine is silky in texture. Of all the aspects of a wine's *taste* (the overall sensory impression we get from a wine), its *flavors* and aromas seem to be the most interesting to wine drinkers today.

(Some people, including some scientists, use the term *flavor* to refer to the total experience of a wine, and they limit the word *taste* to the five basic tastes, which we discuss later in this chapter. We have chosen to use *taste* for the total experience, because we find that it makes sense to more people.)

Considering that wine is a food, to focus on flavors is logical. The Aroma Wheel, developed by Professor A.C. Noble at the University of California at Davis, raised awareness of aromatics considerably among those in the wine trade as well as wine drinkers who became familiar with the wheel. We came to understand that *fruity*, for example, is just the simplest term for a whole family of aromas and flavors that includes fresh fruit, dried fruit, tree fruits, berries, citrus fruits, and so on. Likewise, *vegetative* is an umbrella term for aromas of fresh vegetables such as bell pepper or cooked vegetables such as boiled asparagus. But, as fascinating and complex as aromatics are, they alone do not constitute a wine's style; they are merely part of it.

In fact, *which* aromas and flavors a wine has—whether it's black-peppery or plummy or citrusy—tells only part of the story of a wine's aroma/flavor profile. Just as important an aspect of a wine's taste is the *intensity* of those aromas and flavors. Some wines shout out their aromas and are very flavorful in your mouth, while others make you work to identify their subtle scents and flavors. A wine's flavor intensity is a key aspect of its style. It's one of the reasons why you might like a wine (or not), and it definitely matters in matching wine with food.

Wine aromatics also vary according to their development, that is, how youthful and fresh or how mature they seem. This is mainly a function of the age of the wine and how it was stored. Put it all together, and two vastly different stylistic expressions of wine aromatics might be intense, fresh, fruity wines compared to subtle, developed, vegetal wines. In the descriptions alone, you can almost taste the difference.

STRUCTURE

We sometimes resort to metaphors to explain wine structure, and how it relates to a wine's aromatics. A wine's structure is like the shape, size, and materials of a house; aromatics are what color the house is painted. A wine's structure is like your body; its aromatics are the clothes you wear. And so on.

In these metaphors, the structural elements underpin the aromatics, and the aromatics—the colors, the clothes—would be useless without the structure. The same is true for wine. A wine's structure is its weight, its size, and most of its presence in your mouth. Its aromatics are the icing on the cake.

The building blocks of wine structure are:

- **Alcohol** (formed during fermentation)
- **Sugar** (mainly from the grapes themselves; much of the sugar present in the grapes is transformed into alcohol during the fermentation process; what remains in the finished wine and contributes to the structure is called residual sugar—often abbreviated by wine pros as RS)
- **Acid** (mainly tartaric acid, from grapes)
- **Tannin** (a substance in the skins, seeds, and stems of grapes, as well as in wood casks or barrels that the wine might age in)

These structural components correspond to three of our five basic tastes—sweetness, sourness, and bitterness. Each of a wine's structural components relates to one of these:

- Alcohol is perceived mainly as sweetness.
- Any residual sugar in a wine is perceived as sweetness.

THE INGREDIENTS OF WINE

*W*ine is an amazingly complex liquid. It contains hundreds of aromatic compounds and trace minerals—so many that no one is quite sure of the number. In many cases, except for a small amount of sulfur dioxide that's added as a preservative, and whatever compounds a wine might absorb from sitting in oak barrels, everything in wine either comes from the grapes themselves, or is formed during the fermentation process. (Some winemakers do add sugar, which ferments to alcohol, or add acid, to compensate for nature's deficiency; they can also add tannin or coloring, but this occurs mainly for inexpensive, mass-market wines.) Here are some of the components of wine, with very approximate percentages they might represent in a table wine:

Water	80–90 percent
Alcohol	8–15 percent
Glycerol	0.5–1.0 percent
Tartaric acid	0.5–0.8 percent
Other acids	0.1–0.5 percent
Residual sugar	0.1–2.0 percent
Tannin and coloring matter	0.05–0.40 percent

Wine also contains minerals, mineral salts, dissolved gases, and other elements.

- Acid is perceived as sourness.
- Tannin is perceived mainly as bitterness.

Saltiness, a fourth basic taste, is irrelevant in wine. Umami is now known to be a fifth basic taste (the perception of savoriness); it is relevant to wine mainly in terms of how wines themselves relate to foods with strong umami character.

When you taste a wine, its alcohol, sugar, acid, and tannin

register on your tongue and the different tactile sensations interact to create an impression that's more or less sweet, more or less acidic (*sour* is a term that's not used in wine circles), and more or less bitter.

But the dynamic created by the interaction of a wine's structural components is more complex than that. Together, the structural components create an impression of fullness, depth, weight, and texture in the wine. How full, heavy, and richly textured a wine seems to be depends on its structural components and the balance they strike.

Have you ever heard a red wine described as "firm"? Such wines are probably fairly high in tannin. Do you enjoy white wines that feel "crisp" in your mouth? They have high acidity, which enlivens them and gives them a slightly brittle texture. "Soft" wines taste that way because they lack enough acidity or tannin to make them taste firm or crisp. Likewise, velvety texture, silkiness, depth (a sense of verticality that some wines give in your mouth), and length (the impression of a wine's persistence across the whole length of your tongue), all derive from a wine's structure.

AROMATICS + STRUCTURE = STYLE

Every wine has its own combination of aromatic compounds, which forms the particular aroma/flavor profile of the wine. Every wine also has its own combination of structural components, which forms the wine's weight, texture, dryness, depth, and so on. These two forces work together to create the total impression the wine gives you.

Most of the time when you taste a wine, you won't stop to think about aromatics as one element of the wine and structure as another. You'll either notice individual characteristics of the wine—aromas of grapefruit peel, or crisp acidity, for example—or respond to the wine in a general way, forming the opinion that you like it or dislike it, and how much. But knowing the dynamics of a wine's taste is helpful when you want to figure out exactly what you like about a wine, or when you want to critique a wine.

How to Taste Wine

*S*ee, smell, sip, and spit (or swallow). This simple sequence sums up the act of tasting a wine (as opposed to just drinking it). In case you're not familiar with this sequence, here's how it goes:

See. Tilt a (half-full) glass against a white background and look at the surface of the wine. Notice what color it is, how deep the color is, and (mainly for red wines) whether it fades at the rim, where the wine meets the glass, or even has a slightly different hue at the rim.

Smell. Rotate your glass on the table so that the wine swirls around in the glass and mixes with air. Then stick your nose into the airspace of the glass and inhale the wine's aroma. Notice whether the aroma is subtle, medium, or intense, and whether it is fruity, floral, herbal, vegetal, spicy, earthy, animal-like (such as meat or leather), or chemical.

Sip. Take a moderate amount of wine into your mouth—more than just a sip, but less than a mouthful. Hold it in your mouth while you draw in some air (to release the wine's volatile flavor molecules), and move the wine around in your mouth a bit; notice whatever characteristics the wine expresses to you. If you're not in the habit of tasting wine thoughtfully, you might not notice much besides particular flavors that you might recognize, whether the wine tastes sweet or not, and whether its texture feels smooth or rough. With experience, you'll be able to gauge the wine's *body* (how weighty it feels in your mouth), its *length* and *depth* (impressions that the wine's taste extends all the way to the back of your mouth instead of stopping halfway, and that it doesn't feel flat and shallow on your tongue), and its *balance* (the relationship of the four structural components). Get in the habit of holding a wine in your mouth long enough to notice what it has to say.

Spit or swallow. Unless you're attending a professional wine tasting of six or more wines, just swallow the wine in your mouth. But be sure to notice the wine's finish—the aftermath of its flavors. Does the wine's fruitiness or spiciness linger even after the wine is no longer in your mouth? (In a great wine, it does.)

SUBJECTIVE REALITY

*Y*ou might notice, as you read this book, that we seem to favor the words *impression* and *suggestion* when we discuss how wine tastes. For example, we describe a wine's body as the impression of weight that a wine gives you in your mouth. That's because tasting wine is a totally subjective exercise. Your mouth is not a laboratory that can measure a wine's acidity or the intensity of its flavors; rather, it is the highly personal equipment with which you form an impression of various aspects of a wine.

When you first begin tasting wine thoughtfully, the calibration of your impressions is limited by your lack of experience. Medium-bodied reds are likely to taste full-bodied, for example, if all you ever drink is light-bodied whites. Tasting wine with more experienced people can help you establish parameters, as can tasting wines from all the different styles. The characteristics of each style become part of a mental yardstick against which you can perceive the characteristics of wines in other styles. With experience, you develop a complete frame of reference for body, texture, sweetness, and so forth. Anyone can develop this frame of reference by tasting thoughtfully.

When you look at a wine's color; smell its aromas; feel its texture, weight, and energy in your mouth; and taste its flavors, you come face-to-face with that wine's style. If you like the wine, you will probably enjoy other wines of a similar style.

Much of this book is devoted to describing the fundamental styles of wine. But first we discuss wine quality, an issue that's hard to ignore when you buy wine in wine shops or read about wine.

QUALITY CRITERIA

We have yet to meet a wine drinker who doesn't want to become a better taster and know how to rate the quality of wines. Our discussion of quality markers in wine will help you do that. If you keep these characteristics in mind when you taste a wine, you'll become a thinker and not just a drinker. That's a good thing, because the more you think about what you are tasting, the better you'll become at knowing what you really like, and why.

Don't worry: thinking about wine as you taste it won't take the pleasure out of drinking wine. You can taste a wine thoughtfully (as opposed to just drinking it) only when you want to—for example, the first time that you try a new wine. And you might discover that the thinking part is as much fun as the drinking!

The principal quality markers in wine are balance, depth, length, and concentration. We explain each of these characteristics in the following sections. We also discuss flavor intensity, which is a more controversial quality marker.

Balance

All wine experts agree that a wine must be balanced to be good. But balance is one of the most subjective of all quality criteria because it hinges on personal tolerances.

Balance is an impression created by the relationship among the four structural components of wine. Alcohol, sugar, acid, and tannin all affect the total impression a wine gives you in your mouth, and each one also affects the way you perceive the other three components. The final effect determines the balance of the wine.

Here's how balance happens. Acid and tannin both make a wine firm, while any sugar in the wine makes a wine soft; alcohol can soften a wine or do just the opposite—cause a hard, sharp impression in your mouth—depending on how high it is relative to the other three components.

When a wine is in your mouth, these substances interplay to affect your perception of them:

- The firming components, acid and tannin, accentuate each other if both are present in significant quantity.

- Any residual sugar that's left in the wine after fermentation counterbalances the effect of the acid and tannin and is counterbalanced by them.

- A high alcohol content can contribute a feeling of viscosity and sometimes a sense of sweetness; these impressions contrast with and balance the firming effect of the wine's acid and tannin.

- A very high alcohol content can give the wine a hard, edgy character (some people perceive this as what they call a burning sensation) that plays to an impression of firmness.

When a wine is balanced, its firming components and softening components interact in such a way that no individual element stands out as objectionable in your mouth.

Sometimes you might encounter a wine that seems to be perfectly balanced. That's an indication of high quality—and it's too special to expect of every wine. (In fact, we often use grander words than just balance to describe these wines, such as *harmony* or *grace*.) Most wines have a balance that's skewed a bit toward either firmness or softness; they're still considered balanced as long as neither impression is extreme.

Many red wines today strike an unusual balance by being soft in the front of your mouth but hard in the rear of the mouth. If you drink them quickly, without thinking, the two impressions come together nicely, but when you taste slowly and analytically, you get the sense that the wine is disjointed. In some wines, this effect diminishes with aging. When a wine has ideal balance, you perceive the softness and firmness simultaneously, not separately.

Not every wine is balanced. Many Chardonnays, for example, are so high in alcohol that they are unbalanced in that direction; their alcohol makes them sweet and also often gives a burning sensation at the rear of your mouth. Such wines can be commercially successful, but they are not technically high in quality.

We each have personal thresholds beyond which we experience sugar, acid, alcohol, or tannin more acutely. If your threshold for sugar is low, for example—let's say you don't normally eat sweets—

you are more likely to perceive sweetness in a wine as excessive. That's why the perception of balance in a wine is very personal.

Depth

A wine's depth matters mainly when it is absent, and the wine gives an impression of flatness (which suggests a poorly made wine), or when it is particularly evident (a quality trait). Most wines—the decent, normal, good-but-not-great wines of the world—fall between these two extremes.

Depth is one of the most difficult aspects of wine for us to describe, because we know that we risk sounding ridiculously abstract or metaphysical. Each wine has a shape in your mouth, and depth is an impression of verticality. (Sorry—we tried to warn you!)

Think about this the next time you have wine in your mouth: does the wine give you the impression that it's just a liquid film sitting there on your tongue —or does it suggest some form or shape? Many people perceive wines to have some thickness, and as a wine moves around in their mouth they get an impression of roundness or angularity, of breadth or depth, as if the wine had a shape.

The impression of verticality in a wine derives mainly from the wine's acidity—not just how much acid the wine has, but how its acidity figures in the balance with the other three structural components. A wine that has particularly good depth seems to have an extra dimension to its taste compared to most other wines. Wines without depth can be pleasant in some aspects—they can have attractive flavors, for example, or a nice, smooth texture—but they give an impression of being one-dimensional.

Length

Like depth, a wine's length is a spatial impression in your mouth, but it requires less imagination to perceive. A wine with length expresses itself across the full length of your tongue: you feel the wine—its texture, its weight, its flavors—not just in the front of your mouth but also in the middle and back.

When you swallow a mouthful of wine, of course the wine touches the full length of your tongue on the way to your gullet. But do you get a full sense of the wine the whole way? Many wines today make a big initial impression in the front of your mouth but have little or nothing to say afterward. A wine with length has a different kind of energy. It holds your attention all the way back, and is inherently more intriguing.

Acidity drives the wine's energy across your tongue; overly high alcohol or tannin can cut the wine's taste short and deprive the wine of length.

If you just drink a wine the way you would drink orange juice—quickly, and without thinking—you won't notice a wine's length or lack of it. (For that matter, you won't notice balance, depth, or any of the other quality markers of wine.) In fact, when you drink wine quickly like that, a wine that packs an immediate impression will probably be more pleasing to you, even if it could be criticized for not having length. Consumer research commissioned by a major winery a few years ago determined that the market prefers wines without length. But fine wines must conform to a different standard than mass-market wines, and for them, length is still a critical measure of quality.

Wines without length are often described as "up-front" or "forward," to put a positive spin on their front-palate impression. In professional judgings, such wines are called "short." (Sometimes, if a wine is unpleasant, a judge might remark, "Thankfully, it's short.")

Concentration

When we critique a wine, concentration is often the swing characteristic that determines whether we elevate its score to the next level of quality. Concentration alone does not constitute quality, but without concentration, a wine can never be truly great.

So what is concentration, exactly? It's the impression that a wine is not dilute. When a wine is concentrated, its essence is tightly knit rather than spread thin. Think of a photo printed with a simple color printer compared to one printed with a sophisticated machine that

GRAPES TO WINE: A QUICK COURSE

The nature of the grapes that make a wine has a lot to do with the style of the final wine. The variety of grape—whether it's Cabernet Sauvignon, or Chardonnay, or Pinot Noir—influences the wine, of course, but how the grapes grow, and how ripe they get, also makes a difference. Here's a brief review of some of the variables and how they generally affect wine.

- As grapes ripen they lose acidity and gain sugar; the more sugar in the grapes, the higher the alcohol and lower the acid in the wine.

- For red grapes, the riper they are, the softer and less biting their natural tannin becomes.

- The riper that grapes become, the more that their flavors generally suggest cooked or processed fruit (such as jam, baked fruit, or dried fruit), rather than fresh fruit.

- Winemakers can promote ripeness to some extent by trellising their vines in certain ways or by reducing the number of grape bunches on each vine.

- Winemakers can add acid or tannin to grape juice or wine to create a structure that the grapes don't provide; as a result, wines can have, for example, very ripe, jammy flavors and yet the acidity of less ripe grapes. Alternatively, winemakers can add sugar to the juice, which ferments into alcohol, giving the wine a higher level of alcohol than the grapes are naturally disposed to give.

- Grapes that grow in large industrially farmed, irrigated vineyards with rich soils in warm climates tend to have less character than grapes that grow in poor soil on hillside vineyards.

imprints far more dots per inch. A wine with good concentration has more dots per inch, so to speak, than the next wine.

Using a visual analogy such as a photo might suggest that we are referring to the color of a wine, but we aren't. True, some wines are more saturated with color than other wines—their color is more concentrated, you might say—but color is not the measure of a wine's concentration. (For one thing, some grape varieties simply deliver more color than others, and grape variety is not a quality determinant.) We are referring to something you perceive in your mouth, an impression that the wine has lots of the stuff of its grapes in it. That "stuff" includes the wine's aromatic compounds—its flavors—as well as structural components such as tannin, alcohol, and acid. But because winemakers can manipulate a wine's alcohol, acid, or tannin content, the determination of how much stuff-of-the-grapes a wine has often boils down to a judgment about its aromatic compounds.

The issue in determining a wine's concentration is not how flavorful the wine is—that's what we call its *intensity*, discussed in the next section. The issue is how pure and focused the flavors are, and their relationship to the total impression the wine gives you. Depending on how youthful or mature the wine is, its concentration could express itself as a tight kernel of flavor that will open over time (in a youthful wine) or as a saturation of flavor throughout the wine. (Remember, we're talking about the stuff-of-the-grapes, not the flavor of oak barrels.) In some young wines that have a long life ahead, we perceive a grappa-like essence to the wine, the flavors being concentrated enough to seem as if they were distilled.

Most experts believe that a wine's concentration is a function of its *yield*—the size of the grape crop per acre of land: the lower the yield (the fewer grapes per acre), the more concentrated the wine. The reverse is certainly true—industrially farmed vineyards yielding huge crops usually make wines that are somewhat dilute in flavor.

The word *concentration* has another meaning in wine. It's a process that some winemakers are now using to remove liquid from wine, thereby literally concentrating the remaining components. (Read more about this in the section "Power on Demand" in the "Powerful Reds" chapter.) A wine that has been concentrated in this way can taste impressive enough to earn high grades from some critics. But this unnatural concentration is not what we refer to when we say that concentration is an indicator of quality. Perhaps in time, mechanical concentration will make natural concentration insignificant as a quality marker, because concentration will become a routine trait in wine rather than a special one.

Flavor Intensity

When we first got into wine, no one ever talked about aroma and flavor intensity, because few wines had it. Today, some (not all) experts consider intensity to be a necessary characteristic of high-quality wines—maybe because intensely flavorful wines are currently a dominant style.

Flavor intensity in a wine is like volume in music. Some people like music to be so loud that it reverberates; others like it quiet, so they can listen and think at the same time. In the end, intensity does not correlate to the quality of the music or the wine. We believe that a wine with quiet, subtle aromas and flavors can be just as good as one that's very aromatic and very flavorful. We see intensity as a stylistic issue, not a quality indicator.

Other Quality Criteria

Two other quality criteria—age-worthiness and typicity—are somewhat questionable today. In the past, only wines that had the ability to improve with aging were considered of very high quality. Good wines were also expected to typify their region or grape variety. But many wines today have neither of these characteristics: they are at their most enjoyable when they are young, and their taste speaks to a modern, international standard rather than to a specific grape or region.

When we encounter a wine that is supremely typical of what it is, or one that in our experience has the potential to blossom into greatness over time, we give it credit for those attributes. But to expect every high-quality wine today to have age-worthiness and typicity is unrealistic.

Getting Down to the Styles

Twelve wine—four for white wine, four for red, two for

rosé, and two for sparkling wine—styles plus two

overarching stylistic influences

*W*ine tastes different today than it used to. We're not talking about the wines of ancient Rome here; the collective taste of today's wines is significantly different from that of wines made just two or three decades ago.

More wines today fall into certain popular, best-selling styles, such as full-bodied, oaky white wines, or powerful reds. Styles that were popular in the 1970s—such as crisp, light-bodied whites without any oaky flavor, or subtle, medium-bodied reds—are less common, although they still exist.

Shifts in power (so to speak) from some styles to others happen because over time, outside factors influence the way winemakers grow their grapes and make their wine. Issues such as critics' preferences, for example, can gradually cause winemakers to make a different style of wine, as can changes in winemaking know-how, or market performance of certain types or styles of wine.

The styles themselves are fundamental. Each style of wine that we name in this chapter, and describe in the chapters that follow, is a prototype of how some wines can (and do) taste.

When you have a good grasp of the various styles, you'll know generally what to expect every time you pull the cork on a bottle of wine.

As trends in wine come and go, however, the wines within a style can shift in taste slightly. For example, as fuller and richer wines become popular, wines in a lighter style can become slightly richer than they once were. (Producers tend to alter their winemaking slightly to bring their wines closer to the popular style.) But those wines are still light compared to wines in the richer and fuller style. The differentiation between one style and the next remains the same.

When you have a good grasp of the various styles, you'll know generally what to expect every time you pull the cork on a bottle of wine. And you'll be able to choose the kind of wine you want to drink—whether it conforms to the most popular style or not.

THE WINES OF THE WORLD IN TWELVE STYLES

The more carefully a serious wine taster analyzes a wine while tasting it, the more he can perceive its individual character—the particular nuances of aromatics and structure that distinguish that wine from every other. But when the taster moves his perspective outward from the minute details of the wine's taste to its more general characteristics, he can describe the wine's style. The style of a wine revolves around the most obvious characteristics that the wine shares with other wines.

WHITE WINE STYLES

When we consider how the white wines of the world taste, we see certain characteristics that unify some wines into groups and distinguish them from other white wines. These stylistic markers are flavor intensity, amount of acidity, weight, and the presence or absence of oaky character. These characteristics separate white wines into four styles:

Which Is the Best Style?

*S*ome styles of wine are more popular than others, but no style is inherently better or more valid than the next. The wines of each style are simply different from those of other styles. Each style has its place—with different wine drinkers, or in different seasons, or with different foods.

- **Fresh, unoaked whites.** Generally the lightest and least complex of all dry whites, but also the most refreshing, these wines are crisp, and their aromatic intensity ranges from neutral to mild; they adapt easily to food. Inexpensive Italian Pinot Grigio is a typical wine in this style.

- **Earthy whites.** Representing a middle ground between the first and the fourth styles, these wines are fuller-bodied and more substantial than the first but less flavorful than the fourth, and lack obvious oakiness; they have fairly subtle flavors, often of an earthy or minerally nature, as well as broad, substantial structure. Mâcon is a typical wine in this style.

- **Aromatic whites.** These wines have lots of flavor, but it is flavor that comes from their grapes rather than from oak; they vary in weight from fairly light to rich, and in sweetness from bone dry to medium sweet; they are some of the most food-friendly wines around. German Riesling is a typical wine in this style.

- **Rich, oaky whites.** At the opposite end of the spectrum from the first style in terms of their weight and their flavor intensity, these wines are just about the richest white wines that you can find, apart from sweet dessert wines; smoky/toasty oak character is a common chord for these wines. California Chardonnay is a typical wine in this style.

Within each style are thousands of unique, individual wines—but these individuals all share certain family traits, and relate predictably to certain foods. You might favor the wines of one particular style, or you might like all four styles but prefer one to the others depending on the circumstances. When you're eating a delicate filet of sole, for example, a rich, oaky white will probably be too heavy, while a fresh, unoaked white or a dry, aromatic white could be ideal.

You might favor the wines of one particular style, or you might like all the styles but prefer one to the others depending on the circumstances.

In the next four chapters, we describe these four white wine styles in more detail, name the types of wine that fall into each style, tell you how to recognize quality for each style, and discuss food and wine pairings for each style.

RED WINE STYLES

The amount and nature of a red wine's tannin is a factor in delineating red wine styles. Almost all red wines have some tannin, because tannin exists in dark grape skins, which winemakers need to use for color. Depending on how much *extraction* of tannin occurs during winemaking (the transfer of tannin from the skins into the wine; see "Soaking Up Sturdiness" in the "Powerful Reds" chapter), a red wine could be soft and easy to drink or firm and foreboding until it ages for a decade or more—two widely different styles.

Another determinant of red wine style is how flavorful the wines are and how fruity those flavors are. Fruitiness and flavor impact seem to be the whole point of some reds, while others are distinctly unfruity—and not all that intense in flavor, either.

Based on these characteristics, red wines fall into four styles:

- **Mild-mannered reds.** These wines have aromas and flavors that are not particularly intense, and they have a gentle character; most of them are fairly smooth and not very

Muscadets, inexpensive
white Bordeaux wines,
most Pinot Grigios,
and various other
European whites

Rhône wines, Mâcons,
Vouvrays, many Semillons,
and similar wines

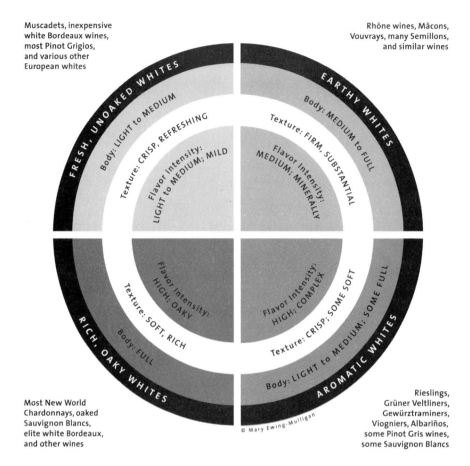

FRESH, UNOAKED WHITES

Body: LIGHT to MEDIUM

Texture: CRISP, REFRESHING

Flavor Intensity:
LIGHT to MEDIUM; MILD

EARTHY WHITES

Body: MEDIUM to FULL

Texture: FIRM, SUBSTANTIAL

Flavor Intensity:
MEDIUM; MINERALLY

Flavor Intensity:
HIGH; OAKY

Texture: SOFT, RICH

Body: FULL

RICH, OAKY WHITES

Flavor Intensity:
HIGH; COMPLEX

Texture: CRISP; SOME SOFT

Body: LIGHT to MEDIUM; SOME FULL

AROMATIC WHITES

© Mary Ewing-Mulligan

Most New World
Chardonnays, oaked
Sauvignon Blancs,
elite white Bordeaux,
and other wines

Rieslings,
Grüner Veltliners,
Gewürztraminers,
Viogniers, Albariños,
some Pinot Gris wines,
some Sauvignon Blancs

WINE STYLE WHEELS

To make it easy to grasp the telltale signs of each of the styles and how each style is similar to and different from the other styles, we created two wine wheels: one for white wines and one for red wines.

WINE STYLE WHEEL: WHITE WINES

The four styles of white wine are not isolated expressions of wine's taste, but parts of a taste continuum. The wines of one style segue into the next, sharing common characteristics with some other styles while remaining distinct in other characteristics. The styles progress in weight from fresh, unoaked whites—the lightest wines—to rich, oaky wines, and from low aroma and flavor intensity to high, varying in texture along the way.

Inexpensive Bordeaux reds, traditional Rioja reds, Northeastern Italian Merlots and Cabernets, simple Chiantis, and similar wines

Most Beaujolais; many Southern Rhône reds; some Southern Italian reds; some Pinot Noirs; some U.S. Merlots; inexpensive reds from the U.S., South America, and Australia; and similar wines

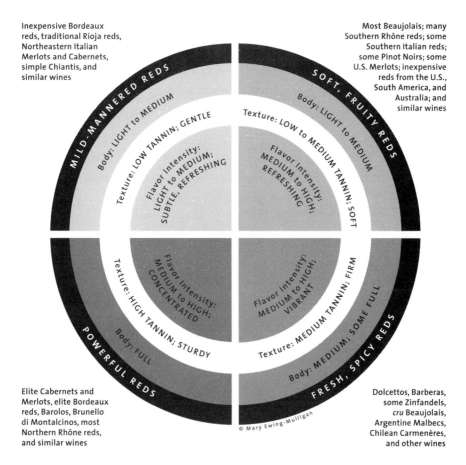

MILD-MANNERED REDS
Body: LIGHT to MEDIUM
Texture: LOW TANNIN; GENTLE
Flavor Intensity: LIGHT to MEDIUM; SUBTLE, REFRESHING

SOFT, FRUITY REDS
Body: LIGHT to MEDIUM
Texture: LOW to MEDIUM TANNIN; SOFT
Flavor Intensity: MEDIUM to HIGH; REFRESHING

POWERFUL REDS
Texture: HIGH TANNIN; STURDY
Body: FULL
Flavor Intensity: MEDIUM to HIGH; CONCENTRATED

FRESH, SPICY REDS
Texture: MEDIUM TANNIN; FIRM
Body: MEDIUM; SOME FULL
Flavor Intensity: MEDIUM to HIGH; VIBRANT

© Mary Ewing-Mulligan

Elite Cabernets and Merlots, elite Bordeaux reds, Barolos, Brunello di Montalcinos, most Northern Rhône reds, and similar wines

Dolcettos, Barberas, some Zinfandels, *cru* Beaujolais, Argentine Malbecs, Chilean Carmenères, and other wines

WINE STYLE WHEEL: RED WINES

Every red wine that you encounter will fall squarely into one style or onto the fringes of a style, sharing characteristics with another style.

Our Red Wine Style Wheel depicts the flow of red wine tastes from mild-mannered reds—light in body, low in tannin, and subtle in aroma and flavor—through to maxed-out powerful reds. The wheel details each style according to its body, texture (particularly its tannins), and its flavor intensity, which are the fundamental stylistic markers that distinguish wines of one taste profile from another.

fruity. Inexpensive Bordeaux is a typical wine in this style.

- **Soft and fruity reds.** These young, ready-to-drink, light- or medium-bodied wines express fruity aromas and flavors and don't have much tannin. Basic Beaujolais is a typical wine in this style.

- **Fresh, spicy reds.** Generally fairly intense in aromatics (and those aromas and flavors often have a spicy note to them), these wines also have substantial structure and a certain edginess of personality. Dolcetto, from Italy, is a typical wine in this style.

- **Powerful reds.** Wines of this style are full-bodied and also have concentrated aromas and flavors, as well as considerable tannic structure; some of them need bottle age to reach their optimum expression. Napa Valley Cabernet Sauvignon is a typical wine in this style.

Some wine drinkers strongly dislike any dryness of texture in red wine, and for them, soft and fruity reds are the best choice among red wines. Other people might choose their style of wine according to the situation: a powerful red for a special occasion, a spicy red for flavorful foods, a mild-mannered red for delicate dishes, and a soft, fruity red for a picnic.

Some wine drinkers strongly dislike any dryness of texture in red wine, and for them, soft and fruity reds are the best choice.

In the chapters on red wine styles, we describe each style in detail and tell you which types of wine fall into each style. We also give plenty of food-pairing suggestions and explain the quality markers for wines in each style.

ROSÉ AND SPARKLING WINE STYLES

Stylistic similarities and differences don't end when you leave the world of white and red wines. Pink—or rosé—wines have specific styles, and so do sparkling wines.

For pink wines, the degree of sweetness is the key demarcation between the two styles. The two styles of rosé wine are:

- **Blush wines.** These pink wines range from slightly sweet to sweet, and they are usually soft and fruity. White Zinfandel is a typical wine in this style.

- **Dry rosé wines.** These wines can be bone dry or they can have a very slight sweetness, less than blush wines; they also have fairly firm structure, from crisp acidity or a small amount of tannin. Rosado from Spain's Navarra region is a typical wine in this style.

For sparkling wines, the key issue is how fresh and fruity a wine is as opposed to how earthy and aged it is; a great tradition exists for both styles of bubbly. Sparkling wine's two styles are:

- **Fruit-driven bubblies.** These wines can be overtly fruity and fresh, or less so, but they are less rich than those in the complex sparkling wine style, and their aromas and flavors are less developed. Sparkling Prosecco is a typical wine in this style.

- **Complex sparkling wines.** Bubblies with earthy, rich flavors that have developed during long aging at the winery fall into this style. Champagne, from France, is a typical wine in this style.

The last two chapters in the book describe these styles of rosé and sparkling wines.

THE META-STYLES

It's almost impossible for us to discuss our twelve different styles of wine without referring to two overarching stylistic influences that affect most wines:

PERSONALITIES OF WINE

*W*hen the great psychologist, psychotherapist, and personality theorist Carl Jung wrote his epic work *Psychological Types*, describing eight personality frameworks, he was careful to point out that no one person neatly fits into any one personality type (such as extrovert thinking, introvert feeling, extrovert intuitive, and so forth). One set of characteristics might predominate, but under certain circumstances other characteristics might emerge. In other words, one pure type does not exist.

The same is true with wines that we peg as certain styles. We might call a wine a fresh, unoaked white, but yes, it can have an earthy side to it as well. We place wines in their most obvious style, with the understanding that styles can intertwine in the same wine, just as personality types do in people.

- The climate in which the grapes for a wine grew
- Winemaking intent (the taste profile the winemaker had in mind when he or she was making a wine)

All wine professionals acknowledge the presence of these two stylistic markers throughout the wines of the world—even those who prefer to classify wines in traditional ways, according to grape variety or region of production, rather than by style. By understanding how these influences affect the taste of a wine, you'll be able to use a particular stylistic lingo in talking with sommeliers or your wine merchant—and you'll understand what they mean when they use particular terms.

In terms of climate, the personality and taste of some wines derive from the fact that their grapes grew in a fairly cool climate, while some other wines display traits that derive from warm-climate agriculture. These wines are described as *cool-climate wines* and *warm-climate wines*, respectively.

Regardless of the grape-growing climate, some wines exhibit a distinctly modern style—fruity and flavorful—and wine professionals describe them as *New World wines*. Other wines taste more classic and traditional—with aromas and flavors that are earthy rather than fruity, for example, and are relatively subtle—and these are often tagged *Old World wines*.

These terms inevitably crop up as we describe our twelve wine styles. When we talk about "mild-mannered red wines," for example, we can't help but mention that most of them come from relatively cool climates and that they lack the overt fruitiness of New World wines.

Here's a synopsis of what wine experts mean when they talk about New World and Old World wines, and cool-climate or warm-climate wines. Just a word of caution: we describe the extremes represented by these terms, and in reality, plenty of middle ground exists.

Location as Destiny

Grapes that grow in cool climates can't ripen as much as grapes that grow in warm climates, because of insufficient heat or sunshine, and sometimes too much rain. At harvest time, they contain less sugar and more acid than they would if they had been able to ripen more. Wines made from these grapes are therefore relatively high in acid and low in alcohol (the amount of sugar in the grapes dictates the wine's alcohol content, unless the winemaker sugars the juice). Conversely, grapes grown in warm climates can ripen easily, and their juice can make soft, high-alcohol wines.

- **Cool-climate wines.** These wines tend to be fairly light-bodied. Their aromas and flavors generally fall toward the "green" or underripe end of the flavor spectrum—think green apple as opposed to papaya, or green peppers as opposed to portobello mushrooms. Their crisp acidity and relatively light body make them easy to drink with food because they don't dominate the flavors of the food.

- **Warm-climate wines.** Just the opposite, these wines are full-bodied, high in alcohol, and low in acid (unless the winemaker adds acid, which is often the case). They sport aromas and flavors of very ripe, plump fruits, or even over-ripe fruits, and are less refreshing, but they're easier to like when you taste them on their own, without food.

The prototypical cool-climate wines are white, because white grapes grow best in the coolest climates. Wines such as Muscadet and dry German Rieslings are classic examples. But the cool-climate influence exists among red wines, too; inexpensive Cabernets from Northern Italy are examples.

Red grapes dominate in very warm climates; a typical warm-climate red would be a rich, high-alcohol Zinfandel from California. Many inexpensive Chardonnays from California or Australia show warm-climate trademarks in white wine.

Winemaking Schools of Thought

The Old World of wine is Europe. Countries such as France and Italy have millennia-old winemaking cultures, and most of the wine grape varieties used throughout the world originated there. European wines were the only game in town until a few decades ago, and still today, two-thirds of the world's wine comes from Europe.

Stylistically, the terms Old World *and* New World *don't refer just to the origin of a wine. They refer to schools of winemaking philosophy.*

Non-European countries that produce wine are the so-called New World wine countries. These include the United States, Australia, and New Zealand, which have relatively short winemaking histories, and also countries such as Chile and South Africa, where winemaking dates back 400-plus years.

But stylistically, the terms *Old World* and *New World* don't refer just to the origin of a wine. They refer to schools of winemaking philosophy.

In Europe, national regulations usually dictate which grape

varieties a winemaker can plant, how long he or she must age the wine, and even the general parameters of the wine's taste. In many cases, the goal of the winemaker is to express in his or her wine the particular personality of the place where the grapes grew—what are called *terroir* characteristics. (*Terroir* is the unique combination of growing conditions that a vineyard has; Chapter 4 of *Wine For Dummies*, 3rd edition, explains this concept.) Although modern winemaking equipment is common in Europe, innovative technique often takes a backseat to traditional methods and objectives. Some wine producers even eschew the title of winemaker; they prefer to call themselves "wine growers," because they believe that it is the vineyard, not the person, that makes the wine.

Outside Europe, grape growing and winemaking are wide open: anyone can plant any grape variety anywhere. In many cases, the goal of winemakers is to capture the personality and flavor of the grape variety in the wine. The notion that a wine should be fruity (because it is made from fruit) probably originated among New World winemakers. With some exceptions, the personality of the land is secondary, if it figures at all in the winemaking goal. This is understandable, because so many New World vineyards are young, and what the land brings to the wine is not yet apparent. Another aspect of New World winemaking is technical expertise.

How are these two different winemaking influences expressed in the taste of a wine?

- **New World wines.** These wines are all about the fruit. They're also very flavorful (the main flavor being fruitiness), and they tend to express themselves immediately, as soon as you put them in your mouth. They're usually technically correct wines—although that's an aspect that's more for wine pros, rather than wine drinkers, to determine.

- **Old World wines.** Not only less fruity—maybe showing earthy, vegetal, or even animal-like aromas and flavors (such as leather or meat)—these wines are also more subtle aromatically. In the balance between aromatics and structure, it's often their structure that dominates. When you put them in your mouth, their characteristics tend to unfold gradually, as the wines cross your tongue, rather than suddenly, in the front of your mouth.

The characteristics we describe are labeled New World traits and Old World traits, respectively, because each set of descriptors is most common in the wines from that origin. But what really matters is the wine's style, not its origin. Not every European winemaker makes classically Old World wines, and not every Californian or Aussie winemaker makes distinctly New World wines. Whether a wine shows either Old World or New World style depends on the winemaker's philosophy—the characteristics he or she is trying to achieve in the wine—and not on the country where the wine is made.

Style Makers, Not Styles

Climate and winemaking intent are influential in forging the style of a wine, but they are not sufficient to be complete styles in their own right. If you were to ask for a warm-climate, New World white wine, you might get an oaky California Chardonnay, an unoaked Australian Chardonnay, or a Viognier from Southern France (which could taste New Worldish even though it's European)—three very different-tasting wines.

Our twelve styles describe wines more precisely, so that you have better odds of getting the taste you want in a wine. But the chords of New World/Old World and cool-climate/warm-climate run through them.

Fresh, Unoaked White Wines

Light, crisp, refreshing whites with fairly subdued

aromas and flavors, such as Muscadets, inexpensive

white Bordeaux wines, Pinot Grigios, and various

other European whites

*I*f you frequent Italian restaurants and order white wine there, then you're already familiar with the fresh, unoaked style of white wine, because this happens to be the dominant style of white wine made in Italy. One reason this style is so prevalent in Italy is that Italian wines are made to go with food, and fresh, unoaked whites excel at that. Their crisp texture and unassertive aromatics accommodate the flavors of food rather than go head-to-head with them.

Other countries make fresh, unoaked whites, too—including France, Spain, Greece, and the United States. Some of these wines are surprisingly inexpensive, because they are "everyday" wines, but others carry heftier price tags, either because they are more famous or because their quality is quite high.

Wines in this category will never win a contest for their intensity of aroma or flavor, but they prove that there's more to a wine than just fruitiness. They are extremely refreshing to drink and are among the food-friendliest wines around.

IT'S WAKE-UP TIME FOR YOUR PALATE!

We could have called this style by many other names—just "fresh," for example, or "light," or "zing!"—but we believe that "fresh, unoaked whites" is the most straightforward label for the wines whose taste characteristics put them into this group. (If you're one of the millions of wine drinkers who have never given the slightest thought to whether your wine is oaked or not, please don't be put off by this technical term in the name of this wine style.)

Wines in the fresh, unoaked style are refreshing to drink and are among the food-friendliest wines around.

What are those taste characteristics? Wines of this style are dry and light-bodied or medium-bodied, with crisp texture and a refreshing, thirst-quenching personality. They can have various aromas and flavors, depending mainly on which grape variety they come from, but these aromas and flavors are just medium pronounced at most. These wines don't provoke you to put your nose into the glass again and again in search of exotic new complexities. For some wines, the general smell of wine might be the only thing that you notice. But at the richer end of the fresh, unoaked spectrum, some wines have distinct minerally, tart-fruity, or nutty aromas and flavors.

The simplest examples of these wines are all about uncomplicated drinking. A fresh, unoaked white is easy to drink because of its fairly light body and relatively low alcohol content compared to many white wines. And it goes very well with food because of its high acidity. Every time you sip it, it cleanses and refreshes your mouth, so that you can enjoy your next mouthful of food.

Many fresh, unoaked whites, when they are young, have a tiny bit of carbon dioxide that you can feel as a prickle on your tongue when the wine is first poured. Winemakers retain this CO_2 in the wine at the time of bottling to keep the wine fresh and refreshing. It dissipates quickly as the wine sits in your glass. You usually can't see this CO_2 in the wine, because it is a far smaller amount than

STYLISTIC SIBLINGS

*F*resh, unoaked whites are the lightest-bodied and crispest of all white wines, and the most subtle in aroma and flavor. Here's how the other three styles of white wine compare to them:

- Like fresh, unoaked whites, wines in the earthy white style are dry, and often their aromas and flavors are somewhat subdued. But earthy whites are fuller-bodied and more substantial in structure, with a more serious, characterful personality.

- Dry aromatic white wines are more intense in aroma and flavor and can be fuller-bodied and richer in texture; the slightly sweet aromatic whites are also sweeter than fresh, unoaked whites.

- Rich, oaky whites are the complete opposites of fresh, unoaked whites: fuller-bodied, more intense in aroma and flavor, and oaky, too.

what you see as bubbles and foam in a sparkling or semi-sparkling wine.

Wines in this style are lean, but that leanness—a textural and weight impression that the wine is spare rather than generous—varies. Some wines are almost austere, while others have a little flesh on their high-acid bones but are still crisp and refreshing.

At their finest, wines in the fresh, unoaked style have enough concentration and complexity of flavor to earn the approval of serious tasters. While the majority of wines in this style are most enjoyable when they are very young, the very best of them can improve with a couple of years of aging; the agers are the exception, however.

The issue of oak comes in for this style because together with crisp acidity, the lack of oaky character is the single most distinctive characteristic of these wines compared to other dry whites.

WHY SOME WINES ARE OAKED AND OTHERS AREN'T

Fresh, unoaked whites taste the way they do for a combination of reasons having to do with their grape varieties, the climate of the vineyards, the natural tendencies of the grapes in a particular area, and the winemakers' grand plans in making the wines. But one issue, the absence of oak barrels or other oak sources in the wine-making process, is critical to this style of wine.

Why is oak a factor in winemaking? Once upon a time in the history of winemaking—sometime after the primitive era of goatskin sacks but before the modern age of shiny stainless-steel tanks—wooden barrels and casks were the containers that held wine (and grape juice about to become wine) in wineries and even on boats that transported wine to buyers overseas. These barrels were made of chestnut, oak, or whatever other type of wood was available. Some wines that were stored in certain types of oak con-tainers developed certain taste characteristics that people liked. As other containers, such as glass-lined concrete vats and fiberglass tanks, came and went, oak hung in there.

Today, when winemakers incorporate oak into their winemak-ing for white wines, it's usually because they want the oak to con-tribute some of its aroma and flavor to the wine. Typical charac-teristics that come from oak are a toasted or smoky aroma and fla-vor, a slightly burnt or charry character, caramel notes, vanilla, and even coconut and dill nuances.

All of these aromas and flavors can be very attractive in a wine—provided that the wine is full-bodied enough and rich enough in flavor to support the additional flavor of oak. If it's not, the oaky character will overpower the wine itself, and you might think you're drinking fermented oak juice instead of grape juice.

When a wine is meant to be fairly light-bodied or delicate in flavor—as fresh, unoaked whites are—the winemaker does not use any oak. The result is a totally different style of wine, one that's much less imposing than that of oaked white wines. (We describe the oaky style in the "Rich, Oaky Whites" chapter.)

THE USER-FRIENDLY WINE

*F*resh, unoaked wines are famously easy to drink. In fact, their approachability is one of their strongest assets. When wine distributors pitch these wines to restaurant owners, they often argue that four diners can easily polish off two full bottles of this kind of wine but would struggle to drink much more than a glass each of a richer, more flavorful white. When you want a white wine that's easy and uncomplicated and doesn't compete with the food, reach for a Pinot Grigio, a Muscadet, or another wine in this style—and test this hypothesis for yourself.

The use of oak is a key issue in winemaking today. Winemakers and other wine professionals can recite the pros and cons of letting wine come into contact with wood during production—not only whether or not the winemaker should use oak but for how long, using which species of oak, and what the size and condition of the oak containers should be. It's a fascinating aspect of winemaking for those inclined to bark up that tree. To get the kind of wine that you want to drink, though, you don't have to know anything about these technical issues. It's enough to know that the freshest, lightest white wines are not oaked. The word *unoaked,* when you use it to describe the style of wine you want, is an instant communication between you and the person taking your order in a restaurant (or a wine store salesperson) that will steer him or her toward wines of this style.

THE GRAPES OF FRESH, UNOAKED WHITES

Many fresh, unoaked whites come from fairly neutral grape varieties—varieties that do not have strong aromatic compounds. They also come from grapes that are high in acidity. Some of these grapes are fairly obscure, and their names don't appear much on wine labels. A few of these varieties are the following:

- **Trebbiano,** a white grape very common throughout Italy
- **Catarratto,** a Sicilian grape
- **Melon de Bourgogne,** the grape that makes Muscadet
- Spain's **Viura,** also known as **Macabeo**
- **Pinot Blanc,** which grows in Italy, France, and elsewhere
- Portugal's **Arinto,** which is particularly high in acid
- **Assyrtiko,** a native Greek variety

Sauvignon Blanc grapes can make fresh, unoaked white wines, even though this variety does have an assertive aroma. That's because in some places, Sauvignon Blanc seems to be less expressive. A prime example is in the vineyards of Bordeaux, where this variety makes clean and refreshing white wines with a piercing but not pronounced aroma that's extremely tame compared to that of Sauvignon Blanc wines from New Zealand or South Africa. In the vineyards of Sancerre, the aromatic assertiveness of this grape is also restrained enough to place some wines into this style.

Another grape variety whose wines could fall into this style or not, depending on how and where the grapes are grown, is **Pinot Gris**. As inexpensive Pinot Grigio, it has just a bit of aroma and flavor, generally because the crop size in the vineyards is large, which delays ripening and inhibits flavor development in the grapes. But as Alsace Pinot Gris, the wine is so flavorful it could fall into the more powerful aromatic white style. The same is true for **Chenin Blanc**, which in its top examples as a dry wine has the weight of an earthy white but in other cases makes fresh, unoaked whites.

Chardonnay—the grape variety that dominates our chapter on rich, oaky white wines—can also make wines in the fresh, unoaked style. A prime example is Chablis, from the Burgundy region of France. Some producers use no oak for their Chablis wines, others oak only their best wines, and a few ferment all their Chablis in oak. When the wine is not oaked, it expresses tart apple, citrus, and mineral flavors, along with crisp acidity. In Australia, too, some Chardonnays are made "unwooded," as they say.

AROUND THE WORLD OF FRESH, UNOAKED WHITES

Wines in the fresh, unoaked style can come from anywhere, but usually they hail from relatively cool climates, for several reasons:

- In cooler wine regions, grapes retain a high amount of acidity at harvest time, and high acidity is a key component of this style.

- Grapes from cooler regions make wines that are relatively light in body, another key feature of this style.

- Many white grape varieties suitable for cool climates are delicate in flavor and therefore are not compatible with oak aging.

In warmer climates, most grapes get ripe enough that they can produce fairly rich, full-bodied white wines of the sort that are perfect for oak aging, and that's a whole different style of wine. Or they get ripe enough to have richness and weight that would place them in the earthy white style. But exceptions do exist. In **Sicily,** for example, a relatively warm region, many whites based on native grape varieties are unoaked and fall into this style.

Many wines of this style also hail from European vineyards. That's because European wines tend to have fairly subdued aromas and flavors and are therefore natural candidates for this style. Europe also has many cool-climate wine districts ideal for such wines. Most winemakers who have a commitment to expressing strong fruitiness in their wines, as many New World winemakers do, would probably not be satisfied to make a wine in this fresh, unoaked, fairly mild-tasting style.

As we mentioned earlier, Italy is a prime breeding ground for fresh, unoaked whites. The three regions of **Northeastern Italy** (**Trentino–Alto Adige, Veneto,** and **Friuli–Venezia Giulia**) make their share of wines in this style, particularly inexpensive Pinot Grigio wines. **Central Italy** also makes dozens of wines in this style; these include **Orvieto, Frascati, Trebbiano d'Abruzzo,** and other wines that are based mainly on the Trebbiano grape.

France's **Bordeaux** region is another key territory for this style. The top tier of dry white wines from Bordeaux have such character and weight that they express the earthy white style (discussed in "Earthy Whites") or are oaked to the point of being rich, oaky whites—but the less expensive wines fall into the fresh, unoaked style, thanks to crisp acidity and fairly subtle aromas and flavors.

The **Muscadet** district of the **Loire Valley** also makes this style. The cool, damp Atlantic-influenced weather plus the neutral aromatics of the Melon de Bourgogne grape, which is grown here, dictate this style. In the interior Loire Valley, some wines made from Sauvignon Blanc—such as **Sancerre** and **Pouilly-Fumé**—express the fresh, unoaked style in their lightest examples.

Some **Chablis** wines fall into this style, particularly the least expensive wines and those from cool vintages such as 2002.

Spain and **Portugal** also make some fresh, unoaked whites. A key example is **Rioja** Blanco, based on the Viura grape—although these wines tend to occupy the softer, less austere end of this style's spectrum. Some white wines of Spain's **Rueda** region also fall into this style, at its more flavorful end, particularly those made from Verdejo rather than Sauvignon Blanc; some Rueda whites are oaked, however. In Portugal, various wines from native grape varieties are fresh and unoaked, particularly those made from the Arinto grape, in **Bucelas** and **Ribatejo**, and those made from the Bical grape, in **Bairrada** and **Dão**.

Greece makes a few fresh, unoaked whites, such as those from the island of **Santorini**. These wines are made from the Assyrtiko grape, which retains its acidity well, even in warm years.

Beyond Europe, this style exists more as occasional examples than as a fairly region-wide stamp. For example, **South Africa** makes some Chenin Blanc wines—sometimes called Steen—that are fresh, crisp, unoaked, and not extremely intense in flavor, but far more South African whites are either oaky or aromatic in style. From **Australia**, wines made from the Verdelho grape can be in this style, although at the somewhat more flavorful end of the spectrum.

WHEN THEY ARE GOOD . . .

Many of the wines that fall into the fresh, unoaked white wine style are inexpensive wines. One simple reason for this is that their prices don't have to cover the cost of expensive oak barrels! Besides the cost-of-oak factor, the wines can be inexpensive because they come from high-yielding vineyards that enjoy a favorable economy of scale. A critical third factor is that critics don't tend to get excited about most wines of this style (except to remark what good values they are), and without the glamour of a high point score, the wines cannot command a high price.

None of this means that these wines aren't good. Most fresh, unoaked wines range from decent to very good in quality, although—as is true for any style—some are disappointing. Here are some quality parameters for wines in the fresh, unoaked style.

The single, most important indicator of quality in a wine of this style is concentration of aromas and flavors; conversely, the typical weakness is dilution. The best wines give you the sense, in your mouth, that their flavors are well knit, even if they are subtle. (See the "Concentration" section in the chapter "Tasting Wine for Quality and Style" for a discussion of this characteristic.) Poor wines of this style taste watery and thin.

The best white wines in the fresh, unoaked style are truly dry, with a good concentration of flavor and a strong backbone of acidity that's balanced by their alcohol.

Fresh, unoaked whites are generally high in acidity, but they must be well balanced all the same. If a wine is so high in acid that it seems astringent, then the winemaker has not executed this style successfully. Bear in mind, of course, that some people have a lower tolerance for acidity than others, and a wine that you consider too severe might seem balanced to someone else. Also remember that a wine that tastes overly acidic on its own sometimes is delicious when you drink it with food.

These wines should be dry. Sometimes, in an effort to make a

YOUTH IS EVERYTHING

*A*lways drink fresh, unoaked whites young—within one or two years of the vintage date. When they get older, they lose their freshness and, with it, their appeal. (If you see a wine in the fresh, unoaked style in a bargain bin at your wine shop, it's probably no bargain.) When a wine in this style has a somewhat deep color and tastes flat rather than refreshing, you know that it's too old.

wine softer and less austere, winemakers will allow the wine to have a small amount of sweetness—not enough to change the style, but enough to muddle it. If an otherwise fresh, unoaked white gives us a slightly sugary impression, we give it a lower quality rating. Similarly, some wines in this style can be high enough in alcohol to have a slight sweetness and a viscous texture, which detract from the style a bit.

Wines in this style do not have much aromatic intensity, but the better wines have at least *some* aroma and flavor. We particularly admire those wines that taste minerally, as if the chalky, slate-like, or stony characters of their soil were infused in the wine—such as you can find in a basic Chablis or Sancerre from a cool vintage.

The best white wines in the fresh, unoaked style are truly dry, with a good concentration of flavor and a strong backbone of acidity that's balanced by their alcohol. The poorest examples of this style are watery, thin, flavorless, and sometimes a bit sugary.

THE FOODS AND THE MOODS FOR FRESH, UNOAKED WHITES

The operative characteristic of fresh, unoaked whites is their lightness, both in body and in flavor. In deciding when to drink or serve them, think light, as in light foods; light, casual occasions; and times when you feel like having something light to drink, such as during summer.

Although these wines don't have much flavor impact, they can be appropriate for parties because of their fairly light body and relatively low alcohol content. They are good as apéritif wines—the first wine in a meal, or the wine that precedes the meal—and are not rich enough to follow other white wines. Remember the classic advice for serving wine: "white before red, light before rich" and so forth.

Fresh, unoaked whites are particularly good with fish and seafood. Some of them, such as Muscadet, are legendary as companions to raw seafood. And there's nothing better with a simple filet of flounder or sole; the acidity of these wines brings out the flavor of the fish much the way a squirt of lemon does, and the delicate flavors of this style don't compete with the fish.

Non-competitiveness, in fact, is a key trait of these wines. At the table, they accommodate the flavors of whatever foods they're served with, rather than assert their own flavor or personality. We can't think of a single dish that would be overwhelmed by a fresh, unoaked white. Oddly enough, these wines go well with many richer dishes, too. If you're serving roast chicken, mushroom risotto, or a spicy pork stir-fry, these wines would not be the ideal choice—but they wouldn't be terrible. Dishes such as sweet Italian sausages and peppers, grilled swordfish or tuna, fried chicken, and portobello mushrooms are in the same category. These more richly flavored foods will neutralize the wine's subtle flavors, but the crisp acidity of the wine will make the food more enjoyable all the same.

SERVING TIP: TWEAKING THE TEMP

*I*f you want to get maximum flavor from a fresh, unoaked white, don't chill it too much. The colder these wines are, the crisper and more bracing the taste—but the more their aromas and flavors become muted by the cold. If you're serving an inexpensive, popular, mass-market brand on a hot day, though, you might care more about the bracing effect and less about the aromas and flavors—and in that case, chill away!

PAIRINGS: FRESH, UNOAKED WHITES WITH . . .

Baked filet of flounder or sole

Fried fish

Fried calamari

Shellfish dishes, except with lobster

Risotto with seafood

Pasta with vegetables and cheese

Sautéed chicken breast filets

Curried chicken

Brothy soups

Main-course salads, especially Niçoise salad

Mushroom omelet

Sandwiches (anything except PB&J!)

Goat cheese

Soft ripened cheeses such as Brie or Camembert

FRESH, UNOAKED WHITES: WINES TO TRY

Most of the fresh, unoaked white wines that we're recommending happen to come from France and Italy; not only do these two countries have lots of cool wine regions that can produce this style of wine, but also this part of the world philosophically and historically has always championed fresh, unoaked whites as great food wines.

Our recommended Italian wines represent some of the highest-quality wines in this category. Hundreds more fresh, unoaked Italian whites are available than what we list here. Here are some Italian wines that we recommend in alphabetical order.

WINE	PRODUCER/BRAND	REGION	COUNTRY
Bianco di Custoza	Cavalchina ▪ Lamberti ▪ Montresor	Veneto	Italy
Frascati	Gotto d'Oro ▪ Villa Simone	Latium	Italy
Gavi	Bergaglio ▪ Broglia ▪ La Scolca	Piedmont	Italy
Lacryma Christi del Vesuvio	Mastroberardino	Campania	Italy
Müller-Thurgau	Pojer & Sandri ▪ Tiefenbrunner	Trentino–Alto Adige	Italy
Orvieto Classico (secco)	Antinori ▪ Barberani ▪ La Carraia ▪ Palazzone ▪ Salviano ▪ Tenuta Le Velette	Umbria	Italy
Pinot Bianco	Jermann ▪ Pierpaolo Pecorari ▪ Russiz Superiore ▪ Mario Schiopetto ▪ Roberto Scubla ▪ Venica & Venica ▪ Villa Russiz	Friuli	Italy
Pinot Bianco	Alois Lageder ▪ Hofstätter ▪ Tiefenbrunner ▪ Elena Walch ▪ Roberto Zeni	Trentino–Alto Adige	Italy
Pinot Grigio	Abbazia di Novacella ▪ Alois Lageder ▪ Josef Brigl ▪ Maso Poli ▪ Peter Zemmer ▪ San Michele Appiano (Castel San Valentino) ▪ Tiefenbrunner	Trentino–Alto Adige	Italy
Soave	Anselmi ▪ Bertani ▪ Campagnola ▪ Gini ▪ Guerrieri-Rizzardi ▪ Inama ▪ La Cappuccina ▪ Lamberti ▪ Pieropan ▪ Pra ▪ Sartori ▪ Suavia	Veneto	Italy
Trebbiano d'Abruzzo	Cataldi Madonna ▪ Marramiero ▪ Masciarelli ▪ Eduardo Valentini	Abruzzo	Italy
Verdicchio	Bisci ▪ Bonci ▪ Bucci ▪ Fattoria Coroncino ▪ Fazi Battaglia ▪ Garofoli ▪ La Monacesca ▪ Marchetti ▪ Monte Schiavo ▪ Santa Barbara ▪ Sartarelli ▪ Tavignano ▪ Umani Ronchi	Marche	Italy
Vernaccia di San Gimignano	Baroncini ▪ Ca' del Vispo ▪ Calcinaie ▪ Falchini ▪ Fontaleoni ▪ Melini ▪ Montenidoli ▪ Mormoraia ▪ San Quirico ▪ Signano Azienda ▪ Strozzi ▪ Teruzzi & Puthod ▪ Vagnoni	Tuscany	Italy

France's fresh, unoaked whites come mainly from cool-climate regions such as the Loire Valley, Bordeaux, and the northern reaches of Burgundy. From the eastern Loire Valley—the part nearest to Paris— Sauvignon Blanc makes light- to medium-bodied, crisp, lively wines with mineral and citrus flavors; Sancerre and Pouilly-Fumé are the most famous wines, and many, but not all, of them fit into this style. (Exceptions include the more expensive Pouilly-Fumés from producers whose wines are barrel-fermented and oak-aged.) Here are some French wines we recommend.

WINE	PRODUCER/BRAND	REGION	COUNTRY
Bouzeron Aligoté	A & P de Villaine ▪ Verget	Burgundy	France
Chablis (all their wines)	Jean-Marc Brocard ▪ Jean Durop ▪ Long-Depaquit ▪ Louis Michel ▪ A. Régnard (aka Albert Pic)	Chablis	France
Chablis (basic AC-level)	Jean Collet ▪ Jean Dauvissat ▪ Jean-Paul Droin ▪ William Fèvre ▪ Domaine Laroche ▪ Christian Moreau	Chablis	France
Ménétou-Salon	Domaine de Chatenoy ▪ Domaine Fournier ▪ Henri Pelle	Loire Valley	France
Muscadet	Chérau-Carré ▪ Château du Cléray (Sauvion) ▪ Domaine de l'Ecu ▪ Domaine de la Louvetrie ▪ Domaine la Quilla ▪ Domaine Michel Bregeon ▪ Louis Métaireau ▪ Marquis de Goulaine	Loire Valley	France
Pinot Blanc	Léon Beyer ▪ Paul Blanck ▪ Trimbach	Alsace	France
Pouilly-Fumé	Michel Bailly ▪ Château de Tracy ▪ Jean-Claude Chatelain ▪ Serge Dagueneau ▪ Domaine Cailbourdin ▪ Ladoucette ▪ Michel Redde ▪ Guy Saget	Loire Valley	France
Quincy	Domaine Denis Jaumier ▪ Domaine Mardon ▪ Domaine Sorbe ▪ Philippe Portier	Loire Valley	France
Reuilly	Claude Lafond ▪ Domaine Reuilly ▪ Domaine Sorbe	Loire Valley	France

Sancerre	Domaine Bailly-Reverdy ▪ Domaine Henri Bourgeois ▪ Comte Lafond ▪ Cotat Frères ▪ Lucien Crochet ▪ Domaine Vincent Delaporte ▪ Domaine Hippolyte-Reverdy ▪ Alphonse Mellot ▪ Domaine de la Rossignole ▪ Vacheron	Loire Valley	France
St.-Bris Sauvignon Blanc	Jean-Marc Brocard	Burgundy	France
White Bordeaux	Château Couhins-Lurton ▪ Château de Cruzeau	Péssac-Léognan	France
White Bordeaux	Château Chantegrive	Graves	France
White Bordeaux	Château Bonnet	Entre-Deux-Mers	France

France and Italy don't have a monopoly on this style, however. Here are a few recommendations from around the world.

WINE	PRODUCER/BRAND	REGION	COUNTRY
Chardonnay (their basic); Sauvignon Blanc	Annie's Lane ▪ Deakin Estate ▪ Wolf Blass	Victoria	Australia
Verdelho	Hope Estate	Hunter Valley	Australia
Pinot Blanc	Biegler	Thermenregion	Austria
Pinot Blanc	Höpler	Burgenland	Austria
Sauvignon Blanc; Chardonnay	Carmen ▪ Casa Lapostolle ▪ Errazuriz ▪ Montes (Leyda Valley)	Casablanca; Leyda	Chile
Assyrtiko	Boutari ▪ Sigalas	Santorini	Greece
Chenin Blanc	Bradgate ▪ Mulderbosch ▪ Vinum Africa	Stellenbosch	South Africa
Chenin Blanc	Groote Post	Darling	South Africa

WINE	PRODUCER/BRAND	REGION	COUNTRY
Chenin Blanc	KWV Steen	Western Cape	South Africa
Verdejo	Marqués de Riscal ▪ Martinsancho	Rueda	Spain
Pinot Gris	Elk Cove Vineyards ▪ The Eyrie Vineyards ▪ Montinore Vineyards	Willamette Valley (OR)	USA

WINES ON THE MOVE: THE CHALLENGES OF DELICACY

In today's bigger-is-better wine culture, wines in the fresh, unoaked style are definitely underdogs. To some extent, the popularity of richer, fuller-bodied, more flavorful white wines (not to mention red wines) threatens the continued existence of this style. Some wine producers are beginning to make their fresh, unoaked whites slightly softer than previously, and sometimes the wines are not truly dry. Eventually, the parameters of this style will probably shift somewhat in the direction of greater richness.

Another factor influencing this style is the weather. Many of the world's wine regions are experiencing unprecedented heat during the grape-growing season, which makes their wines richer, fuller-bodied, and softer than they traditionally were, even if the wines are still unoaked. In some cases, the riper grapes are bringing distinctly fruity aromas and flavors to wines that were previously not at all fruity.

We love more traditional, less ripe, bone-dry wines, and we will miss them if they ever succumb completely to the joint forces of the market and the weather. But philosophers claim that change is good—and in any case, it's inevitable. Fortunately, so is the swing of the pendulum.

Earthy Whites

Unoaked or gently oaked wines with broad,

earthy flavors, such as Rhône whites, Mâcons,

Vouvrays, and similar wines

We can just see the spread in the lifestyle magazine:

Choose your wine according to your personality! Can you relate to the following statements?

- My home is decorated in earth tones.
- Stone surfaces are sexy.
- People describe me as a salt-of-the-earth type.
- Flashy isn't classy.

If this sounds like you, then earthy white wines are what you've been longing to drink! Earthy whites are subdued and unpretentious, just like you. They convey a sense of genuineness that will warm your heart!

What provoked this daydream is the range of connotations that the word *earthy* carries in our culture. Some of those common connotations—such as genuine, rustic, hearty, or pragmatic—can be apt associations for the word's use in the world of wine. The literal meaning—having characteristics of the earth, such as minerality—is also appropriate for wines. Earthy white wines are substantial, dry wines, sometimes characterized by minerally or soil-related aromatics, that have a no-nonsense personality. They have a statement to make, but they make it in a somewhat low-key way, without being very fruity or floral or particularly toasty and oaky.

STURDY AND SUBSTANTIAL

Wines that share the earthy white style are dry wines with fairly full body and medium aromatic intensity. They could be unoaked or they might be oaked—but gently, so that the effects of oak do not become a major part of their expression. They are mouth-filling in a broad way, suggesting substance more than sheer force.

Some earthy whites have earthy aromatics, but others don't. Aromas and flavors of damp earth or dry soil are considered earthy, as are woodsy notes and mineral aromas, such as suggestions of stone, chalk, or slate. Sometimes these earthy aromas and flavors coexist with a mildly smoky or spicy character from oak; with fruity, floral or herbal notes; or even with animal notes. (Wet wool and lanolin, both aromas of animal origin, are two descriptors sometimes applied to certain wines in this category.) But whatever their actual aromas and flavors are, earthy white wines have less forthcoming, pronounced aromatics than the wines we cover in the next chapter, aromatic whites.

Earthy whites have considerable structure, based on medium to high alcohol, a solid component of acidity, sometimes phenolics (mainly tannins) derived from oak or grape skins, and sometimes a richness of texture from lees aging (refer to "Leesy Does It," later in this chapter, for an explanation of this). Although you can often detect clear, specific aromas from these wines, the aromatics do not dominate the structure.

STYLISTIC SIBLINGS

*H*ere's how earthy whites fit into the universe of our four white wine styles:

- Fresh, unoaked whites are less flavorful, lighter-bodied, leaner, and less substantial than earthy whites (but the lightest earthy whites are not far from the richest of the fresh, unoaked whites).

- Aromatic whites are more overtly flavorful than earthy whites; they are also generally lighter-bodied, and their structure is a less defining aspect of their taste.

- Rich, oaky whites have more aroma and flavor intensity and are fuller-bodied than earthy whites, and many of them are softer in texture, but the most restrained oaky whites are close in style to the richest earthy whites.

What defines wines in this style is a balance between aromatics and structure that creates an impression of substance, weight, and solidity in the wine. Another key characteristic is that wines in this style tend to taste natural, as opposed to tasting (to the trained palate) of their winemaking. Telltale winemaking characteristics such as overt oakiness or candied-fruit character derived from certain fermentation techniques are largely absent in these wines.

Earthy white wine is not the most popular style, nor is it the most marketable to a mass audience of wine drinkers. The fairly subtle flavor of wines in this style and their lack of overt fruitiness suit them instead to somewhat sophisticated wine lovers. Those who love earthy whites understand that they have to meet these wines halfway—that is, they have to pause a moment and pay attention to the way such a wine tastes, appreciating its structure, balance, and somewhat reserved flavors. It's possible to enjoy wines in the other three white wine styles by drinking without thinking, but if you approach earthy whites like that, they'll probably leave you cold.

In their own way, earthy whites can be delicious and compelling. Wines in this style are the beverage of choice for many discriminating wine lovers. And some earthy whites are great wines—legendary, even. But they're probably not what you'd choose to serve at a large party, or recommend to friends or relatives who are just getting started in wine.

THE WHERE AND WHY OF EARTHY WHITES

So which types of wines are earthy whites, and where do they come from? They are Mâcon wines, from the southern part of France's Burgundy region, white wines from the Rhône Valley, those from Vouvray, and some wines from Chablis, to name a few.

Generally, earthy whites are not varietal wines, possibly because many of the grapes that make these wines are somewhat obscure varieties whose names wouldn't be recognized by many wine drinkers. Also, many wines of this style are blended wines, made from several different grape varieties, which don't qualify for varietal naming. Of course, some exceptions exist; for example, you can find varietal Chenin Blancs from California or Washington that qualify as earthy whites, as well as some Pinot Gris wines from Alsace, and Semillons from Australia.

More than being associated with a particular grape variety—as the rich, oaky style is associated with Chardonnay—earthy whites are associated with a place: They spring from the Old World and its winemaking mind-set. These are traditional wines that predate the modern notion that wines should be fruity. They usually express their *terroirs*—the combination of growing conditions that influence a wine—rather than their grape varieties in the abstract.

As we mention in the chapter "Getting Down to the Styles," the meta-styles of Old World and New World apply to the philosophy of the winemaker and not just to the origin of the wines. Many winemakers in California, Australia, Washington, and other New World wine regions subscribe to the Old World notion that a fine wine should express the soil and climate that spawned it—that a Chardonnay from one vineyard should taste different from that of

LEESY DOES IT

*T*he effect of lees contact in winemaking is another technical issue that you really don't need to get into unless you want to be able to converse with the pros or understand why your favorite style of wine tastes the way it does. Lees are solids that either form during fermentation (such as yeast cells) or are in the juice to begin with (such as pulp). When fermentation ends, these solids gradually fall to the bottom of the tank or barrel. At that point, the winemaker can choose to separate the clear wine from the solids, or remove just the largest particles and let the fine, yeast cells interact with the wine for a while.

The longer that the lees remain in contact with a white wine, the more they affect the wine. They consume oxygen, and they enable certain undesirable substances to precipitate out naturally, so that subsequent processing of the wine is avoided. They encourage malolactic fermentation (see "Nuances of Power" in the chapter on rich, oaky whites). Ultimately, lees contact results in a less fresh-and-fruity wine, with greater textural richness and occasionally a slightly nutty flavor.

Lees contact is most common in barrel-fermented white wines, but some tank-fermented wines undergo the process. It's a very traditional practice for certain wines, and although it is a winemaking technique, it creates a "natural" effect in the wine more than a manipulated "winemaking" effect.

another vineyard, for example. Some of them make wines in the earthy white style.

Besides either coming from Europe or being made by European-inspired winemakers, earthy white wines tend to come from climates that are not extremely cool. Very cool climates make white wines that are high in acidity, and this acidity slants the wine's taste toward other styles, particularly fresh, unoaked whites and aromatic whites. Warmer climates give wines the breadth and fullness typical of this style, generally speaking.

Because many earthy whites express a minerality of flavor, we're tempted to say that they come from wine regions with particular types of soil—mineral-rich, relatively infertile soils, for example. That is true of some wines. The particular soil of much of the Chablis area, for example, contributes a distinctly mineral note to the best Chablis wines. But other styles of white wine can also express minerality (particularly aromatic whites, discussed in the next chapter), and not all earthy whites do. Therefore the association of soil types with earthy whites is not convincing.

THE GRAPES OF EARTHY WHITES

Just about the only white grape varieties that can't make wines in the earthy style are those whose aromatics are so intense that their wines automatically place out of this style, such as Gewürztraminer, Muscat, and some other varieties that we discuss in the chapter "Aromatic Whites." That leaves the field of grape varieties for earthy whites wide open.

Relatively low-acid grapes that tend to ripen to high sugar levels are probably the most common in this style; **Grenache Blanc**, a grape variety grown in the Southern Rhône Valley and in Spain, is an example. Grapes whose aromatics are not intense are also likely to be found in earthy white wines.

Chardonnays in the earthy style tend to come from Europe, especially parts of the Burgundy region of France.

Despite its dominance of the rich, oaky white style, **Chardonnay** also makes several earthy whites. Chardonnay's own aromas and flavors (as opposed to those contributed by oak) can be fairly quiet when the grape grows in climates that are not very warm, and Chardonnay often brings a broadness of structure to its wine—earthy white characteristics on both counts. Chardonnays in the earthy style tend to come from Europe, especially parts of the Burgundy region of France.

Chenin Blanc makes earthy whites, except for its lemon-lime, candied-fruit, mass-market versions in California and other places. Good examples are the wines of the central Loire Valley, in France.

Here are some other grape varieties that you'll find in earthy white wines:

- **Sémillon,** grown in the Bordeaux region of France, Australia, and elsewhere
- **Marsanne,** a Rhône grape that is increasingly popular outside of France, though still at tiny production levels
- **Chasselas,** a grape making excellent dry wines in Switzerland
- **Xarel-lo,** a Spanish sparkling-wine variety that's beginning to make table wines
- **Tocai Friulano** and **Greco,** local varieties in the Italian regions of Friuli and Campania (and elsewhere in the south), respectively.
- **Pinot Gris,** in its more expressive but not most expressive versions
- **Sylvaner,** aka **Silvaner,** a variety that makes fresh, unoaked whites in Germany but also some earthy whites in Alsace and Switzerland

AROUND THE WORLD OF EARTHY WHITES

If we had to name a quintessential type of wine for this style, we'd probably choose **Mâcon**. These white wines from the southern part of the **Burgundy** region, in France, are dry and fairly full-bodied, with an earthy, minerally flavor and substantial structure. They're made from Chardonnay, as almost all white Burgundies are, but they're less refined than other, more famous white Burgundies. *Rustic* and *coarse* are descriptors that you might occasionally hear or see for these wines, but these are not pejorative terms—just another way of describing the gritty, down-to-earth personality of these wines.

Numerous white wines fall into the general Mâcon category.

The most basic of these are simply labeled Mâcon; others carry the **Mâcon-Villages** appellation, while others—climbing the ladder of quality and price—carry the name of a specific village, such as **Pouilly-Vinzelles** or **St.-Véran.** The most famous wine of the area is **Pouilly-Fuissé**, named after two towns.

With the exception of Pouilly-Fuissé, wines from the Mâcon district are generally not oaked. (Some Pouilly-Fuissé wines are oaky enough that they fall into the rich, oaky white style.) But even wine professionals can be fooled into thinking that these wines are made in oak, because they are so substantial.

If you want to try an earthy white, we recommend starting with Mâcon because these wines are widely available at many price and quality levels.

The extreme northern part of the Burgundy region also makes earthy whites, in the form of **Chablis.** Made entirely from Chardonnay, Chablis wines are sometimes unoaked and sometimes gently oaked (occasionally you can even find a rich, oaky one). Some producers oak their best wines—those from the best vineyard sites, *premier cru* and *grand cru* vineyards—and not their basic Chablis wines. For more on the hierarchy of vineyard sites in Burgundy, refer to *Wine For Dummies*, 3rd edition.

Many Chablis wines have a vein of minerality running through their taste; they can also have an apple-like fruitiness or even a slight citrus character, but they are not overtly fruity. Despite the high acidity of their fairly cool growing region, the higher-pedigree wines come across as broad in your mouth, thanks to the weight and substance of Chardonnay.

The rest of the white wines of Burgundy walk the line between earthy whites and rich, oaky whites. Meursaults will most often be in the rich, oaky style, as will the *cru* wines of Puligny-Montrachet and Chassagne-Montrachet. Straight **Bourgogne Blanc**—the most basic white wine of the region—usually expresses the earthy style. Whites from the **Côte Chalonnaise** district, just north of the

If you want to try an earthy white, we recommend starting with Mâcon beacuse they are available at many price and quality levels.

Mâcon area—such as **Mercurey, Givry,** and **Rully**—are often earthy whites. A lot hinges on the producer (how oaky he or she likes to make the wines) and the vintage (riper vintages giving richer wines that are more likely to be oaky). Your wine merchant can guide you, as can our list of recommended wines at the end of this chapter. Just remember: even when a white Burgundy crosses over into the rich, oaky style, it's still at the more reserved end of that style, compared to many New World Chardonnays brimming with tropical fruit flavors and smoky, butterscotchy oak.

Another hotbed of earthy white wines is the **Rhône Valley**. Red wines outnumber whites dramatically, but most of those whites that you do find are in the earthy style. (Exceptions are those wines made from the aromatic Viognier variety, such as Condrieu.) These wines are generally blends of grape varieties such as Grenache Blanc, Marsanne, Roussanne, and Bourboulenc. They are full-bodied, broad, characterful, dry wines with fairly subdued aromas and flavors. This style is almost universal in the region, whether you're talking about white wines from the southern part of the Rhône—those labeled **Côtes du Rhône** Blanc or **Châteauneuf-du-Pape** Blanc, for example—or from the northern part, such as **Hermitage** Blanc or **Crozes-Hermitage** Blanc. Some Rhône whites use a small amount of Viognier or Rolle grapes, both aromatic varieties, and this makes the wines more flavorful but does not skew them into the aromatic white style. The "satellite" wine districts south and east of the Rhône Valley, such as **Côtes du Lubéron, Côtes du Ventoux,** and **Coteaux du Tricastin,** also make wines in the earthy style.

And then there's the **Loire**. The dry wines made from Chenin Blanc vary somewhat from one district and winemaker to another, but they almost all fall somewhere within the earthy white style. **Savennières** is a classic example: dry, minerally, and firm, with aromas and flavors that are not very pronounced. **Vouvray** wines can be dry, off-dry, or sweet; they have an earthy spirit, but the sweetest of them are dessert wines rather than earthy whites.

Finally, some **Alsace** whites are in this style—specifically the leaner of the Pinot Gris wines and Sylvaners.

Although **Italy** dominates the fresh, unoaked style of white wine, it also makes earthy whites. These are high-quality whites that have more concentration than wines in the fresh, unoaked styles but don't take the route of oak aging to express their quality. Some examples include the following:

- Top-quality Pinot Grigio wines from the **Friuli** and **Trentino–Alto Adige** regions, which are richer and more substantial than inexpensive, mass-market Pinot Grigios
- Many Tocai Friulano wines
- **Greco di Tufo** from **Campania**
- Rich versions of **Vernaccia di San Gimignano**
- Better Verdicchio wines, from **Marche**

Australia has some earthy whites in its unoaked **Hunter Valley** Semillons, especially when the wines have a few years of age. Some Chardonnays that come from specific wine districts, particularly **Yarra Valley** in **Victoria** (as opposed to the inexpensive Chardonnays that hail from Southeastern Australia), can be in the earthy white style, even if they are produced in oak, because they are more restrained than flamboyant.

You can also find earthy whites from **Chile** and **Argentina**, but these tend to be isolated examples rather than regional clusters of the style. Some South African Chenin Blancs—sometimes called Steen—are in this style, but others are not; these wines are inexpensive, though, so a little trial and error won't set you back a bundle.

QUALITY ISSUES AND INDICATORS

You might occasionally hear fairly knowledgeable wine people use the term "earthy" as a euphemism for wines that are not cleanly made and have some funkiness to them. The source of this characteristic could be microbial or it could come from bad storage of the wine, such as in excessive heat. Some wines with microbial funkiness can actually be pleasing to some people if the so-called funk is not very strong. But this type of characteristic is not related to what we call the earthy style of white wine. White wines of any style that express uncleanness or dirtiness are, technically, inferior in quality.

Positive quality indications in earthy white wines include the usual quality markers for wine, such as balance and length. Depth is a less critical element in this style than in some others, because the impression of broadness that these wines give your mouth can compensate for a less pronounced impression of the verticality that defines depth.

One characteristic that distinguishes the best earthy whites is concentration of aromas or flavors.

One characteristic that distinguishes the best earthy whites from the more ordinary wines is concentration of aromatics. The aromas and flavors of wines in this style are not intense—but that doesn't mean that they should be dilute. When you're judging the quality of a wine in this style, think about how tightly knit the aromatics seem to be; wines that enable you to perceive a tight kernel of aroma or flavor when you smell or taste them are higher in quality than those with aromatics that seem to have no center of gravity.

A slight expression of bitterness is not a flaw in earthy white wines. These wines often are high in extract (the non-volatile, non-sugar components of a wine), which is part of what gives these wines a certain grip in your mouth. Of course, if you don't like this characteristic, this style of wine might not be for you.

Some wines in this style can be very high in alcohol, to the point of diluting the wines' concentration and making them seem hollow. This can be a flaw, but the perception of it depends on your personal alcohol threshold.

Sweetness is not a typical characteristic of the earthy white style, but some of the wines in this category, such as Vouvray, do come in off-dry versions that are not dessert wines. You can't fault these wines for being somewhat sweet (that's what they're intended to be), but you can decide that you prefer a dryer version. On the other hand, if you encounter sweetness in an earthy white that's billed as a dry wine—such as a Mâcon or a Verdicchio—then you can downgrade the wine for its sweetness.

SERVING TIP: NOT TOO COOL

If you like your white wines very cold, you'll find that you can still appreciate earthy whites for their structure, but the cold will diminish their rather subtle flavor. We chill them just a little (no more than an hour in the fridge) and serve them out of large Bordeaux glasses (glasses with fairly straight-sided bowls as opposed to round, balloon-type bowls). In very hot weather, when we want a cold, refreshing white, we tend not to reach for earthy whites, because they seem too big—but that's okay, because we also tend not to be eating cassoulet!

EARTHY EATS

Wines in the earthy white style are terrific food wines. They are generally big enough in structure to stand up to fairly substantial foods. They're also subtle enough in aroma and flavor to not dominate a food's flavor, and yet characterful enough to not be overwhelmed by food. Although they are less powerful than rich, oaky whites, they, too, can accompany many of the foods that you might consider having with red wine.

Reach for an earthy white when you have a fairly substantial dish whose flavors are not very fresh or lively.

We particularly enjoy drinking earthy whites with what we consider earthy foods, such as portobello mushrooms, green leafy vegetables (their natural bitterness is no problem for these wines), mushroom risotto, squid-ink pasta, or cassoulet. The wines match these foods not only in flavor intensity but also in personality.

Lack of fruitiness and fairly subtle flavor intensity gives these wines a chameleon-like advantage with poultry, veal, and pork dishes. We recommend them equally with simple roast chicken (although we generally opt for a soft, fruity red), veal piccata, smoked pork chops, or stuffed veal roast.

Foods with any fruitiness to them tend to taste incongruous with earthy whites. Very complex, spicy dishes, such as you find in many Asian cuisines, are not a terrible combination, because the wine becomes a neutral backdrop to the dish. But an aromatic white (see the chapter on that style) is a better choice. Likewise, spicy, flavorful Southwestern dishes—picture a cheesy chicken quesadilla with scallions and fresh cilantro and a side of refried beans—could find better mates. Bottom line: reach for an earthy white when you have a fairly substantial dish whose flavors are not very fresh or lively.

PAIRINGS: EARTHY WHITES WITH . . .

Manchego cheese and other sheep's-milk cheeses

Hearty white bean soup

Grilled portobello mushrooms

Mushroom quiche

Portuguese kale and potato soup

Grilled chicken Caesar salad

Turkey burgers

Veal chop milanese with arugula and tomatoes

Risotto with mushrooms

Grilled swordfish

Oyster stew

Cassoulet

Pheasant

EARTHY WHITES: WINES TO TRY

France produces more earthy white wines than any other country. In fact, our prototype earthy white is Mâcon/Mâcon-Villages from Southern Burgundy. The entire Mâconnais region, as well as the villages north of Mâcon in the Côte Chalonnaise (Mercurey, Rully, Givry, and Montagny), and to some extent Chablis all figure in our earthy white recommendations from Burgundy.

WINE	PRODUCER/BRAND	REGION	COUNTRY
Bourgogne Blanc	Domaine A & P de Villaine ▪ Domaine Patrick Javillier ▪ Domaine François Jobard ▪ Domaine Leflaive ▪ Domaine Ramonet	Burgundy	France
Chablis (Grand or Premier Cru)	Billaud-Simon ▪ Domaine Jean Collet ▪ Domaine Jean Dauvissat ▪ Domaine Daniel-Etienne Defaix ▪ Domaine Jean-Paul Droin ▪ Joseph Drouhin ▪ William Fèvre ▪ Domaine Jean-Pierre Grossot ▪ Domaine Laroche ▪ Domaine Christian Moreau Père et Fils ▪ Verget	Chablis (Burgundy)	France
Mâcon-Villages	Domaine Daniel Barraud ▪ Joseph Drouhin ▪ Domaine Guffens-Heynen ▪ Louis Jadot ▪ Louis Latour ▪ Verget	Mâcon (Burgundy)	France
Montagny; Givry Blanc	Domaine Bertrand ▪ René Bourgeon ▪ J. Faiveley ▪ Louis Latour	Côte Chalonnaise (Burgundy)	France
Pouilly-Fuissé	Domaine Daniel Barraud ▪ Château Fuissé ▪ Domaine Robert Denogent ▪ Roger Lassarat	Mâcon (Burgundy)	France
Rully Blanc; Mercurey Blanc	Domaine A & P de Villaine ▪ Antonin Rodet ▪ J. Faiveley ▪ Domaine de la Folie ▪ Domaine Michel Juillot ▪ Louis Latour ▪ Olivier Leflaive Frères	Côte Chalonnaise (Burgundy)	France
St.-Véran	Domaine Daniel Barraud ▪ Château Fuissé ▪ Louis Jadot ▪ Roger Lassarat ▪ Verget	Mâcon (Burgundy)	France
Viré-Clessé	Domaine André Bonhomme ▪ Jean Rijckaert	Mâcon (Burgundy)	France

France's other classic regions for earthy whites include the Rhône Valley, Provence, Alsace, and surely the Loire Valley. In fact, Chenin Blanc, the noble white variety that rules the central Loire, is one of the key players for earthy whites, and nowhere does it perform better than in the Loire. Savennières, the dry, minerally Chenin Blanc wine from the Loire Valley's Anjou district, has always been one of our favorite white wines in the world. A few Bordeaux wines also fall into this category.

WINE	PRODUCER/BRAND	REGION	COUNTRY
Bandol Blanc	Domaine Tempier	Provence	France
Bordeaux Blanc	Aîle d'Argent	Bordeaux	France
Cassis Blanc	Clos Ste.-Magdeleine	Provence	France
Châteauneuf-du-Pape Blanc	Château de Beaucastel ▪ Les Cailloux ▪ Domaine Font de Michelle ▪ Domaine de la Janasse ▪ Paul Jaboulet Aîné ▪ Domaine de Marcoux ▪ Clos du Mont-Olivet ▪ Château Mont-Redon ▪ Château de La Nerthe ▪ Clos des Papes ▪ Château Rayas ▪ Domaine du Vieux-Télégraphe	Rhône Valley	France
Coteaux d'Aix-en-Provence	Chapoutier "Les Beatines"	Provence	France
Côtes du Rhône Blanc; Côtes du Rhône-Villages Blanc	Château de Beaucastel "Coudoulet" ▪ Domaine du Caillou ▪ Jean-Luc Colombo ▪ Guigal ▪ Paul Jaboulet Aîné ▪ Château St.-Cosme ▪ Domaine Santa Duc	Rhône Valley	France
Côtes du Ventoux Blanc	Domaine Fondreche ▪ Domaine Santa Duc	Rhône Valley	France
Crozes Hermitage Blanc	Domaine Albert Belle ▪ Chapoutier ▪ Delas Frères ▪ Ferraton ▪ Paul Jaboulet Aîné ▪ Domaine des Rémizières ▪ René Rostaing ▪ Domaine Marc Sorrel	Rhône Valley	France
Graves	Clos Floridene ▪ Château Rahoul	Bordeaux	France

WINE	PRODUCER/BRAND	REGION	COUNTRY
Hermitage Blanc	Domaine Albert Belle ▪ Chapoutier ▪ Domaine Jean-Louis Chave ▪ Jean-Luc Colombo ▪ Delas Frères ▪ Ferraton ▪ Guigal ▪ Paul Jaboulet Ainé ▪ Domaine des Rémizières ▪ Domaine Marc Sorrel	Rhône Valley	France
Montlouis	Domaine François Chidaine ▪ Domaine Délétang	Loire Valley	France
Péssac-Léognan	Château Carbonnieux; ▪ Château Fieuzal ▪ Château La Tour-Martillac ▪ Château Pape-Clément	Bordeaux	France
Provence Whites	Jean-Luc Colombo "Les Pins Couchés" ▪ Château Routas "Coquelicot" and "Wild Boar White" ▪ Domaine de Triennes Viognier	Provence	France
Saumur Blanc	Château de Villeneuve	Loire Valley	France
Savennières	Domaine des Baumard ▪ Domaine du Closel ▪ Château d'Epiré ▪ Domaine Laffourcade ▪ Nicolas Joly	Loire Valley	France
St.-Joseph Blanc	Chapoutier ▪ Domaine Louis Chèze ▪ Domaine Yves Cuilleron ▪ Delas Frères ▪ Domaine Philippe Faury ▪ Ferraton ▪ Guigal ▪ Paul Jaboulet Ainé ▪ Domaine François Villard	Rhône Valley	France
Sylvaner	Domaine Paul Blanck ▪ Domaine Dirler-Cadé ▪ Muré/Clos St.-Landelin ▪ Domaine Ostertag ▪ Domaine Charles Schleret ▪ Domaine Weinbach	Alsace	France
Tokay–Pinot Gris/Pinot Gris	Léon Beyer ▪ Trimbach	Alsace	France
Vouvray	Domaine Allias ▪ Domaine des Aubusières ▪ Domaine Bourillon-d'Orléans ▪ Marc Brédif ▪ Domaine Didier Champalou ▪ Domaine du Clos Naudin ▪ Domaine Le Haut Lieu ▪ Domaine François Pinon	Loire Valley	France

We conclude our earthy white wine recommendations with some of our favorites from Italy, as well as a few wines from the United States, Switzerland's Chasselas variety, and Xarel-lo, a unique wine from Spain.

WINE	PRODUCER/BRAND	REGION	COUNTRY
Greco di Tufo	Feudi di San Gregorio ▪ Mastroberardino ▪ Terredora	Campania	Italy
Pinot Grigio	Giralamo Dorigo ▪ Doro Princic ▪ Livio Felluga ▪ Marco Felluga ▪ Jermann ▪ Pierpaolo Pecorari ▪ Pighin (Collio) ▪ Plozner ▪ Puiatti ▪ Ronco del Gelso ▪ Ronco del Gnemiz ▪ Russiz Superiore ▪ Sant'Elena ▪ Mario Schiopetto ▪ Venica & Venica ▪ Vie de Romans ▪ Villa del Borgo ▪ Villa Russiz ▪ Villanova ▪ Volpe Pasini ▪ Zamò & Zamò	Friuli	Italy
Pinot Grigio	Bottega Vinaia	Trentino	Italy
Tocai Friulano	Doro Princic ▪ Livio Felluga ▪ Plozner ▪ Ronco del Gelso ▪ Ronco del Gnemiz ▪ Mario Schiopetto ▪ Venica & Venica ▪ Villa Russiz ▪ Zamò & Zamò	Friuli	Italy
Verdicchio	Colonnara	Marche	Italy
Xarel-lo	Segura Viudas "Creu de Lavit"	Penedès	Spain
Chasselas	Gilliard Fendant ▪ Gilliard "Fendant Les Murettes"	Valais	Switzerland
Chasselas	Badoux "Aigle Les Murailles"	Vaud	Switzerland
Dézaley	Testuz "Dezaley L'Arbalette"	Vaud	Switzerland
Neuchatel	Château d'Auvernier	Neuchatel	Switzerland
Roussanne	McCrea Cellars	Red Mountain (WA)	USA
Roussanne	Alban Vineyards ▪ Qupé	Edna Valley (CA)	USA
Sémillon	Hogue Cellars	Yakima Valley (WA)	USA
Sémillon	L'Ecole No. 41 ▪ Waterbrook	Walla Walla (WA)	USA

WINE	PRODUCER/BRAND	REGION	COUNTRY
Sémillon	Barnard Griffin ▪ Chinook	Yakima Valley (WA)	USA
Sémillon	Chateau Ste. Michelle ▪ Columbia ▪ Columbia Crest	Columbia Valley (WA)	USA

WINES ON THE MOVE: RIPENESS FOR RIPENESS' SAKE

We're not sure whether to blame it on global warming or the tendency of winemakers to make wines in styles that critics prefer, but whatever the reason, many wines today taste as if they've been made from riper grapes than in the past. Chablis wines are softer and (dare we say?) sweeter than they used to be; some Alsace Pinot Gris wines are downright dessert-like; Mâcons, at least from some producers in some vintages, are more creamy than firm in texture, or overtly fruity.

We have no reason to believe that this trend won't continue. Global warming will increasingly give Burgundy a Rhône-like climate, and short of a regime change among wine critics, winemakers will continue to worship at the altar of "ripeness above all." As time goes by, the earthy white style will therefore shift toward greater richness of texture and weight (due to increased alcohol levels from riper grapes), riper flavors, and more frequent perception of sweetness. In other words, these wines will veer toward the rich, oaky white style, except without the overt aromatics of oak.

Aromatic Whites

Flavorful, unoaked whites from aromatic grapes,

such as Rieslings, Grüner Veltliners, Gewürztraminers,

Viogniers, Albariños, some Pinot Gris wines, some

Sauvignon Blancs

*I*magine a white wine that has real flavor—lots of flavor, but not the smoky/toasty/butterscotchy flavor of oak. This wine might smell like flowers, or it might taste like a bowl of fresh mixed fruit. It could have aromas and flavors of orange peel, or ripe peaches, or dried apricots—maybe with an herbal note, or white pepper spiciness, or minerally accents. When you sip it, its flavors engage your mind as well as satisfying your mouth. You're not sure whether to talk about it or just relax and enjoy it.

A wine like this would fall into the aromatic white style. This is a broad taste category that encompasses wines of various weights, textures, and sweetness levels (but not those sweet enough to be classified as dessert wines). Wines in this category all have a lot of natural aroma and flavor from their grapes, and range in intensity from medium-plus to oh-my-God intense.

In some ways, these are the perfect white wines. They taste delicious alone, and yet they have a remarkable ability to accompany food, especially difficult cuisines that challenge other styles of white wine.

GARDENS AND SPICE CABINETS OF FLAVOR

Aromatic white wines come from aromatic white grapes—that is, grapes that have strong aroma/flavor signatures. The salient, identifying characteristic of these wines is their perfume, which of course comes across as flavor when you have the wine in your mouth.

Aromatic whites have a remarkable ability to accompany food, especially dishes from difficult cuisines that challenge other styles of white wine.

Other than their common chord of aroma and flavor, aromatic whites are a diverse lot. Not only do these wines come from many different grape varieties, but also many of these grape varieties are vinified in several ways, depending on where those grapes grow as well as on the winemakers' intentions. For example, some Riesling wines are made in an off-dry, low-alcohol style, while other Rieslings have medium to full alcohol and are bone dry. Although dry wines and off-dry wines do taste different, and you might have a general preference for one over the other, we combine them both in this category because we believe that the wines' sweetness (or lack of it) is secondary to the general personality of these wines. They are about flavor, unmuddled by oakiness.

Many of the wines of this style are fruity, but we don't label the style with that term for two reasons:

- You can find fruitiness to some extent in white wines of other styles—for example, a rich, oaky California Chardonnay that has flavors of tropical fruits along with toasty oak character.
- Not every aromatic white is fruity.

Those that are fruity can have aromas and flavors of fresh fruits, dried fruits, fruit skins (as in lemon zest or peach skins), or preserved fruits (as in orange marmalade).

Floral aromas and flavors—rose, lavender, honeysuckle, pear blossom, and the like—characterize some aromatic whites. Others are commonly said to have spicy aromatics, sometimes along with fruity or floral notes; this spiciness can be literal, as in white pepper or cumin aromas, or it can be figurative, referring to a certain liveliness of aroma and flavor.

Mineral aromas and flavors are also common in wines of this style. Unlike for earthy whites, however, this minerality is not a dominant character in the wine but an additional, complexity-adding note. You'll certainly also find some wines that have herbaceous aromatics, such as the fresh, green grass character of some Sauvignon Blancs.

Structurally, aromatic whites can be slim, through a combination of relatively low alcohol and high acidity. Or they can be generous, from high alcohol and relatively low acid, along with intense flavors. Some Albariño wines—wines from a grape of the same name, grown in Northwestern Spain—typify the lighter-bodied, crisper end of this style's spectrum, while very ripe Gewurztraminer wines from Alsace exemplify the softer, fuller-bodied wines. Between these two extremes are many medium- to full-bodied wines that have a viscous, slightly oily texture.

The range of sweetness for this style extends from totally dry to medium sweet. (Really sweet dessert wines are not part of this style.) But you don't always fully perceive the sweetness of an aromatic white, if any exists: many wines with fairly high residual sugar levels have such high acidity that the acidity offsets the impression of sweetness. When you stop to think about it, you might agree that such a wine has sweetness, but otherwise, you're likely just to enjoy it without particularly noticing the wine's residual sugar.

One aspect of aromatic white wines that's fairly constant is their lack of oak in winemaking. Oak fermentation or aging would suppress the flavors of the grape and are therefore illogical for wines of this style. You can occasionally come across a wine from an aromatic grape, such as Viognier, that has been barrel-fermented; whether the wine still tastes like an aromatic white or whether

STYLISTIC SIBLINGS

ere's how the other styles of white wine relate to aromatic whites:

- Like most aromatic whites, fresh, unoaked whites tend to be high in acidity and do not have oaky aromas and flavors. But aromatic whites are entirely more flavorful than fresh, unoaked whites, and many of them are richer in texture.

- Earthy whites have minerally aromas and flavors, as many aromatic whites do, but aromatic whites have more pronounced aromatics, and minerality is just one aspect of those aromatics.

- Both aromatic whites and rich, oaky whites are fairly intense in aroma and flavor, but oaky whites tend to be fuller-bodied. And, of course, the flavor of oaky whites is mainly oakiness.

the oak has given it the characteristic of another style depends on the taste of that wine.

Every style of wine encompasses a range of expressions, but the aromatic white style is the most diverse. Maybe that's one reason why it is becoming so popular with connoisseurs. Many sommeliers routinely feature several aromatic white wines among their wine-by-the-glass selections, and many hard-core wine lovers (present company included) count aromatic whites among their favorite white wines.

SWEETNESS AND DRYNESS

Our favorite wines in the aromatic white style are the so-called dry aromatic whites. We say "so-called" because—as happens in all white wine styles—one person's dry is another's slightly sweet. We know lots of winemakers who assert that one half of one percent of residual sugar in a wine is the perceptible threshold at which people detect sweetness. All we can say is that our thresholds are much lower. A complicating issue is that high acidity (as well as a bit of carbon dioxide) can balance out sugar in a wine, so that a wine can taste less sweet than it actually is. A further complicating issue is that high alcohol can contribute its own sweet impression to a wine. In the end, you have to decide what's dry to you, what's off-dry but pleasantly so, and what's too sweet. And, of course, a wine that's too sweet with a certain food or in certain circumstances might be just right in others.

A wine that's too sweet with a certain food or in certain circumstances might be just right in others.

Plenty of aromatic whites are truly dry. Austria is one of the places that champions the dry, aromatic white style in its Rieslings, Grüner Veltliners, and Muscats. Some German producers make dry (labeled *tröcken*) Rieslings, too—but bear in mind that a German Riesling that's dry in one vintage could be less so in the next. Some Alsace producers make dry Riesling, Gewurztraminer, and Pinot Gris wines, but probably the majority these days aim for such ripeness in these wines that we personally perceive them to be sweet. (To our taste, too sweet, because we are so extremely fond of the very dry wines.) Italy's Vermentinos tend to be dry if they're from Liguria or Tuscany, but some of the Sardinian versions have a gentle sweetness to them. Among Spain's Albariño wines, how dry they are depends on the producer.

Ripeness as Style

Ripeness is one of the key determinants of how dry or sweet an aromatic white ends up being. When the grapes' juice is very ripe, it has enough sugar to ferment into high-alcohol wine that gives a sweet impression from its alcohol; ripe juice also gives rich flavors of ripe fruit that enhance the impression of sweetness, whether any residual (unfermented) sugar remains in the wine or not. Less ripe grapes cannot create sweetness in a wine without certain wine-making processes that sweeten the wine. (We discuss those later in this chapter.)

But how ripe the grapes are doesn't just depend on Mother Nature and her sunshine. The ripeness of the grapes also speaks to winemaking intent. Many winemakers who want to make extreme-ly rich aromatic whites grow their grapes in particular ways—reducing their crop size, for example, and harvesting late—to max-imize ripeness. Their wines have some sweetness because they grew the grapes that way. Certain producers in Alsace are prime examples of this facet of aromatic whites.

Extreme ripeness is very fashionable in winemaking these days, but not every winemaker worships at that altar. You can find truly dry aromatic whites if that's what you prefer. If you like the maxed-out style, you'll have abundant pickings in fine wine shops, because these wines are increasingly popular.

Subliminal Sweetness

Some aromatic white wines that are not bone dry almost don't strike you as being the least bit sweet. This phenomenon can occur when the wine's acidity is very strong. In some elite German Rieslings, for example, high acidity forms such a firm backbone for the wine that any sweetness comes across (depend-ing, as always, on your threshold) as richness and flesh rather than as sweetness. In our experience, in fact, it's a rare German Riesling that can taste balanced without a little residual sugar, because in general the acidity levels of these wines are very high. Acid needs either sugar or alcohol to balance it (see "Balance" in the chapter "Tasting Wine for Quality and Style"), and the nat-ural alcohol levels of most German wines are usually not up to the task.

Sweetness can also be subliminal in aromatic whites that are very fruity. In some Albariños, for example, the ripe apple flavors give us the impression that it's just the fruitiness of the wine that seems sweet, when in fact the wine has a bit of residual sugar.

WINE IS AN ACQUIRED TASTE

*W*e read about some research proposing that humans and other primates have an innate, evolutionary taste for alcohol, born from centuries of eating fermented ripe fruit in the wild. Maybe so, but we believe that wine is an acquired taste. We think that lots of people start off with the *idea* of enjoying wine and then learn to enjoy it by finding, through trial and error, wines that appeal to them. Often those first appealing wines are somewhat sweet. Some people stop there, and others keep trying different wines, gradually acquiring a taste for what wine geeks would call fine wine, as in dry wine.

If your own taste is for sweeter wines, then that's what you should drink. If you care to, you can acquire a taste for dryer wines when and if you feel like it.

Off-dry Styling

If you like white wines that have an easygoing sweetness to them, you'll be pleased to know that you can find them in this style.

These wines are intentionally sweet, not as a by-product of ripeness and not just to a subliminal degree. Their winemakers added sweetness to them or purposely retained some of the grapes' natural sugar instead of letting it all convert to alcohol. Often, the winemaking intent is to make a wine that will appeal to people who are new to wine, or who are accustomed to drinking other sweet beverages—and if that sounds like you, you should definitely check out wines in this style.

One way that winemakers create such wines is by back-blending unfermented grape juice into dry wine. The natural sweetness of the juice sweetens the wine and also dilutes its alcohol. In Germany, this process is responsible for the sweetness of many of the inexpensive, mass-market wines. If you read the labels on these wines, you'll see that they have alcohol levels as low as 7.5 per-

OFF-DRY VERSUS SWEET

*T*he term *off-dry* is one of wine's most marvelous contributions to the English language. It enables people to drink sweet wines with dignity in a culture that believes that sweet wines aren't good.

Actually, *off-dry* is a blanket term for table wines (as opposed to dessert wines) that have sweetness. Wine marketers, merchants and writers use this term when they think they might turn people off with the word *sweet*. But *off-dry* doesn't tell you how sweet a wine is.

If you're considering buying a wine that your wine merchant or waiter describes as "off-dry" and you'd like a more precise description of its sweetness, here's some language you can use. Ask him or her if the wine is "just off-dry" (meaning it's just over the edge of dryness), medium-dry, medium-sweet, or sweet.

cent—a bonus side effect for those who want to limit their alcohol consumption.

Wines can also be sweetened by adding concentrated grape juice. This technique doesn't lower the wine's alcohol much because the volume of juice that's added is smaller.

Some white wines made in an intentionally off-dry style also have oaky flavors—for example, many inexpensive New World Chardonnays. Because of their oaky character, those wines fall into the rich, oaky white style—at the sweeter end of it, of course. But if the wine has no oak and does have the flavors of aromatic grape varieties, it falls into this style.

THE GRAPES OF AROMATIC WHITES

It just so happens that many aromatic white wines are varietal wines—but they're not necessarily the usual varietal wines that you see in supermarkets. The grapes that make aromatic white wines include a few well-known varieties, and many more fairly esoteric varieties.

Muscat is one of the most aromatic varieties of all. Have you ever had a bottle of Asti, the famous Italian sparkling wine? (If you're wincing, you probably didn't have a fresh bottle; give the wine another chance.) The grape that gives Asti its captivating floral-fruity aromas and flavors is Muscat: a good Asti tastes exactly like freshly harvested Muscat grapes.

Muscat grows all over the world; in fact, several different Muscat grape varieties exist. It's used for sparkling wines such as Asti, and for dessert wines (see the sidebar "Three Faces of Dessert and Fortified Wines"). And a few Muscat table wines exist, too—notably Italy's fizzy, low-alcohol, off-dry Moscato d'Asti, Austria's dry Muscat wines, and the dry Muscat wines from the Alsace region of France.

Speaking of Alsace, the **Gewurztraminer** grape, which excels in Alsace, is another key aromatic grape. Gewurz (as it's known to its friends) smells and tastes like lychee fruit and roses, an amazingly exotic combination. Besides Alsace, Gewürztraminer grows in Germany, Northern Italy, California, New York, and a few other places. Because this grape does not have high acidity, the wines are often soft and ample, and they sometimes have a very slight earthy bitterness that counters their richness. Unless a winemaker imposes unusual restraint, Gewürztraminer wines are among the biggest and most intense of all white wines.

Viognier, a variety from France's Rhône Valley that's taking off big time in Southern France and California, and also grows in Oregon, Washington, and even Argentina, sometimes has aromas that you could confuse with Gewürztraminer or Muscat—floral, peachy, and perfumed, not unlike a bar of scented soap. Its acidity is marginally higher than Gewürztraminer's, though, which gives its wine a firmer profile in the mouth. As winemakers experiment with this variety, a number of versions are emerging, from outright floral with slight sweetness to aromatically intense but dry, and even rather subdued wines with a touch of gentle oak character.

Riesling is the noblest of all the world's aromatic white varieties. Apart from its legendary, late-harvest dessert wines, this grape makes bone-dry to somewhat sweet wines that have high acidity (assuming the grapes grow in an appropriately cool climate). Riesling wines have aromas and flavors of peaches, peach skins, apricots, citrus, or mixed fruits, along with mineral or delicate floral notes, depending on where they come from. The notion that Riesling wines are too sweet and not serious has somehow become prevalent among wine drinkers who are just getting started in wine, but in fact, Rieslings are among the finest white wines in the world. The grape is at its best in Germany, Austria, and the Alsace region of France; good Rieslings also come from Australia's Clare Valley, New Zealand, New York, Washington, cool pockets of California, and Oregon.

Several other grape varieties that make aromatic white wines are specialties of certain countries; most of these grapes do make varietally labeled wines. The grapes include the following:

- **Albariño**, a variety that grows in Northwestern Spain and (as Alvarinho) in the Vinho Verde region of Portugal. It has floral, citrusy, or ripe apple aromas and flavors, often combined with a vein of minerality, and it has high acidity. The wines range from dry to off-dry.

- **Grüner Veltliner**, an Austrian variety whose aromatics range from spicy to slightly vegetal to fruity (citrus, fig, pear) or minerally. The wines are generally dry, with high acidity.

- **Vermentino**, an Italian variety found mainly in Liguria, Tuscany, and Sardinia. Its aromas and flavors are citrusy, appley, or herbal. The wines tend to have a firm backbone of acidity. In Southern France, this grape is called **Rolle** and is part of many blended whites.

- **Fiano**, an Italian variety from Campania, the region where Naples is located. These wines are broad and fairly soft, with flavors of peaches, peach skins, and sometimes flowers.

- **Arneis**, a native Piedmontese variety that makes floral-scented wines.

- **Müller-Thurgau**, a German variety, is moderately aromatic. This grape mainly makes medium-dry blended whites that sell without a varietal name—such as Liebfraumilch.

- **Torrontés**, an Argentine variety, is extremely intense in aromatics. Like Muscat, Gewürztraminer, and Viognier, its aromas and flavors are very floral; the wines tend to have a very slight sweetness, but some are dry. Some vineyards lie at very high altitudes, where cool climate brings a refreshing acidity to the wines.

- **Moschofilero**, a Greek variety that makes wines with floral perfume but lighter body and higher acidity than Gewürztraminer.

Pinot Gris is technically not an aromatic grape. But some Pinot Gris wines do fall into this style, because in some places the grape makes very flavorful wines. Alsace Pinot Gris wines are generally aromatic whites, and so are some of Oregon's Pinot Gris wines. The great majority of Italian Pinot Grigios are not (they are fresh, unoaked whites, and the richer wines are earthy whites), but occasionally a Pinot Grigio from Friuli crosses the line into this style.

Sauvignon Blanc is another grape that plays it both ways—in fact, it goes in four directions. The grape itself is aromatic, and many of the wines made from it are aromatic whites. But some of its wines are earthy whites (many Pouilly-Fumés), some are fresh, unoaked whites (inexpensive white Bordeaux wines and Sancerres), and some are barrel-fermented, rich, oaky whites. New Zealand Sauvignon Blancs are squarely in the aromatic white style, as are those from South Africa. A few California Sauvignon Blancs and Fumé Blancs are aromatic whites, but usually their aromas are less intense than those of South African or New Zealand wines.

AROUND THE WORLD OF AROMATIC WHITES

Just about every country in the wine world produces at least some aromatic white wines, but this style is a specialty of moderate to cool climates. In warmer climates, aromatic grapes tend to be used instead mainly for producing dessert wines.

Germany and **Austria** excel in these wines. Austria's are almost always dry, with a few exceptions among the least expensive Grüner Veltliners, which can have some subliminal sweetness. Germany's aromatic whites—which are mainly Rieslings, but also include Gewürztraminers and blended whites—can be totally dry, pleasantly off-dry, or fairly sweet, although they always have refreshing acidity.

France's aromatic whites come from fairly warm, dry climates, namely, **Southern France** and **Alsace**. Viogniers from the **Languedoc-Roussillon** area in the south seem to have an almost New World flavor intensity, but the classic Viogniers from the **Rhône Valley** district of **Condrieu** can be somewhat more restrained. Blended whites from **Provence** often have an aromatic note from Viognier or Rolle. In Alsace, with the exception of Pinot Blanc and Sylvaner wines, all the whites fall into this taste category, but they vary wildly in richness, sweetness, and aromatic expression, because the region has so many producers.

With the exception of Muscat-based wines such as Moscato d'Asti, we find **Italy's** aromatic whites to be among the most reserved of this style. Italian winemakers have traditionally preferred to make whites that are fairly neutral in aroma and flavor, and when they do make wines from aromatic varieties, these wines are more restrained than they might be in others' hands. Italy's leading examples are varietally labeled wines from Vermentino, Fiano, Falanghina, Arneis, and sometimes Tocai Friulano.

The **United States** has a history of making inexpensive, rather sweet aromatic whites, usually blends of several grape varieties, for mass-market consumption. These wines have diminished in popularity, but they still exist. Today, the United States produces some fine Rieslings—mainly in **New York, Washington, Oregon,** and the cool edges of **California**. The riper, sweeter versions of Oregon's Pinot Gris wines are also aromatic whites, and you can find a few creditable Gewürztraminers in America, too.

Australia's most significant, serious contribution to the aromatic white category is its Rieslings from **Clare Valley** and nearby areas, which have earned a place in the firmament of great Rieslings. And we can't forget tiny **New Zealand**. Many Sauvignon Blanc wines from the **Marlborough** region redefine the term *aromatic,* so intense are their passionfruit, green citrus, or vegetal aromas and flavors.

This survey of regions producing aromatic whites is by no means exhaustive. As you explore the world of aromatic whites, you're sure to find some from **Portugal, Spain, Greece, Hungary**, and other wine-producing lands.

BALANCE DICTATES QUALITY

In determining the quality of an aromatic white, the first aspect you should consider is the wine's balance. Balance is an important marker of quality for all wines, but for aromatic whites, it is critical. Balance is operative in high-quality aromatic whites in two ways: acid balance and the balance of intensity between a wine's aromatics and its structure.

For wines that have either residual sugar or very high alcohol that contributes an impression of sweetness, quality often hinges on the acid balance. Without sufficient acidity, a very ripe wine can taste clumsy, and a sweet wine can taste cloying. If you are evaluating an aromatic wine that has richness or sweetness, hold the wine in your mouth and try to perceive some depth of acidity in the mid-palate; in the best wines, you'll notice (when you focus on it) that the acidity is high, giving the wine that mid-palate depth impression. When you just drink the wine, you might not even notice the acidity, though, because it operates in the background.

THREE FACES OF DESSERT AND FORTIFIED WINES

*F*or many wine drinkers, "wine" is table wine—regular, non-sparkling red, white, and rosé wines—with just an occasional deviation toward bubblies. Some of the most delicious and fascinating wines fall into another category, however. These are dessert wines and fortified wines. They are delicious and unusual, sometimes rare and expensive but sometimes very affordable. Connoisseurs drink them generally outside the normal course of a meal: either beforehand, as apéritif wines, or after a meal, as dessert or sometimes cheese wines.

Dessert wines are generally white. These sweet wines come from grapes that are unusually rich in sugar—so rich that it's impossible for all the sugar to ferment into alcohol. In some cases, a beneficial fungus called *Botrytis cinerea* infects the grapes, dehydrating them and concentrating their sugar, acidity, and aromatic compounds; Sauternes and the great German late-harvest wines, usually Rieslings, are examples. In other cases, winemakers dry grapes in the sun after harvesting, to desiccate them into near-raisiny richness; this process makes several Sicilian and Greek wines, among others. And some grapes freeze on the vine (or off the vine, with the help of technology) so that when they are pressed, still frozen, much of their water separates out as ice; these are Germany's *eisweins* and the ice wines that Canada excels in. Wines of this general style all have concentrated flavors of dried fruits or fresh fruits and extraordinary sweetness balanced by extremely high acidity. A wine like this can be a dessert unto itself.

You can encounter aromatic whites that are full-bodied and high in alcohol but relatively low in acidity; Gewürztraminer wines that are made from very ripe grapes can be an example. These wines manage to be balanced despite their low acidity because they are so high in extract (a wine's non-volatile solids). The extract

Fortified wines can be dry or sweet. The sweet versions come both red and white. These wines become sweet because of the winemakers' intervention: as the juice ferments, when only some of its sugar has converted to alcohol, the winemaker adds alcohol to the juice ("fortifies" it), stopping the yeasts in their tracks, and leaving natural sweetness in the wine. Port, usually red, is the prime example of this style; it is a very fruity wine that comes in various weights, intensities, degrees of seriousness, and prices, including some excellent under-$20 wines. Several wine zones of Southern France also make this style of wine, from white and red grapes; Muscat Beaumes de Venise is probably the best-known. The sweet types of Madeira are other examples. Sweet Sherries are a variation on this style, being fortified after all their sugar is converted to alcohol, but then sweetened; they are usually less fruity than Port. All these wines generally have about 20 percent alcohol. They excel after dinner, with cheese and dried fruits.

Dry fortified wines are the smallest of the three styles. Typified by fino-type Sherry and other dry Sherries, as well as the dryer Madeiras, these wines are fermented to dryness and left dry. Depending on the type, they are more or less delicate and range from about 15.5 to 20.5 percent alcohol. These are apéritif wines, for sipping with nibbles before dinner, or for drinking with soup.

seems to "ground" the wine in your mouth, giving it a sense of grip that balances the alcohol fullness. But except in these unusual cases, acidity is key.

The second key aspect of balance is the relationship of aromatics to structure. Imagine inhaling the scent of an intensely aromatic white wine, then sipping the wine and tasting the same intensity of flavor but feeling a thin, meager texture and structure. You might

The more intense the aromatics, the more structured the wine needs to be—in body, acidity, alcohol—to be in balance.

enjoy the flavor, but the wine would probably feel out of sync with itself. The more intense the aromatics, the more structured the wine needs to be— in body, acidity, alcohol—to be in balance. Some aromatic whites have fairly delicate structure, and this is not a fault provided that their aromatics do not overwhelm their structure.

Complexity of aromatics is another quality marker for wines of this style. Some wines are so amazingly, outrageously flavorful that it doesn't seem to matter that their aromatics are rather simple and one-dimensional. But you will probably tire of such a wine by the second glass. A really outstanding aromatic white has complex aromas and flavors, more or less intense, that intrigue you more with each sip.

Finally, concentration is necessary for greatness. A tasty but insubstantial wine can give you lots of pleasure, but it can never have the greatness and class of a wine whose flavors are tightly focused.

THE WORLD'S FOOD-FRIENDLIEST WINES?

Aromatic whites can be delicious on their own because they have so much flavor and personality. It's therefore ironic that they are also among the most versatile wines you can have on your dinner table.

White wines in this style excel particularly with cuisines that are challenging for other wines. These include cuisines with some sweetness, such as many Asian cuisines; those that have elements of hot spiciness, with or without sweetness, as some Indian dishes do; and those with sour elements.

Not every aromatic white goes with every challenging cuisine, of course; this is a fairly diverse style, and subsets of wines within it— the dry wines, for example, or Grüner Veltliners specifically—can have potential with certain foods that other aromatic whites don't.

We remember one experience at home that amazed us. Our

THE SOMMELIERS' CHOICE

*W*e know more than one sommelier who believes that Riesling is the food-friendliest wine on the planet. Its fruity flavors work double time to either complement or contrast with the flavors of a dish. It adds a dimension of flavor to simple foods and has enough complexity to work with dishes that are themselves complex. We recommend that you always have a bottle of good dry or off-dry Riesling on hand.

dinner was smoked pork chops, sauerkraut, and sweet caramelized onions, with spicy mustard on the side—four foods so different that we didn't imagine one wine might go well with the combination. We started with an Alsace Pinot Gris and were surprised to realize that it was all we needed for the entire dinner. It had enough flavor of its own to avoid being overwhelmed by the meal's strong flavors, and enough concentration, balance, and character to take on the acid, spice, and sweetness of the meal with aplomb.

Alsace wines in general are great choices when the meal has you wondering what wine could possibly work. Their rich but unoaked flavor and substantial weight can handle the acidity of tomatoes or sauerkraut, the fattiness of sausage, or the richness of cream sauces.

When pairing aromatic whites with food, consider the weight of the dish and the richness of the wine, as well as the sweetness of the wine and food. Pair richer wines with richer foods, and sweeter wines with foods that have either sweetness, spiciness, or fruity flavors. But the wines of this taste profile work with food in a way that seems to defy analysis. Just try an aromatic white, even if you're unsure about it; chances are the wine will surprise you.

When serving aromatic whites, you might want to vary the tem-

Pair richer wines with richer foods, and sweeter wines with foods that have either sweetness, spiciness, or fruity flavors.

perature of the wine according to the wine's sweetness and aromatic intensity. The less cold you serve a wine, the more ample it will taste, and the more flavorful—but it will also taste sweeter, if in fact it has any sweetness. If you have a fairly restrained dry wine, for example, serving it a bit less cool will enable its aromas and flavors to emerge. And if a wine has a tad more sweetness than you like, chilling it down will make its sweetness less noticeable.

PAIRINGS: AROMATIC WHITES WITH . . .

Popcorn

Raw nuts

Green olives, or sauces made with green olives or capers

Salads with bitter greens (spinach, kale, chard)

Mozzarella and tomatoes with olive oil

Soft cow's milk cheeses

German potato salad

Smoked meats or fish

River fish with creamy sauces

Onion tarts

Baked ham

Indian curries

Choucroute garni

Veal roast

AROMATIC WHITES:
WINES TO TRY

Since aromatic wines are most prevalent in moderate to cool climates, it's not surprising that many are produced in classic cool-climate regions, such as Northern Germany, Austria, Northern France, Northern Italy, and Northwestern Spain. Riesling, the uncrowned king of aromatic grape varieties, is at its best in Germany and Alsace—along with Austria—and we focus our aromatic white wine recommendations on this variety. In Austria, we also name several producers of Grüner Veltliner, this country's leading aromatic white. Alsace is chock full of aromatic whites; along with Riesling, the same producers typically make Gewurztraminer, Pinot Gris (sometimes labeled Tokay–Pinot Gris), and Muscat—all of them aromatic.

WINE	PRODUCER/BRAND	REGION	COUNTRY
Grüner Veltliner	Schlossweingut Bockfliess ▪ Brundlmayer ▪ Heidler; Hirsch ▪ Loimer ▪ Nigl ▪ Weingut Pfaffl ▪ Heidi Schrock	Various regions	Austria
Grüner Veltliner; Riesling	Hirtzberger ▪ Knoll ▪ Nikolaihof ▪ Franz Prager ▪ Domaine Wachau	Wachau	Austria
Muscat	Ernest Burn ▪ Marcel Deiss ▪ Domaine Ostertag ▪ Trimbach ▪ Zind-Humbrecht	Alsace	France
Riesling; Gewurztraminer	Jean-Baptiste Adam ▪ Lucien Albrecht ▪ Léon Beyer ▪ Paul Blanck ▪ Marcel Deiss ▪ Hugel ▪ Josmeyer ▪ Marc Kreydenweiss ▪ Kuentz-Bas ▪ Domaine Ostertag ▪ Clos St.-Landelin/Muré ▪ Charles Schleret ▪ Domaine Schlumberger ▪ Trimbach ▪ Domaine Weinbach ▪ Zind-Humbrecht	Alsace	France
Tokay–Pinot Gris	Jean-Baptiste Adam ▪ Lucien Albrecht ▪ Paul Blanck ▪ Marcel Deiss ▪ Hugel ▪ Josmeyer ▪ Marc Kreydenweiss ▪ Kuentz-Bas ▪ Domaine Ostertag ▪ Clos St.-Landelin/Muré ▪ Charles Schleret ▪ Domaine Schlumberger ▪ Domaine Weinbach ▪ Zind-Humbrecht	Alsace	France

WINE	PRODUCER/BRAND	REGION	COUNTRY
Riesling	Dr. Fischer ▪ Karlsmühle ▪ Kerpen ▪ Dr. Loosen Merkelbach ▪ Meulenhof ▪ Egon Müller ▪ J.J. Prüm ▪ Selbach-Oster ▪ Dr. H. Thanisch Erben Mueller-Burggraef ▪ Reichsgraf Von Kesselstatt ▪ Friedrich Wilhelm Gymnasium	Mosel-Saar-Ruwer	Germany
Riesling	Georg Breuer ▪ Leitz Erben Rudesheimer ▪ Knyphausen ▪ Robert Weil	Rheingau	Germany
Riesling	Heyl zu Herrnsheim ▪ Strub	Rheinhessen	Germany
Riesling	Basserman-Jordan ▪ Dr. Burklin-Wolf ▪ Lingenfelder ▪ Müller-Catoir	Pfalz	Germany
Riesling	Prinz zu Salm-Dahlberg ▪ Schloss Wallhausen ▪ Weingut Diel	Nahe	Germany

The Rieslings of the New World, although aromatic, tend to have less acidity than those from European vineyards, mainly because of generally warmer climates. Some of these wines fall into the easy-drinking subset of aromatic whites. Oregon's richer, sometimes sweeter Pinot Gris wines also belong here.

WINE	PRODUCER/ BRAND	REGION	COUNTRY
Riesling	Annie's Lane ▪ Jim Barry ▪ Grosset ▪ Mitchell ▪ Pike ▪ Reilly's	Clare Valley	Australia
Riesling	Henschke ▪ Leeuwin Estates ▪ Petaluma ▪ Pipers Brook ▪ Wolf Blass ▪ Yalumba	Various regions	Australia
Gewürztraminer	Sakonnet Vineyards	Rhode Island	USA
Pinot Gris	Oak Knoll ▪ Panther Creek ▪ Sokol Blosser ▪ Willakenzie Estate	Willamette Valley (OR)	USA
Riesling	Palmer Vineyards ▪ Peconic Bay	North Fork of Long Island (NY)	USA
Riesling	Arbor Crest ▪ Chateau Ste. Michelle "Eroica" and Cold Creek ▪ Hogue Cellars	Columbia Valley (WA)	USA
Riesling	Long Vineyards ▪ Smith Madrone ▪ Trefethen	Napa Valley (CA)	USA

WINE	PRODUCER/BRAND	REGION	COUNTRY
Riesling; Gewürztraminer	Fox Run ▪ Dr. Konstantin Frank ▪ Lamoreaux Landing ▪ Standing Stone ▪ Herman J. Wiemer	Finger Lakes (NY)	USA
Riesling; Gewürztraminer	Elk Cove Vineyards ▪ Montinore Vineyards	Willamette Valley (OR)	USA

Viognier has emerged in the last two decades as one of the most popular aromatic white varieties. It used to be known only by connoisseurs of Condrieu, a 100 percent Viognier wine from France's northern Rhône Valley. Now Viogniers are being made in all three West Coast states in the United States, on Long Island's North Fork, in North Carolina, in Argentina and Chile, in Southern France, in Australia, and in several other wine regions. In short, Viognier has arrived—and deservedly so, because it has one of the most tantalizing aromas of any variety, a blend of flowers, fruits, and herbs that is irresistible.

WINE	PRODUCER/ BRAND	REGION	COUNTRY
Condrieu/ Viognier	Patrick & Christophe Bonnefond ▪ Chapoutier ▪ Domaine Louis Cheze ▪ Jean-Luc Colombo ▪ Domaine Yves Cuilleron ▪ Delas Frères ▪ Domaine Philippe Faury ▪ Gilles-Barge ▪ E. Guigal ▪ Paul Jaboulet Ainé ▪ Domaine Alain Paret ▪ Domaine Georges Vernay	Rhône Valley	France
Viognier	Alamos ▪ Gascon ▪ Santa Julia	Mendoza	Argentina
Viognier	Bedell Cellars	North Fork of Long Island (NY)	USA
Viognier	W.B. Bridgman ▪ Columbia Winery ▪ Hogue Cellars ▪ McCrea	Columbia Valley/Yakima Valley (WA)	USA
Viognier	Griffin Creek	Rogue Valley (OR)	USA
Viognier	Freemark Abbey ▪ Miner Family Vineyards ▪ Turnbull	Napa Valley (CA)	USA
Viognier	Alban Vineyards ▪ Rabbit Ridge ▪ Wattle Creek	Various CA regions	USA

We never appreciated how aromatic Sauvignon Blanc could be until we came across our first New Zealand Sauvignon Blanc. Wow! Cut green grass, asparagus, passionfruit, lime, and more. South Africa also produces wonderful, aromatic Sauvignon Blancs, but they're slightly more subdued than the Sauvignons of New Zealand.

WINE	PRODUCER/BRAND	REGION	COUNTRY
Sauvignon Blanc	Babich ▪ Craggy Range ▪ Kim Crawford ▪ Drylands ▪ Goldwater ▪ Grove Mill ▪ Mount Riley ▪ Nobilo ▪ Selaks ▪ Villa Maria ▪ Wairu River	Marlborough	New Zealand
Sauvignon Blanc	Backsberg Estate ▪ Boschendal ▪ Nederburg ▪ Plaisir de Merle ▪ Seidelberg Estate ▪ Villiera Estate	Paarl	South Africa
Sauvignon Blanc	Groot Constantia ▪ Klein Constantia	Constantia	South Africa
Sauvignon Blanc	Neil Ellis ▪ Clos Malverne ▪ Mulderbosch ▪ Thelema ▪ Zonnebloem	Stellenbosch	South Africa

We conclude our aromatic white recommendations with a selection of Vermentino wines, the new "in" white Italian wine (made in three different Italian regions), as well as other Italian wines, the aromatic and affordable Torrontés wines of Argentina, the red-hot aromatic Albariño from Galicia in Northwestern Spain, and a few Greek wines.

WINE	PRODUCER/BRAND	REGION	COUNTRY
Torrontés	Santa Isabel ▪ Santa Julia ▪ Michel Torino	Mendoza	Argentina
Moschofilero	Antonopoulos ▪ Boutari ▪ Domaine Spiropoulos ▪ Tselepos	Mantinia	Greece
Falanghina	Cantine Farro ▪ Feudi di San Gregorio ▪ Montesole ▪ I Normanni ▪ Terredora ▪ Villa Matilde	Campania	Italy
Fiano di Avellino	De Concilis ▪ Feudi di San Gregorio ▪ Mastroberardino ▪ Terredora	Campania	Italy

WINE	PRODUCER/BRAND	REGION	COUNTRY
Moscato d'Asti	Ceretto "Santo Stefano" ▪ Dante Rivetti ▪ Paolo Sarocco ▪ La Spinetta ▪ Vietti "Cascinetta"	Piedmont	Italy
Vermentino	Colle dei Bardellini ▪ Terre Bianche ▪ Enoteca Bisson ▪ Lupi ▪ Terenzuola	Liguria	Italy
Vermentino	Antinori ▪ Cecchi	Tuscany	Italy
Vermentino	Capichera ▪ Sardus Pater ▪ Sella & Mosca ▪ Cantina del Vermentino	Sardinia	Italy
Albariño	Martin Codax ▪ Fillaboa ▪ Lusco ▪ Bodegas Morgadío ▪ Vionta	Rías Baixas	Spain

WINES ON THE MOVE: HOW INTENSE IS TOO INTENSE?

We feel as if we are repeating ourselves, but this is the reality today: wines are becoming richer, fuller-bodied, riper-tasting, and slightly sweeter than they used to be. This trend can take some aromatic whites over the top, into the realm of excessive weight, richness, and flavor intensity. If you enjoy this richness, then you'll be pleased, but if you prefer more moderate wines, you'll be left with fewer to choose.

But some winemakers who produce dry, firm aromatic whites seem to be truly committed to that style and we believe that they will not cave in to peer pressure to make richer wines. We foresee that the parameters of this style will remain the same at the dry end and stretch a bit in richness at the opposite end, and more wines will populate that richer extreme.

Rich, Oaky Whites

Full-bodied, flavorful whites with oaky character,

such as most New World Chardonnays, oaked

Sauvignon Blancs, elite white Bordeaux wines,

and other wines

The rich, oaky taste profile represents the most popular style of white wine in America today. We feel comfortable making that statement not because anyone ever did a survey of wine drinkers to determine which style they prefer but because Chardonnay—the runaway most popular type of white wine—typifies this style.

It's easy to understand why wine drinkers like rich, oaky whites. They're very flavorful, and they're very full. When you take a taste of a rich, oaky white, there's no doubt about it—you have a lot of wine in your mouth. With certain foods, wines in this style can be too powerful. But when you want a white wine that tastes important, this is the style that fills the bill.

Abundance and Opulence in a Glass

The two words that name this style say it all:

- **Rich.** These are full-bodied, substantial wines with high alcohol, made from very ripe grapes generally grown in warm climates.

- **Oaky.** The toasty, smoky aromas and flavors of oak infuse these wines—gently or assertively, depending on the wine.

It's not just the use of oak that places a wine in this stylistic category; it's also the innate richness of the juice from which the wine was made. As we mention in the "Fresh, Unoaked White Wines" chapter, winemakers tend to use oak treatment for a wine only when the wine is substantial enough to handle oaky character without being overwhelmed by it. (Lighter wines with oak treatment are like a little girl in her mother's oversized shoes and clothes.) For good wines of this style, the richness and the oakiness go hand in hand.

You might have enjoyed many a glass of a rich, oaky white wine without realizing (or caring) about the use of oak in winemaking. But oak is a defining issue in the taste of these wines. If a wine smells toasty or smoky—or charry, vanilla-like, butterscotchy, or even a bit like coconut—and has similar flavors, those characteristics are due to the oak, not the grape variety. Knowing this, you'll be able to ask for such a wine and get it.

Of the four styles of white wine, rich, oaky whites are the most intense and powerful wines.

Of the four styles of white wine, this style encompasses the most intense and powerful wines. But like each of the other styles, it groups together wines with individual differences. Some rich, oaky white wines sit at the extreme of richness and oakiness, while others are a bit less rich or wear their oaky character more subtly. And of course the wines within

STYLISTIC SIBLINGS

*H*ere's how white wines of the other three styles compare to rich, oaky whites.

- Fresh, unoaked whites are polar opposites of rich, oaky whites because they are lighter in body, are less intense in aromas and flavors, and have no oaky character.

- The richest end of the earthy white style can overlap somewhat with the most delicate end of the rich, oaky style, if the earthy wines are slightly oaky. But the earthy wines will be subtler in aroma and flavor and less oaky.

- Aromatic whites are akin to rich, oaky whites in that wines of both styles are fairly high in aroma and flavor intensity—but the aromas and flavors of aromatic whites are fruity or floral rather than oaky. Some aromatic whites also share a similar degree of sweetness with some oaky whites. But aromatic whites are generally lighter in body than rich, oaky whites, and most of them are also crisper and less soft.

this style vary in their aromas and flavors. Some are just toasty/smoky, while others have tropical fruit or other fruity flavors, mineral aromas, or rich, buttery notes.

Some oaky whites are built for aging. This group includes the most expensive Burgundies and Californian Chardonnays, which develop nuances and complexity as they age in bottles. But many rich, oaky whites are made for enjoying young.

NUANCES OF POWER

The white wines of the Burgundy region of France—which are made entirely from Chardonnay grapes—were the original rich, oaky whites. For more than half of the twentieth century, these wines were considered more or less the only great dry white wines in the world, and the best of them commanded the highest prices for dry whites. When winemakers in fledgling wine regions such as California and Australia began making Chardonnay wines, they often modeled their wines after Burgundies.

But outside of Burgundy, the style changed a bit, becoming fruitier, more oaky, sweeter, or simply more flavorful. Today, you can find a range of expressions within this style. The wines extend from the dry, full-bodied, but relatively subtle and relatively austere wines of Burgundy on one end to slightly sweet, tropical-fruity, very flavorful, overtly oaky wines at the other end.

As for all wines, the grape variety matters for this style. But real differences among wines in this style are due to where the grapes grow, what the winemaker has in mind when he or she makes the wine, the type of oak that's used, and the way that the winemaker uses that oak. In fact, taking just one grape variety, Chardonnay, as an example, dozens of variations on the theme of rich, oaky whites exist, depending on *terroir*, winemaking intention, and winemaking technique.

- **Barrel fermentation versus tank fermentation.** Classic white Burgundies are fermented in barrel—juice goes into the barrel, finished wine comes out—but some winemakers in other parts of the world choose instead to ferment the juice in stainless-steel tanks and then put the wine into barrels to age. Wine interacts differently with oak than juice does, and in the end, oakiness is actually more apparent in the taste of the tank-fermented wine.

- **Raw material.** The grape juice that makes the wine, even if it's the same variety—in this case, Chardonnay—is not the same everywhere, because of differences in local growing conditions, such as warmer or cooler climates, the yield of grapes per acre, or soil differences. And that's before we consider different *clones* of Chardonnay. A clone is a subdivision of a grape variety; numerous Chardonnay clones exist, each subtly different from the next in its growth pattern or the taste of its fruit. Some oaked Chardonnays are richer and fruitier than the Burgundian prototype as a result of clonal or vineyard differences.

- **Winemaking intent.** Winemakers in the New World prize flavor intensity in their wines, and a Californian or Australian Chardonnay is therefore more likely to be more overtly flavorful and less subtle than a white Burgundy.

- **Sweetness.** Many rich, oaky whites today have some sweetness to them, even if the wine trade categorizes wines of this style as dry white wines. This is particularly true of inexpensive white wines intended to appeal to a mass market. The sweetness can be due to high alcohol or unfermented sugar in the wine.

- **Malolactic fermentation (ML).** This optional process weakens a wine's acidity, reduces the impression of fruitiness in a wine, and softens the wine. Classic barrel-fermented whites usually go through ML and end up less fruity than they might otherwise be, with a soft, creamy mouth feel and sometimes a slightly buttery flavor. But sometimes winemakers avoid ML for oaked whites, or they use partial malolactic fermentation (letting ML occur in some of the wine but not in all of it). These wines can have a fresh, fruity character, even though they are also oaky. (To read more about ML, see Chapter 5 of *Wine For Dummies*, 3rd edition.)

THE GRAPES OF RICH, OAKY WHITES

So far, we've focused only on **Chardonnay** wines within this style. Chardonnay is by far the main grape variety for wines of this style, but the style also features wines of other grape varieties.

Some **Sauvignon Blanc** producers ferment the juice of this grape in oak. This creates a rich, creamy texture that's unusual for wines from Sauvignon Blanc; it also creates smoky aromas and flavors in the wine that sometimes are so strong that they subjugate the vivacious aromatics of the Sauvignon Blanc grape. If the winemaker oaks only part of the wine (for example, blending unoaked and oaked wines), the wine is less rich and less oaky. Ditto if the winemaker uses older oak barrels that have less oaky character to contribute. In these two cases, the wine could turn out to be a milder example of a rich, oaky white, or it could be an earthy white. Unfortunately, it's difficult to tell which style a Sauvignon Blanc wine has from reading the label. Our list of recommended wines later in this chapter names some that fall squarely into the rich, oaky style.

The top white wines of Bordeaux—which qualify as rich, oaky whites—are made from Sauvignon Blanc, often with some **Sémillon** blended in. Typical of Old World wines, they tend not to be particularly fruity, but they can be quite complex, especially as they age. Again, you can't tell from the label whether a white Bordeaux wine is crisp and unoaked or rich and oaky; generally, wines costing more than $30 a bottle are likely to be in the latter style.

Other grape varieties appear in this style as isolated examples. These include **Viognier,** which more commonly makes aromatic whites, as we describe in the chapter on that style, and **Pinot Gris,** which some Oregon wineries barrel-ferment or barrel-age.

AROUND THE WORLD OF RICH, OAKY WHITES

Whatever diversity the rich, oaky style lacks in terms of grape varieties, it makes up for in regional diversity. Just about every country in the world that grows Chardonnay (which is just about every country that makes wine) produces wine in this style.

Fairly warm wine regions favor the rich, oaky style because they foster very ripe grapes that are inherently rich and can handle the effects of oak. But wine regions with moderate climates can also pro-

HOW WINES GET THEIR OAKY CHARACTER

*W*ine columnist Matt Kramer once wrote that oak is to humans what catnip is to cats. In fact, the scent and flavor created by oak can be almost intoxicating in a wine. But the nature of a wine's oakiness varies according to which technique winemakers use to infuse that oakiness into the wine. These are the main techniques:

Oak barrels. The most natural way for wine and oak to marry is through the fermentation of the juice in oak barrels, or the aging of the wine in oak barrels. While the juice or wine sits in the barrel, it extracts aromas, flavors, tannin, and even certain sugars from the wood. When the juice actually ferments in oak barrels, the wine can also develop a rich texture from the interaction of the juice with the wood. The newer the barrel, the more of its character it has to contribute to the wine; barrels that have been used previously make less-oaky wine. Winemakers use new barrels or older ones—or both—according to the character of the juice or wine they have. They also choose certain types of oak—from specific French forests, for example, or from the Ozarks or even from Hungary—to get the effect they want in the wine. Finally, they select how much toasting or charring (a burning of the insides of the barrels) they want for their wine. All these variables affect the nature of a wine's oaky characteristics.

Oak staves. Barrels are pricey. The cost of one new barrel of French oak translates into more than $2 additional cost per bottle for the

duce wines in this style, in warm vintages or when the grape growers keep their yields low (which gives them riper, richer grapes).

Some key wine regions making wines in the rich, oaky style include **California, Australia,** the **Burgundy** and **Bordeaux** regions of **France, Southern France, Tuscany** and other Italian wine regions, **Chile, Argentina, Spain, Washington,** and **Oregon.**

To list California and Australia as single wine regions is a bit winemaker; that's more than $6 a bottle additional cost by the time the wine finds its way onto the shelf of your wine shop. Oaky whites are so popular that winemakers have had to find other, less expensive ways of achieving this style, and one of them is oak staves. These are planks of oak that are inserted into large stainless-steel tanks to mimic the effect of barrel fermentation or aging.

Oak chips. These are small pieces of wood that soak in the wine in a large "teabag," contributing oaky aromas and flavors to the wine.

Liquid oak extract. This is, in effect, oak flavoring that's added to wine.

Barrel fermentation is the gold standard of oak treatment, because it results in the best integration of oakiness within the wine. Barrel aging of a white wine that was fermented in stainless steel tends to give a slightly harder edge to the oak flavor.

The less expensive a wine, the more likely it is that the winemaker employed a shortcut to make it oaky, such as oak chips or oak extract. These shortcuts are perfectly appropriate for simple, inexpensive, everyday wines. But, as a clever South African winemaker remarked, in terms of quality and taste "there's a big difference between putting wine in oak and oak in wine."

simplistic, because each encompasses a wide variety of growing climates and soils. But oaky white wines (especially Chardonnay) are so prevalent that to list individual regions within each territory would be tedious.

In fact, we can't think of a single wine region within California that does *not* produce oaked Chardonnay. Although they are all the same style, the wines vary a lot in degree of oakiness, flavor intensity, and dryness. These differences are rarely obvious on the labels, other than an occasional reference to Burgundian techniques or barrel fermentation on a back label, which would suggest a dryer, more subtly oaked wine. But price is a fairly reliable indication of where a wine falls within this style.

- The least expensive wines, most of which label their origin as simply "California," generally come from grapes grown in the warm **Central Valley**; these wines often rely on oak chips or oak extract for their toasty, smoky flavor and often have a bit of appealing sweetness.

- California's very priciest Chardonnays—whose grapes come mainly from **Sonoma** and **Napa** counties, as well as the **Santa Barbara** area—are generally dry, barrel-fermented wines made in the Burgundian tradition, although their ripe, fresh fruitiness and sometimes their tropical fruit flavors usually distinguish them from Burgundies.

- In the middle price tiers—wines selling from about $12 to $35 a bottle—are Chardonnays that might have been produced either with barrel fermentation, with stainless-steel fermentation plus barrel aging, with oak-stave fermentation or aging, or with a combination of these methods. These wines vary in dryness and oakiness. You'll need to rely on trial and error—or the advice of a trusted wine merchant or sommelier—to determine which wines are most to your liking.

Other Californian wines in this style include oaked Sauvignon Blancs and Fumé Blancs and white Meritage wines. Meritage wines, made in California and other states, are usually oak-aged, because they emulate the style of the finest white Bordeaux wines.

Australia embraced the toasty, oaky, ripe-fruit style of Chardonnay in the mid-1980s, and plenty of wines still feature this style. But a trend toward unoaked Chardonnays exists, and, in the same spirit, many of the oaked wines show more restraint today than once; the Chardonnays of **Yarra Valley**, such as Green Point's, are particularly restrained. The exceptions to the trend are wines in the inexpensive tier of Chardonnays such as Yellow Tail, which not only are rich and oaky but also are somewhat sweet, to appeal to a mass market.

We mentioned the rich, oaked whites of Burgundy and Bordeaux—based on Chardonnay and Sauvignon Blanc, respectively—earlier in this chapter. Within Burgundy are two exceptions to this style: unoaked Chablis wines, which express either the fresh, unoaked style or the earthy style, depending on the particular wine, and the wines of the Mâcon district in southernmost Burgundy, which are mainly earthy whites. But **Pouilly-Fuissé**, the most elite of **Mâcon** whites, is usually rich and oaked. Southern France makes varietally labeled Chardonnays that are rich and oaky, but being European wines and fairly inexpensive, they tend to fall into the more restrained end of this style spectrum. In France's **Loire Valley**, this style is not common, but a few producers do make rich, oaky **Pouilly-Fumés**, which derive from Sauvignon Blanc.

Italian Chardonnays are often very dry and lean, with crisp acidity and a somewhat austere oakiness that comes from barrel aging, as opposed to barrel fermentation (although some fine barrel-fermented wines do exist). But inexpensive (under $10) Chardonnays from Northeastern Italy are sometimes not oaky at all. You can find an occasional oaked Sauvignon Blanc, such as the excellent Alteni di Brassica of Angelo Gaja, but many more unoaked Sauvignons. Italy does not have a tradition of barrel fermentation or aging for white wines, and its entries in this style are therefore relatively limited.

Other countries making at least a few rich, oaky whites (usually Chardonnays), in addition to those listed above, include **South Africa, Portugal, Greece, Israel,** and **New Zealand**—and we wouldn't be surprised to find this style in such improbable wine producing countries as India, China, Japan, or Zimbabwe, either, because it is so popular.

QUALITY MARKERS IN RICH, OAKY WHITES

Popularity breeds mediocrity. Many wines in the popular rich, oaky style are of low quality, even though they may be tasty and appealing when you just drink them down and don't pause to analyze their quality. But this style boasts some excellent wines, too. If you are concerned about quality, here are some issues to consider when you taste rich, oaky whites.

One of the main detractors from quality is overly high alcohol. On the positive side, high alcohol can give a wine a pleasant sweetness; a soft, viscous texture, and a mouth-filling generosity. But when it's too high, it overpowers the other elements of the wine, such as the wine's acidity and even its aromas and flavors. It causes the wine to be short (see our discussion of length in the chapter "Tasting Wine for Quality and Style"), and it can create a burning sensation in your mouth, even a slight bitterness and coarseness. Because ripe grapes, rich texture, and rich structure are key elements of the rich, oaky style, high alcohol is naturally part of the picture—but the best wines of this style manage to strike a balance between their high alcohol and their acidity.

Because ripe grapes, rich texture, and rich structure are key elements of the rich, oaky style, high alcohol is naturally part of the picture.

Sweetness is another common flaw in these wines. There's nothing wrong with sweetness in a wine, per se. But lots of winemakers use sweetness as a quick trick to make a wine appealing and to distract your palate from what else the wine has to offer, or not. And wines of this style are supposedly dry wines.

In many inexpensive Chardonnays, sweetness masks the burn and bitterness of overly high alcohol—an artful compounding of flaws that improves the taste of the wine somewhat but has nothing to do with quality. Besides being deceptive, sweetness also really limits the foods that you can enjoy with a wine. Oaky whites with sweetness can taste good when you sip them, but they are cumbersome during a meal.

STOPPING TO SMELL THE ROSES

*Y*ou don't ever have to decide whether a wine is of good quality or not; as long as you enjoy drinking it, that's really all that matters. We discuss the quality markers for each style not because quality is critical to your enjoyment of a wine but because, for us, quality is part of the aesthetic of wine. We believe that paying attention to the details of our wine—as well as our food, clothing, and surroundings—enhances the quality of our lives. But anyone can certainly enjoy wine without worrying about its quality.

High-quality wines in the rich, oaky style can often give an impression of slight sweetness, but that impression derives from factors such as ripe fruitiness, soft acidity, high alcohol (but not too high), and creamy texture from aging on the lees—fermentation deposits, discussed in the chapter "Earthy Whites." In these fine wines, a sweet impression is integral to the wine, not a cover-up that masks the other elements of the wine.

Dilution is a third shortcoming of many rich, oaky wines, and its opposite, concentration, is a real virtue in the better wines. In our experience, full-bodied wines often lack concentration: it takes a lot of stuff-of-the-grapes to fill a big wine, and many a big wine gets by on too little fruit character stretched too thin in the wine's full body and high alcohol. Some rich, oaky whites have a large presence in the mouth but give the impression of having no real center of gravity. They're all about hugeness and lots of oaky flavor, but they're empty in the middle.

The final quality detractor that we'll mention is too much oak. (And then we'll get on to the positive attributes these wines can have; they do indeed exist!) The issue of oakiness is like the glass being half full or half empty: we once heard a man who sells barrels to winemakers state that there's no such thing as an over-oaked wine—just under-wined wines! However you look at it, some wines in this style smell and taste too much of wood—even if it is smoky, exotic, and captivating wood—and not enough of the juice that, let's face it, is the wine. When you evaluate a rich, oaky white, search with your nose and your mouth (and your imagination) to find the wine inside the oak—the fruity, floral, or spicy character of the grapes, the mineral notes of the soil. If you can't perceive it, then the wine is over-oaked—or under-wined.

The quality markers for wines of this style are balance, concentration, and length. Actually, these are just the flip side of the flaws we discuss above. When a rich, oaky white wine is balanced, its alcohol level is not excessive, nor is its sweetness. When it's concentrated, it does not give an impression of being dilute, and it probably has enough fruit character to sustain its oakiness. When it has length, it's usually because that wine is well balanced and not overly high in alcohol.

Because the best wines of this style are capable of aging and developing for quite a few years after you buy them, you can encounter a wine that seems aromatically inexpressive. If it has good concentration and balance, and especially if you can sense a concentration of fruit character on the finish of the wine, it is probably just too young and will become richer in aroma and flavor over time.

The best rich, oaky wines are capable of aging and developing for quite a few years after you buy them.

In the average-quality ranks, most rich, oaky whites will not improve with age and are not meant to. They exist to give pleasure to wine drinkers who like lots of flavor (including the particular flavor of oak) and lots of weight in a white wine. And for that, they can be delicious.

RICH WINES, RICH FOODS

A rich, oaky white needs foods that can match either its weight or its flavor intensity (or both). Think creamy sauces, flavorful preparations such as grilling, and rich dishes such as chowders and stews. Foods that you might think of as swing foods—they could go

SERVING TIP: REIN IN THE POWER

*F*or the biggest, boldest, and sweetest of wines in this style—particularly inexpensive to moderately priced Californian and Australian Chardonnays—you might enjoy serving the wine colder than you'd normally serve a white wine. (Chill it for two or three hours in the coldest part of your refrigerator.) The cold temperature will make the wine's high alcohol less obvious, and will also undercut any sweetness in the wine. As for the wine's flavors, well, they'll also be toned down a bit by the cold, but these wines are often so aromatically intense that you'll still get a lot of flavor out of them. And if a wine is very inexpensive, we're actually not averse to putting a single, small ice cube in the glass; the ice dilutes the high alcohol as it melts.

Another way to tone down a rich, oaky white that's a bit overpowering is to serve it in a fairly narrow, slim wineglass, as opposed to a glass with a big, wide bowl. We can't explain why, but narrower glasses seem to make wines taste less huge and more concentrated.

with either white or red wine—are candidates for these wines, the richest of all dry whites. Foods with some sweetness or fruitiness are good bets for the fruitier New World wines of this style. And salty foods can be good matches because the saltiness agrees with any sweetness that the wine might have.

Because they are so flavorful, rich, oaked whites can be delicious on their own, and some of the richest of them (especially if they have some sweetness) might be better alone than with most foods. But you should be aware how high in alcohol and powerful some wines of this style are; their 14-plus percent alcohol can go right to your head if you're not eating.

We're not big believers in pairing wines and foods according to the flavors that each has. We believe that the weight and flavor intensity of the food and of the wine are more critical than the precise flavors themselves. But if you like to match flavors, by all

The weight and flavor intensity of the food and of the wine are more critical than the precise flavors themselves.

means try wines of this style with smoked meats, which will harmonize with the smoky, toasty flavors of the wine, or with fusion cuisine that incorporates fruity elements. By the same token, drink them with buttery popcorn!

If you're trying to eat lightly, or if warm weather inclines you to eat light, fresh foods, this is not the style of wine that's likely to be ideal. These wines can overpower delicate foods.

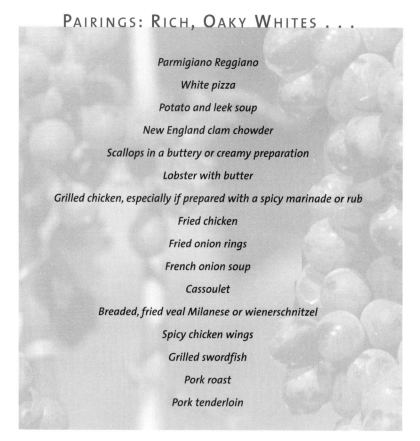

PAIRINGS: RICH, OAKY WHITES . . .

Parmigiano Reggiano

White pizza

Potato and leek soup

New England clam chowder

Scallops in a buttery or creamy preparation

Lobster with butter

Grilled chicken, especially if prepared with a spicy marinade or rub

Fried chicken

Fried onion rings

French onion soup

Cassoulet

Breaded, fried veal Milanese or wienerschnitzel

Spicy chicken wings

Grilled swordfish

Pork roast

Pork tenderloin

RICH, OAKY WHITES: WINES TO TRY

Almost every wine region in the world makes some version of rich, oaky whites, especially wines made from Chardonnay. Rather than recommend an endless list of such wines from around the world, we select a few leading examples, many of which are among our favorite wines of this type. California and the Burgundy region of France set the tone for rich, oaky whites, and therefore many of our recommendations come from these two regions.

WINE	PRODUCER/BRAND	REGION	COUNTRY
Chardonnay	Catena "Alta" ▪ Santa Julia "Reserva"	Mendoza	Argentina
Chardonnay	Casa Lapostolle ▪ Concha y Toro "Amelia" ▪ Errazuriz ▪ Haras de Pirque	Casablanca	Chile
Bâtard-Montrachet, Puligny-Montrachet	Etienne Sauzet	Burgundy	France
Chardonnay	Altera ▪ Faucon Bleu ▪ Fortant de France ▪ Domaine St. Martin de la Garrigue ▪ Réserve St. Martin	Pays d'Oc	France
Chassagne-Montrachet	Domaine Guy Amiot ▪ Domaine Colin-Delégér ▪ Domaine Jean-Noël Gagnard ▪ Bernard Morey ▪ Marc Morey	Burgundy	France
Chevalier-Montrachet, Puligny-Montrachet	Domaine Leflaive	Burgundy	France
Corton-Charlemagne	Bonneau du Martray ▪ Louis Jadot ▪ Louis Latour	Burgundy	France
Meursault	Patrick Javillier ▪ Louis Jadot ▪ Domaine François Jobard ▪ Domaine Olivier Leflaive ▪ Domaine Guy Roulot ▪ Verget	Burgundy	France
Pouilly-Fuissé	Daniel Barraud ▪ Domaine Robert Denogent ▪ Château Fuissé ▪ Domaine Roger Lassarat	Burgundy	France

WINE	PRODUCER/BRAND	REGION	COUNTRY
Chardonnay	Cabreo "La Pietra" ▪ Cervaro della Sala	Tuscany	Italy
Chardonnay	Gaja "Gaia y Rey" ▪ Pio Cesare "L'Altro"	Piedmont	Italy
Chardonnay	Backsberg Estate ▪ Boschendal Estate ▪ Glen Carlou ▪ Nederburg ▪ Plaisir de Merle	Paarl	South Africa
Chardonnay	Klein Constantia	Constantia	South Africa
Chardonnay	Hamilton Russell	Walker Bay	South Africa
Chardonnay	Neil Ellis ▪ Jordan ▪ Louisvale ▪ Thelema	Stellenbosch	South Africa
Chardonnay	Mount Eden Vineyards	Santa Cruz Mountains (CA)	USA
Chardonnay	Domaine Drouhin ▪ Eyrie Vineyards Reserve ▪ Ponzi Vineyards Reserve	Willamette Valley (OR)	USA
Chardonnay	Beringer ▪ Château Montelena ▪ Forman ▪ Grgich Hills ▪ Long Vineyards	Napa Valley (CA)	USA
Chardonnay	Arrowood Vineyards ▪ Château St. Jean ▪ Ferrari-Carano ▪ Fisher Vineyards ▪ Hanzell Vineyards ▪ Kistler ▪ Marimar Torres Estate ▪ Peter Michael ▪ Sonoma-Cutrer	Sonoma County (CA)	USA
Chardonnay	Handley Cellars	Mendocino (CA)	USA
Chardonnay	Chalone ▪ Estancia ▪ Talbott Vineyards	Monterey (CA)	USA
Chardonnay	Au Bon Climat ▪ Byron ▪ Cambria	Santa Barbara (CA)	USA
Chardonnay	Chateau Ste. Michelle Cold Creek Vyd. (also, Canoe Ridge Vyd., Indian Wells Vyd.) ▪ Columbia Winery	Columbia Valley (WA)	USA
Chardonnay	Pellegrini Vineyards ▪ Pindar Vineyards	North Fork of Long Island (NY)	USA

Among wines based on Sauvignon Blanc, many California Sauvignon Blancs and Fumé Blancs exemplify the rich, oaky style, as do a few Pouilly-Fumés from France's Loire Valley. The best white Bordeaux wines (which are usually a blend of Sauvignon Blanc and Sémillon) are subtler versions of this style.

WINE	PRODUCER/BRAND	REGION	COUNTRY
Bordeaux Blanc	Domaine de Chevalier ▪ Château La Louvière ▪ Château Malartic-Lagravière ▪ Château Smith-Haut-Lafitte	Péssac-Léognan	France
Pouilly-Fumé	Didier Dagueneau ▪ La Doucette	Loire Valley	France
Sauvignon Blanc	Rudd Estate ▪ Selene	Napa Valley (CA)	USA
Sauvignon Blanc	Chalk Hill ▪ Kalin Cellars ▪ Matanzas Creek	Sonoma (CA)	USA
Sauvignon Blanc	Bernardus	Monterey (CA)	USA
Sauvignon Blanc	Babcock ▪ Brander ▪ Fiddlehead ▪ Gainey ▪ Sanford ▪ Flora Springs "Soliloquy"	Santa Barbara (CA)	USA
Sauvignon Blanc	Raphael	North Fork of Long Island (NY)	USA

Chablis and Viognier are two types of wine that can have different styles, depending on who makes the wine. In the chapters on fresh, unoaked whites and earthy whites, we suggest some Chablis wines made in the fresh, unoaked style or the earthy style; here we recommend two very fine Chablis wines that are superb rich, oaky whites. Viognier is generally an aromatic white, but here we name one Californian rendition in the rich, oaky style.

WINE	PRODUCER/BRAND	REGION	COUNTRY
Chablis	René & Vincent Dauvissat ▪ Raveneau	Burgundy	France
Viognier	Calera	Mt. Harlan (CA)	USA

WINES ON THE MOVE: IF OAKINESS WENT OUT OF FASHION . . .

Oak will always be used to make the top white Burgundies and other elite wines of this style, because winemakers believe that it enhances quality. But for inexpensive and mid-priced Chardonnays and similar wines, oak is used mainly because wine drinkers like oaky wines and buy them. If the mass market were to move away from oaky wines, we bet that many winemakers would abandon their oak chips, staves, and liquid extract faster than you can say "fresh, unoaked whites." This trend has begun, to some extent, in Australia, where some Chardonnays are unoaked and some others are fairly restrained in their oakiness.

As the fashion of wine moves in this less oak-emphatic direction, wine drinkers who love the rich, oaky style will still find plenty of wines to enjoy. The wines might be less opulent and less smoky/toasty than they are now, but they'll still be rich and flavorful compared to most other white wines.

Mild-mannered Reds

Easy-drinking, subtle reds, such as inexpensive

red Bordeaux wines, traditional Rioja wines,

Northeastern Italian Merlots and Cabernets,

simple Chiantis, and similar wines

You're tired. It's been a long day, and you just want to relax over dinner. You don't want a wine that challenges you. What you'd like is a dry red wine that's pleasant and easy to drink without making any demands on your attention or your energy, like a familiar friend. Well, that's exactly what the wines that we call "mild-mannered reds" are all about.

Unlike most of our other style categories, this one has a name that's more fanciful than it is part of real-world wine lingo. If we were to ask people in the wine trade what they would call this style, most of them would probably say "light reds." That term doesn't satisfy us because some wine drinkers might think it refers to a wine's color (which it sometimes also does, but not necessarily) and because it focuses on a single taste aspect, a wine's body. Wines in this category are somewhat light and unimposing in other ways besides their body; for example, they generally have fairly subdued aromas and flavors, and they are not very tannic.

So we reached back into our pasts—way back, to the days of

STYLISTIC SIBLINGS

*I*n the spectrum of red wines, mild-mannered reds are the lightest, the mildest in flavor, and structurally the least aggressive. Here's how the other three styles of red wine compare.

- Soft, fruity reds have more aroma and flavor intensity than these wines, and their aromatics are more overtly fruity.

- Spicy reds also have more pronounced aromas and flavors, as well as slightly more weight, denser texture, and, especially, an angularity of mouth feel as opposed to the suppleness of mild-mannered reds.

- Powerful reds have more force and presence in your mouth, due to their fuller body, higher tannin, and, generally, their more intense flavor.

Superman comics—and came up with this Clark Kent metaphor for this wine style. Which is appropriate on another front: like Clark Kent, these wines are not necessarily the insignificant weaklings that some people might think they are. They can be legitimately good wines, but milder, more considerate, and mannerly.

ELEGANCE AND FINESSE, FOR CIVILIZED TASTES

Appreciating mild-mannered reds requires a certain sensitivity. Those who are accustomed to bolder, more flavorful wines will probably find these wines lacking in intensity—flavor intensity as well as intensity of personality—but other wine drinkers will find that they strike just the right balance. For certain foods and certain occasions, they are certainly the appropriate choice.

Generally, mild-mannered reds are light- to medium-bodied and truly dry, with a low to medium amount of tannin that is not drying or astringent. Their specific aromas and flavors vary according to grape variety and the individual wine; they are not overtly, unmistakably fruity, the way that those of soft, fruity reds are, but they can in fact be fruity. They can also be vegetal or herbal, or earthy. Whatever the aromas and flavors are, their intensity is subtle. You could drink a glass of one of these wines without ever stopping to think about what the flavors are; they are pleasant, that's all.

Whatever the aromas and flavors are, their intensity is subtle.

Mild-mannered reds range in texture from thin (remember, this is a characteristic, not a flaw) to slightly fleshy or slightly velvety. If you prefer wines that are dense and richly textured, you're more likely to find what you're looking for in the other three red wine styles.

When you taste a mild-mannered red, rather than describing its flavors per se, you might be inclined to describe its weight, texture, or overall impression—remarking that it's a smooth wine, for example, or that it's elegant. The composite personality of these wines—gentle, easygoing, and full of finesse—is what characterizes them best.

These are wines that suit simple foods, simply prepared. They would be overwhelmed by a steak smothered with spicy steak sauce, but they're terrific with a plain steak or simple grilled lamb chops. They are classic wines for classic foods—nothing too ethnic or avant-garde.

Mild-mannered reds are classic wines for classic foods— nothing too ethnic or avant-garde.

COOL CLIMATES AND A GENTLE TOUCH

Mild-mannered red wines tend to come from wine regions with mild climates. Bordeaux is the classic example—a region with a temperate climate buffered by the maritime influence of the Atlantic Ocean. In mild climates, grapes don't get so incredibly ripe that they automatically make robust, high-alcohol reds. With lower levels of natural sugar than they would have in warmer climates, the grapes make wines of more restrained alcohol levels, generally from 12 to 13 percent, and light to medium body. The tannins of these grapes might not have the chance to ripen and soften the way that they could in warmer climates, and that means these wines can have some perceptible tannin. The relatively high

WHO SAYS WINES HAVE TO BE FRUITY?

*O*nce upon a time, the only wines that were intense in aroma and flavor were fortified wines such as Ports, aromatic whites such as German Rieslings and Alsace Gewurztraminers, and great old Bordeaux reds. That was in the days when European wines were the only game in town. Then along came California, Australia, and other young whippersnappers, and suddenly the world was full of intensely flavored wines. University-educated winemakers decreed that wines should be fruity. (This is presumably because they're made from fruit—grapes—but if that's the reason, why is it acceptable for them to taste like cherries?) Procter & Gamble–trained marketers decreed that wines should have lots of flavor, in keeping with consumer demand for ever more flavorful fast foods. Now, wines that are subtle in flavor or not fruity are second-class citizens.

Of course we exaggerate. But frankly, we sometimes get bored with the fruity, flavorful sameness that pervades red wine production today. If you find that you like the style of a mild-mannered, subtle red, don't let any wine insider tell you that it's not really very good, because it "lacks fruit." Just enjoy it and applaud yourself for helping to support diversity in red wines.

acidity of the grapes—another effect of the mild climate—works with the tannin to give these wines a lean, linear profile in the mouth. But despite this structure, the wines are not really all that tannic by today's standards. That's because mild-mannered reds usually don't age in new oak barrels. The wines have tannin of their own, but not additional oak tannin.

Two other factors can govern this style. One is high crop levels. When vines are cultivated in such a way that an acre of land yields a large quantity of grapes, those grapes are generally less ripe (have lower sugar levels, leading to lower-alcohol wines, and have higher acidity and leaner tannins) than they would be if crop levels were kept lower. Many mild-mannered reds in fact come from wine regions where crop levels are fairly high. A favorable consequence, besides creating this style of wine, is that large yields make less expensive wines.

The final factor giving birth to mild-mannered reds is the mind-set of the grape grower and winemaker. Wines of this style generally don't come from winemakers schooled in the creed of fruit-driven wines. In the industrially farmed vineyards of California's Central Valley, for example, crop levels are very high, but the wines tend not to be mild-mannered reds (more likely they're in the soft, fruity style) because the meteorological climate and the winemaking climate both favor ripe fruit and flavorful wines. Mild-mannered reds tend to come from Old World regions where a tradition of subtle, food-friendly, fairly light red wines guides winemakers.

THE GRAPES OF MILD-MANNERED REDS

We bet that you could make a mild-mannered red wine from just about any red grape variety, but certain varieties seem disposed to this style. Principal among these are **Cabernet Sauvignon** and **Merlot**.

If you are familiar mainly with high-quality Napa Valley and Sonoma Cabs and Merlots, you might think we're crazy, because those wines are anything but subtle. Actually, California's top wines from these varieties are in a class by themselves and are not typical of how Cabernet Sauvignon and Merlot perform elsewhere in the world. And remember, oaky character is a big factor in the taste of those California wines; remove oak from the equation, and you have far less flavorful wines, although still powerfully structured.

The Cabernet grape, as it manifests itself in most of the wine world, is not rich in aroma and flavor. Textbooks say that black currant is the typical aromatic of Cabernet, and sometimes you can actually detect that. In some regions, Cab has a slightly minty character. When the grapes are somewhat underripe, the aromas of the wine are vegetal, like green peppers. Not exactly a huge array of aromas and flavors, is it? Without a blending grape or two to give the wine a little pizzazz, or oak barrels to contribute spiciness and perfume, or age to give it complex earthy and leathery notes, Cabernet is fairly one-dimensional, aromatically speaking. That's why many mild-mannered reds happen to be made from Cabernet.

Merlot has a richer aromatic profile than Cabernet does, but still a sedate one compared to many other grape varieties for red wine. Plums, tea leaves, and dried herbs are typical, and some people say that Merlot smells or tastes somewhat like chocolate. When the grapes are underripe—as they can be when crop levels are high—the aromatics veer toward the herbal and vegetal, rather than the fruity. Without the extra oomph of oak, all these aromatics are rather quiet, the way fans of mild-mannered reds like them.

Grenache is another grape predisposed to this style of wine, at least as it is grown in most vineyards. Old-vine Grenache wines from Australia are powerful reds, as are those few Châteauneuf-du-Pape wines that rely on intensely flavored Grenache grapes grown at very small crop levels. But typically, Grenache dilutes both the aromatic intensity and the tannin of wines with which it's blended, making the wines milder.

Sangiovese is another candidate, provided that it is (a) grown in Italy and (b) grown at high crop levels to make inexpensive wine. Wines made from such Sangiovese grapes tend to be thin in texture, and this is a typical characteristic of mild-mannered reds. And all Sangiovese wines tend to be fairly restrained in aroma apart from oak aromas and flavors, showing just a bit of tart cherry and sometimes nutty character.

Because most mild-mannered red wines are European, they often carry place names rather than grape variety names.

Other grape varieties that you'll encounter when you drink mild-mannered reds include Spain's **Tempranillo** (which can make wines in all four styles), Italy's **Nebbiolo**, and various lesser-known varieties. Because most mild-mannered red wines are European, they often carry place names rather than grape variety names. (You can read about wine names in Chapter 4 of *Wine For Dummies*, 3rd edition.) We discuss these wines in our geographic survey of mild-mannered reds, in the next section.

AROUND THE WORLD OF MILD-MANNERED REDS

One of the first wine regions that comes to mind when we think about mild-mannered reds is **Bordeaux**. But Bordeaux produces a huge amount of red wine, and not all of it is the same style. The less expensive Bordeaux reds are the mild-mannered ones; the elite, expensive Bordeaux reds tend to be powerful reds (see the chapter on that style).

These less expensive wines include regional Bordeaux wines—those that bear the region-wide appellations "Bordeaux" or "Bordeaux Supérieure"—as well as some *petits châteaux* wines from specific areas within the region, such as **Médoc**. (Refer to Chapters 4 and 5 of *French Wine For Dummies* for a rundown of the geography and winery structure of Bordeaux.) We list a few specific Bordeaux wines later in this chapter; your wine merchant should be able to recommend others. Ask for a generic Bordeaux red (the least expensive wines), or a wine from an unclassified château (fairly inexpensive wines), and be sure to say that you want something that's not very fruity or intense.

Although the **Southern Rhône Valley** of France is a warm wine region, some inexpensive **Côtes du Rhône** wines qualify as subtle, mild-mannered reds. A large quantity of red wine exists under the Côtes du Rhône name; because these are blended wines from several grape varieties—gentle Grenache, spicy and flavorful Syrah, meaty Mourvèdre, supple Cinsault, and so on—the wines vary in style according to their grape blend. They also vary according to their winemaking: some winemakers strive for a fruity, modern style, while others favor a less intense, traditional style. We recommend some mild-mannered Côtes du Rhône reds in the section "Wines to Try" later in this chapter.

Red wines from **Northeastern Italy** also come to mind. Just as in Bordeaux, it is the least expensive wines from this area that tend to be in the gentle, mild-mannered style; producers who want top dollar for their wines tend to make either powerful reds or spicy reds. Many Cabernets and Merlots from the regions of **Veneto, Trentino–Alto Adige,** and **Friuli** share this style; often, the wines come from grapes of more than one region and carry the designation *IGT* (Indicazione Geografica Tipica) *delle Venezie.*

You can also find wines of this style from elsewhere in Italy, with the exception of the southern regions, such as Puglia, where warm weather predisposes the wines to a more powerful taste profile. The wines of the Valtellina area, in the **Lombardy** region, for example, are generally mild despite being made from the powerful Nebbiolo grape; the northerly situation of the vineyards prevents the wines from being ripe enough to be powerful. But in our experience, the mild-mannered style is widespread only among inexpensive Northeastern Italian reds.

It is the least expensive wines from [Bordeaux] that tend to be in the gentle, mild-mannered style.

Ten years ago, **Chianti** wines typified this style, but today richness seems to be the winemakers' goal more than finesse. This change is due to new clones of the Sangiovese grape that achieve a higher degree of ripeness, the use of new oak barrels to age the wine, warm vintages such as 2000 and 2003, and probably even the use of concentration techniques by some winemakers. (The sidebar "Power on Demand" in the chapter on powerful reds describes these techniques and their effect on the wines.) Despite the shift in style among many winemakers, lots of Chianti wines are still in the mild-mannered style, however. These will be the least expensive wines, generally those that cost about $12 or less a bottle, with the geographic designation of simply "Chianti" rather than the more elite "Chianti Classico." Some varietally labeled Sangiovese wines from **Tuscany** also fall into this style—but we're talking value Sangiovese wines here, not elite "Super-Tuscan" wines.

Spain's premier red wine region, **Rioja**, is another place where wine style is shifting away from the gentle and toward the more intense and powerful. Nonetheless, you can find subtle, mild-mannered Riojas from more traditional producers. The fairly intense aromatics that are typical of these wines rank the wines among the most flavorful in this style. You can also find some wines from **Navarra**, blended from Cabernet, Merlot, and Tempranillo, that have this style.

Some **South African** red wines are subtle and mild-mannered. This might be a bit surprising because South Africa is technically part of the New World of wine, and many South African reds are in fact fruity, spicy, or powerful. But you can find wines characterized by subtlety and finesse, particularly blended wines from grape varieties used in Bordeaux—Cabernet Sauvignon, Cabernet Franc, and Merlot.

Defying Today's Notion of Quality

Some of the terms that we've used to describe mild-mannered reds—such as "light," "lean," or "thin"—are often pejorative terms in most wine circles. Today's concept of wine quality doesn't favor wines that are not fruity, flavorful, and concentrated, and characteristics such as thin texture or relatively light body are therefore considered negatives. In fact, most wines in the mild-mannered red style probably don't receive particularly high grades from most wine critics. (Many of these wines score in the mid-80s on a 100-point scale.) They are like dusty-pastel or earth-tone rooms in an industry that favors rich mahogany and dark red upholstery.

It's true that today's viticultural and winemaking knowledge could "improve" many of these wines. Smaller crop levels could make the wines richer, removing water from the juice could make them more concentrated, and using new oak barrels could make them more flavorful and intense. Of course, all of these measures would make the wines more expensive, not to mention that they would start to taste more like other wines. In other words, the style would become extinct. That would be a pity for those who enjoy these wines.

The important point to remember is that quality does not count in the absolute. It matters only within the context of style. Your first goal should be to get a wine that has the taste profile you prefer. Secondarily, you can look for the highest-quality wines that style has to offer.

The highest-quality wines in this style are those that are balanced. A little too much tannin relative to their alcohol and weight, a touch of sweetness that the lean structure can't support—these imbalances can be jarring in a wine whose whole personality is

TO AGE OR NOT TO AGE

*M*ost mild-mannered reds are ready to drink when you buy them, especially inexpensive Bordeaux and Northeastern Italian wines. These inexpensive wines are released to the market when they are about two years old, and when you buy them, they will usually be two to three years old. If they are older, be cautious. Oxidation resulting from poor storage is a particular problem for this style of wine because the wines don't have lots of tannin as a line of defense. And wines of this style often don't enjoy the turnover of those in more popular styles.

Some mild-mannered reds can age a bit after you buy them young, and can even improve; examples are mid-priced Bordeaux wines, such as many *cru bourgeois* wines. A rule of thumb is to enjoy these wines within five years of the vintage date, provided that you have good storage for them.

understated. Likewise, aromas and flavors that are intense can overpower a wine's trim structure.

A flaw that mild-mannered reds can have is being tired, lacking freshness. Now, these wines are not particularly vibrant or bright, and those who don't like this style (or who don't approve of it) would characterize them *all* as tired. But even if you like the style, you could encounter a wine that you feel might have tasted better a year ago. It might have dull, slightly cooked flavors of oxidation, or a flatness of structure that's atypical for this style.

Mild-mannered reds should strike you as gentle, easygoing, and undemanding of your palate. If a wine makes you stop and wonder whether it's really balanced, whether it might be too old, then it is not a successful rendition of this style.

HOLD THE SWEETNESS, HOLD THE SPICE

Mild-mannered reds are made to be enjoyed with food, and in fact they taste best that way, because they lack the flavor intensity to stand alone. They can be extremely satisfying with many dishes and very easy to drink.

But if you like foods with lots of flavor—"special recipe" fried chicken, tacos, bacon cheeseburgers, chili, and buffalo chicken wings, for example—you won't find this style of wine very compatible with your food. Not that a mild-mannered red will taste bad with this food: it will just be wiped out by the dish and won't bring much to the table (so to speak) besides the fact that it's liquid. A fruity or spicy red would be far more harmonious with these foods.

The gentle nature of mild-mannered red wines shines when the wines are paired with subtly flavored or simple foods. A rare steak, a perfect lamb chop, a simple hard cheese, a grilled portobello mushroom—foods such as these are equal matches for understated wines.

Although it's best not to overwhelm these wines with very flavorful foods, you can choose foods that contrast with the wines in weight. For example, if you were eating fettuccine with a home-made *ragú bolognese* (a fairly mild-tasting tomato-meat sauce), a mild-mannered red could be fine, despite the fact that the dish is heavier in style than the wine is. In pairings like this, the wine becomes the relief, refreshing your mouth between bites of food and lightening the weight of the meal. Similar pairings would be a mild red with beef stew, cheese-bedecked simple pizza, mushroom risotto, or roasted duck (hold the fruit sauce).

Because they are relatively light in weight, you can enjoy mild-mannered reds in warm weather.

Because they are relatively light in weight, you can enjoy mild-mannered reds in warm weather, if you're inclined to drink red wine rather than white. They are also appropriate for informal occasions because they are generally inexpensive wines rather than pricey, "important"

RETRO REDS

*M*ild-mannered reds are old-fashioned wines, in the sense that they are not the ripe, fruity, concentrated wines that are so common today. If you want a mild-mannered red, tell your wine merchant or restaurant server that you'd like a traditionally made or "retro" red—not a modern wine.

wines. Don't serve them in oversized wineglasses or in wide-bowled balloon-type glasses because these glasses will cause the wine's flavors to seem weaker. Glasses with fairly narrow bowls, of the sort that are traditional for Bordeaux, will cause the flavors to taste more concentrated and will enhance the wines.

PAIRINGS: MILD-MANNERED REDS WITH . . .

Mild cheeses such as Edam, young Gruyère, young Fontina, or young sheep's-milk cheeses

Cobb salad

Chicken salad

Stewed chicken

Sautéed chicken with mushrooms

Toasted ham and cheese sandwiches

Lamb shish kebabs

Pork roast

Grilled swordfish

Grilled vegetables

Risotto of almost any kind, except with fish

MILD-MANNERED REDS: WINES TO TRY

Although you can find examples of this style all over the world, most mild-mannered red wines come from temperate climates in the Old World, and so many of our recommended wines in this category are from France and Italy.

Good places to begin your search are the Bordeaux region of France, the neighboring wine districts of Southwest France, and the Rhône Valley. Look for inexpensive red Bordeaux; they will not have been aged in new oak barrels, we guarantee, because that would make the wine too expensive. Côtes du Rhône wines are also inexpensive, and are mild-mannered enough to go with all sorts of everyday cuisine, such as salads, sandwiches, or roasted meats and vegetables.

WINE	PRODUCER/BRAND	REGION	COUNTRY
Bordeaux	Château Bonnet (Rouge) ▪ Château Lauretan ▪ Michel Lynch Cabernet Sauvignon ▪ Michel Lynch Merlot ▪ Mouton-Cadet Rouge	Bordeaux	France
Côtes de Bourg	Château Roc de Cambes	Bordeaux	France
Côtes de Castillon	Château Cap de Faugères	Bordeaux	France
Côtes du Rhône	Château Beauchêne ▪ Domaine Brusset ▪ Domaine de la Buissonne ▪ Domaine Gramenon ▪ Domaine de la Guicharde ▪ Château des Tours	Rhône Valley	France
Gascon Rouge	Domaine du Mage Rouge	Southwest France	France
Haut-Médoc	Château Bel-Air ▪ Château Coufran	Bordeaux	France
Margaux	Château Clairefont	Bordeaux	France
Premières Côtes de Blaye	Château La Tonnelle	Bordeaux	France
St.-Julien	Château Gloria	Bordeaux	France

Italy makes lots of mild-mannered red wines, most of which are inexpensive. Try any of our recommended Italian reds below, such as a Merlot or a Sangiovese, to capture the mild-mannered Italian experience. Needless to say, these wines are a natural when accompanying classic Italian cuisine.

WINE	PRODUCER/BRAND	REGION	COUNTRY
Cabernet Sauvignon	Josef Brigl ▪ Cavit ▪ Kettmeir	Trentino–Alto Adige	Italy
Carmignano Riserva	Capezzana	Tuscany	Italy
Chianti (not Classico)	Badia a Coltibuono "Cetamura" ▪ Cecchi ▪ Melini "Borghi d'Elsa" ▪ Ruffino "Aziano"	Tuscany	Italy
Merlot	Alois Lageder ▪ Josef Brigl ▪ Cavit ▪ Kettmeir ▪ La Vis ▪ Torre di Luna	Trentino–Alto Adige	Italy
Merlot	Borgo Conventi ▪ Le Due Terre ▪ Pierpaolo Pecorari ▪ Plozner ▪ La Roncaia ▪ Ronco del Gelso ▪ Villa del Borgo ▪ Vistorta ▪ Volpe Pasini ▪ Zamò & Zamò	Friuli	Italy
Sangiovese (inexpensive)	Badia a Coltibuono "Cancelli" ▪ Melini	Tuscany	Italy
Sassella, Grumello, Inferno, Valgella	Nino Negri, Rainoldi	Valtellina (Lombardy)	Italy

We conclude our mild-mannered red wine recommendations with a couple of choices from Spain, a classic Old World country, and a few selections from South Africa, a New World country with strong Old World roots, which these wines reflect.

WINE	PRODUCER/BRAND	REGION	COUNTRY
Cabernet Sauvignon	Klein Constantia	Constantia	South Africa
Cabernet Sauvignon	Nederburg	Paarl	South Africa

WINE	PRODUCER/BRAND	REGION	COUNTRY
Cabernet Sauvignon	Louisvale	Stellenbosch	South Africa
Cabernet/ Merlot blend	Rozendal ▪ Villiera Estate	Paarl, Stellenbosch	South Africa
Merlot	Meerlust ▪ Zonnebloem	Stellenbosch	South Africa
Navarra	Bodegas Guelbenzu "Evo"	Navarra	Spain
Rioja	El Coto "Crianza" ▪ Bodegas Montecillo "Crianza"	Rioja	Spain
Tempranillo	Bodegas Ramón Bilbao	Rioja	Spain

WINES ON THE MOVE: THE QUEST FOR POWER

Producing wine is a business. Winemakers all over the world need a market for their wines, either in their home countries or abroad. Because the United States is the largest market for wine in the world, in terms of dollar value, wineries everywhere eye this market and try to gear their production to the tastes of this market.

What are those tastes? Power, richness, flavor intensity. Dark-colored reds with rich, soft texture and a bit of sweet, ripe fruitiness. In other words, the opposite of mild-mannered, subtle reds.

We have already seen some lean, subtle reds become fleshier and softer in recent vintages, and we expect this trend to continue, as long as critics harbor a fondness for huge, rich wines. We don't believe that the types of wine that we discuss in this chapter will ever become overtly fruity, at least not any time soon, because that would be a jarring departure from what they are. But more weight, softer texture, and more denseness are undoubtedly on the horizon for today's mild-mannered reds.

If you really like the lightest and leanest of these wines and in the future they become harder to find, consider drinking dry rosés, which will veer into this style if they, too, become more substantial.

Soft and Fruity Reds

Uncomplicated, youthful reds, such as most Beaujolais

wines, many Southern Rhône wines, some Southern

Italian reds, some Pinot Noirs from the New World,

some U.S. Merlots, and inexpensive American and

Australian reds

Ever since *60 Minutes* aired its report on the "French paradox" in 1991, which suggested that red wine is healthful, red wines have gained in popularity at a faster pace than white wines in the United States. The skins of grapes, which are necessary for making red wine (but not white wine), contain substances that have proven to have beneficial health effects. But healthfulness aside, many wine drinkers prefer red wines because they are generally more substantial than white wines, and often more flavorful.

The red wines that fall into the soft and fruity style are the easiest red wines to drink. They have delicious fruity flavors—such as cherries, berries, or plums—and they are fairly soft in texture, without a lot of the mouth-drying tannin that you can find in some other styles of red wine. (See the chapter "Tasting Wine for Quality and Style" for information on tannin.)

Soft, fruity reds are the best red wines for those who are just getting into wine or those who usually drink white wine. But even serious red wine drinkers who prefer wines of power and character can enjoy the wines in this easier style as a change of pace for casual occasions, or when hot weather makes a richer red taste too heavy.

As Easy as Red Can Get

Most red wines have fruity aromas and flavors when they are young. But in many wines, that fruitiness mingles with earthy notes, a spicy quality, vegetal aromas and flavors, or—especially in the case of powerful reds (see the chapter on that style)—the charry, smoky character of oak. What distinguishes the wines in this category is that their fruitiness is their salient flavor characteristic. Unlike wines in the other three styles, these wines are fruity for fruitiness' sake. The most typical examples of soft, fruity reds can have aromas and flavors of red berries, dark berries, cherries, plums, currants, and other fruits.

Even wine drinkers who prefer wines of power and character can enjoy soft, fruity reds as a change of pace.

Some soft, fruity reds can have a slight hint of oak in their aroma and flavor—a gentle vanilla note, for example—that doesn't overpower their fruitiness. These wines don't have mouth-drying oak tannins, however. When the exposure between wine and oak is brief, such as when oak chips are used for flavor, a wine can be oaked and yet turn out soft and fruity.

Wines in this style are fairly low in tannin, which makes them soft and smooth for red wines. Some wines in this category can have a backbone of acidity that renders them less soft and fleshy than others—Bardolino, a red wine from Italy, comes to mind—but they are nevertheless not very tannic. Other wines can be slightly sweet, within the range of sweetness that today qualifies as dry wine, but many of them are bone dry. However, they are not dry in *texture*, thanks to their low tannin.

In terms of weight, most wines in the soft, fruity style range

STYLISTIC SIBLINGS

*H*ere's how the other three red wine styles compare to soft, fruity reds:

- Mild-mannered reds are simply less fruity than wines of this style, and their aromas and flavors are less intense. They can be similar structurally—in their light to medium weight, and in their low tannin profile—but aromatically, they are quite different.

- Spicy reds are less smooth and soft, more angular in your mouth rather than round; they grip your tongue in a way that soft, fruity reds don't. Their aromas and flavors are as intense as those of fruity reds, but they are more focused and vibrant, and their fruity aromatics are strictly those of fresh fruits, not baked or candied fruits.

- Powerful reds are fuller-bodied and far more tannic. Those that are fruity can be similar to soft, fruity reds in their aromatics, but they are also oaky in aroma and flavor, and their fruity character is often compact, tightly knit, and less obvious.

from light-bodied to medium-bodied. Some wines from warm climates are made from such ripe grapes that they have fairly high alcohol, up to about 13.5 percent, and this alcohol gives them weight and fullness. But they are still low in tannin, and of course they're fruity.

When you taste a soft, fruity red, you could fault it for not tasting important enough, like a serious, age-worthy red wine. But you'd have to admit that it's tasty and easy to drink. And that's what these wines aim to be.

A STYLE IS BORN

Many more soft, fruity reds exist today than twenty years ago. This is an inherently modern style of wine that many wine drinkers have found extremely appealing, and winemakers all over the world are scrambling to make more and more red wines in this style.

Some wines like this have been around seemingly forever, such as Beaujolais and Valpolicella. But the style has exploded thanks to New World winemakers who believe that a fruit-driven, approachable taste profile is exactly what most red wines should have—apart from elite, super-premium wines that are naturally more powerful. Most inexpensive New World wines today sport this style, and many inexpensive European wines emulate it, showing more fruitiness today than they traditionally have.

The primary requirement for soft, fruity reds is nicely ripe grapes, so that their flavors are fruity and their tannins are fairly soft. This gives an edge to wine regions that are warm enough to get good ripeness in their grapes year after year, such as California, Washington, and Australia.

Another requirement is that winemaking minimize tannin, or maximize fruitiness so that it outweighs the wine's tannin. Just about all dark grapes have tannin in their skins and seeds (and stems). Red wines need those skins to get color—therefore red wine has tannin. But winemakers can limit the amount of tannin in a wine. For example, controlling the length of time when the skins intermingle with the juice during fermentation can reduce the amount of tannin that actually finds its way into the wine. And using little or no oak prevents the leaching of strong wood tannins into the wine. To make low-tannin reds, winemakers can also choose a grape variety that's relatively low in tannin, such as Pinot Noir.

Most wines that fall into the soft and fruity category are made using techniques such as these so that the wines are not particularly tannic or dry-textured. This gives an edge to large wineries with state-of-the-art technology. These wineries churn out large quantities of popularly priced wines under best-selling brands.

Many wines in this style come not from grapes grown in small, specific wine districts but large viticultural areas. For example, you're much more likely to see "California" or "Southeastern Australia" on the labels of these wines than "Dry Creek" or "Yarra

Valley." That's probably because when the producer's aim is to express the fruitiness of the grapes, nuances of *terroir* that come from specific districts are irrelevant. Also, declaring a larger territory as the wine's origin enables producers more leeway in purchasing grapes, which keeps the taste consistent and prices down.

In our experience, most European wines that qualify as soft and fruity fall into the somewhat less fruity and less aromatically intense end of this style's spectrum—with the obvious exception of Beaujolais Nouveau. And the few South American wines that fall into this style are less overtly fruity, slightly more tannic, and less fresh and bright in personality than North American and Australian wines of this style.

THE GRAPES OF SOFT AND FRUITY REDS

Some white grape varieties seem destined from birth to become fresh, unoaked white wines or aromatic whites, but the destiny of red grape varieties is more dependant on upbringing than genes.

Red grape varieties that are naturally tannic can make wines that are not particularly tannic if the winemaker carefully controls the skin contact—the process of soaking the dark skins in the grapes' juice. Conversely, red grape varieties that are fairly low in tannin can become tannic, fairly powerful red wines if the wine ages in oak barrels that contribute wood tannin.

Some red grape varieties, particularly **Pinot Noir**, have very fruity aromas and flavors that predispose them to the soft, fruity style of wine. But in general the intensity of fruitiness in red wines depends less on the specific grape variety and more on how the grapes grew. Take **Grenache**, for instance. This variety has fabulous raspberry character, but in many large vineyards in the Southern Rhône Valley, the crop levels are so high that the wines lack sufficient concentration and are not very fruity at all. Another example is **Cabernet Sauvignon**, which tends to be more vegetal than fruity when grown in the typical Bordeaux vineyard but usually expresses a real fruitiness when grown in California.

All of this means that choosing a wine according to its grape variety is not a reliable method for finding soft and fruity reds: This style cuts too easily across grape variety lines. But if you have a favorite red grape variety, chances are that you can find it in a soft, fruity style wine. Here are some examples.

- **Merlot.** As a grape, Merlot is not very tannic, and it can have fruity plum flavors when the grapes are ripe enough. But "important" Merlot wines—the expensive wines—are aged in oak barrels, and all that oak tannin makes them more powerful than soft. Inexpensive Merlots, especially from New World areas such as California and Washington, are more likely to be soft and fruity. Look for Merlots that cost about $12 or less a bottle.

- **Cabernet Sauvignon.** Just what we said for Merlot, except that this variety is innately tannic. Nevertheless, inexpensive versions are often soft and fruity. Value-priced Californian and Australian Cabs are particularly good bets.

- **Syrah.** Forget the pricey Syrahs and Shirazes that win wine competitions and score high with the critics, because they are usually powerful reds. Focus on $15-and-under wines, especially Shiraz wines from Australia.

- **Pinot Noir.** You'll find lots of good pickings with this variety, as long as you steer clear of the most expensive wines—say, $35 and up. Again, New World versions, from the United States and Australia, are more likely to be in the soft, fruity style. Some Bourgogne Rouge wines—the basic red wine from France's Burgundy region, made entirely of Pinot Noir—are fruity and others are less so, but most of them are fairly low in tannin; higher-pedigree reds from Burgundy tend to fall into the spicy or powerful styles. Likewise, some New World Pinots are unpredictable, because they could have been made with a relatively high amount of oak.

- **Zinfandel.** Many a red Zin falls into this style. Just avoid the single-vineyard Zinfandels and those produced in small lots from old vines. Your basic $8 to $20 Zin will give you all the fruitiness and softness that your mouth desires—although some can lie on the stylistic cusp between fruity and spicy reds, because of Zin's herbal notes.

- **Sangiovese.** Many Italian wineries make an inexpensive, varietal Sangiovese in the soft, fruity style, although some Sangioveses can be mild-mannered instead; producers with a more modern bent tend to make the fruitier wines. Californian Sangiovese wines, on the other hand, tend to be either spicy or powerful in style.

Price is a better indicator of a soft and fruity style wine than grape variety is.

In every case, price is a better indicator of a soft and fruity style wine than grape variety is. You might not consider yourself a typical wine drinker, but if you like soft and fruity reds, you should seek out inexpensive, mass-market brands made for the typical consumer.

AROUND THE WORLD OF SOFT, FRUITY REDS

Some red wines that are classic examples of the soft, fruity style do not carry grape variety names but are named instead for the European wine regions where they come from.

Rouge à la Française

Beaujolais is one of them. Not only that, but Beaujolais is the quintessential soft and fruity red. If you like this style, you owe it to yourself to explore Beaujolais wines. Beaujolais is made entirely from the Gamay grape. It's often said that Gamay is not a tannic variety. Actually, Gamay is tannic—but most of the time, Beaujolais is not a tannic wine because of how it is made. Winemakers often

Shortcuts to Finding Soft, Fruity Reds

*W*hen you don't have the benefit of a good wine merchant or sommelier to guide you, you can better your odds of finding a soft, fruity red by remembering these general guidelines:

- Look for inexpensive wines, as they are less likely to be oaked—and even those that are made using some sort of barrel alternative, such as oak chips, aren't particularly tannic because the chips contribute the aroma and flavor of oak more than its tannin.

- Look for New World wines, especially those from California and Australia, which pride themselves on being "fruit-forward."

- Look for young wines, not more than three years old.

- Among European wines, look for wines from warm climates, such as Southern Italy, Central Spain, and Southern France.

- Look for the word *bright* (as in "bright cherry flavors," for example) on the back label of a wine; it's a descriptor commonly used by those who market wines in this style.

use a particular method called carbonic maceration to ferment Gamay (see "Fermenting Inside-out" in this chapter); this method accentuates fruitiness and diminishes tannin, to make flavorful, fruity wines that are enjoyable when they're young. Beaujolais Nouveau, the young wine released in late November every year, is always in this style. Many wines labeled "Beaujolais" or "Beaujolais-Villages" are also soft and fruity, although not to the extreme of the Nouveau wines. The top wines of the Beaujolais region—which are named for specific vineyard areas, such as **Brouilly** or **Juliénas**—can fall into the spicy red style instead. But the largest producer, Georges Duboeuf, makes almost all of his Beaujolais wines in the soft, fruity style.

Another region that produces soft, fruity reds is the **Southern**

Rhône Valley of **France**. The basic red wines here are called **Côtes du Rhône** and are blends of several grape varieties, primarily Grenache, Syrah, Mourvèdre, and Cinsault. They can be more or less fruity, depending on their specific grape blend, how the grapes grew (see our comment on Grenache in the section "The Grapes of Soft and Fruity Reds," earlier in this chapter), and how the wine was made. Some winemakers use carbonic maceration, the Beaujolais technique, to reduce the tannin of the Syrah component, for example. Generally, Côtes du Rhône reds won't ever be as fruity as a typical, inexpensive Californian or Australian red. They occupy the somewhat more restrained end of the fruity, soft style, and are fairly reliably low in tannin.

Many of the simplest red **Burgundies** are soft, fruity reds. These are labeled **"Bourgogne Rouge"** and sometimes also have the grape variety name, Pinot Noir, on their labels. As a group they tend to be less intense in aroma and flavor and less fruity than

FERMENTING INSIDE-OUT

The technique that many winemakers in Beaujolais use to reduce tannin and accentuate fruitiness in their wines—carbonic maceration—is now practiced in many wine regions of the world, using many different grape varieties. In this process, the grapes are not crushed to make a "soup" of grape solids and juice that ferment together in a big vat, as would be the normal procedure. Instead, whole bunches of red grapes are left to ferment, with their juice still intact within the grape berries. Fermentation occurs from the inside out, triggered not by yeasts on the outside of the skins but by chemical processes inside the grapes. This process draws lots of fruity aromas and flavors from the grapes, but not the tannins that result from normal fermentations. Sometimes wines made in this method have a characteristic youthful, grapey aroma.

Pinot Noir wines from **California, Oregon,** or **Australia**. They occupy the dryest, most restrained end of this style's spectrum.

Rosso and Tinto

Southern Italy has its share of fruit-driven, low-tannin reds. These wines are generally made from native Italian grape varieties that are fairly obscure to most wine drinkers, such as Negroamaro, Primitivo, and Nero d'Avola. They often have regional names, such as **Salice Salentino**, rather than grape variety names. What makes these wines fruity is not so much a concerted effort on the part of winemakers to produce a fruity, clean, modern style of wine as much as the high level of ripeness that naturally occurs in the grapes under the warm southern sun. For inexpensive wines, winemakers generally do not use much oak, if any, and the wines are therefore not very tannic. Sometimes their high alcohol can put them on the cusp of the powerful red style, however. Later in this chapter we mention several Southern Italian reds to try.

Northern Italian reds tend to be leaner and less soft than Southern Italian wines, but some of them do fall into the soft and fruity category. **Bardolino** and **Valpolicella** are prime examples. Both are made from native Italian varieties, in neighboring vineyard areas around the city of Verona; of the two types, Bardolino is the lighter-bodied. Each can have a good backbone of acidity, which makes them less soft than some wines in this style, but they are not very tannic, and they have aromas and flavors of fresh, tart red fruits. Valpolicella wines that are made using a process called *ripasso*—a second fermentation of sorts—can be quite fruity, but they are often rich enough that they are barrel-aged and oaky; as a general guideline, look for Valpolicellas that cost less than $18 a bottle if you're going for the fruity style.

The youngest, freshest wines from Spain's **Rioja** region are usually soft and fruity. These wines, made mainly from Tempranillo grapes, might be labeled "Crianza," which means that they've had some wood aging at the winery, but not much compared to the

Reserva and Gran Reserva wines of the region. You can also find wines of this style from other Spanish regions such as **Navarra** or **Toro**. But beware of Spain's tendency to make wines that are firm from oak and high in acidity, for a combined effect that's not soft; when in doubt, ask your retailer.

Oz and Apple Pie

A real treasure trove of soft fruity reds comes from Australia. The Australians are geniuses in knowing what kind of wine people like to drink, and determining how to make it. They pioneered a technique of very short skin contact for red wines that prevents harsh tannins from entering the wine but still gives the wines plenty of color. (The secret is a rotating fermentation tank that mixes the juice and skins well enough to get color quickly, before the tannins can dissolve into the juice.) And the fruitiness of the wines is a given, considering Australia's many warm climate zones and the shared belief of most of the winemakers that wines ought to express the fruity characteristics of their grapes. If you are a fan of soft, fruity reds, by all means try just about any inexpensive Australian red. The more expensive wines are still fruity, but they can have so much oak tannin that they fall squarely into the powerful red style. And some mid-priced Shirazes are spicy reds.

California's less expensive red wines are made in the same spirit of fruitiness, freshness, and drinkability as Australia's are. Wines costing less than $12 are probably in this style, almost regardless of grape variety, while wines costing between $12 and $15 might be or not, depending on their oak treatment and tannin content. The same is true of Washington's wines and many other U.S. wines.

Oregon makes plenty of soft and fruity reds because its **Willamette Valley** region is such a gifted area for growing Pinot Noir grapes. Even Oregon's top Pinots can appeal to lovers of this wine style—but the less expensive the wine, the better the odds that it will not be very oaky.

Can a Soft, Fruity Red Be Seriously Good?

Because red wines in the soft and fruity style are usually inexpensive, always easy to enjoy, and often targeted to the mass-market wine consumer, they generally don't get high scores from wine critics. These are the kinds of wines that critics will say are "good quality for the price" or will describe as "well made," rather than wax poetic about their attributes. But remember: it's a wine's taste characteristics that determine whether you enjoy a wine, not its quality rating from a critic. Wines in this style can be delicious, even if they are not serious enough to be in the ranks of the world's greatest wines.

In fact, the best wines in this style have all the positive characteristics of quality wine: length, depth, balance, concentration, and so forth, as discussed in the chapter "Tasting Wine for Quality and Style." All they lack is age-worthiness—the ability to improve over several years—and the sophistication that subtlety can bring. Soft, fruity reds are best when they are young, while they still express their fresh, primary-fruit character. (After all, isn't that the reason you like them in the first place?)

Soft, fruity reds are best when they are young, while they still express their fresh, primary-fruit character.

Overt sweetness is an occasional flaw in wines of this style. What do we mean by "overt"? Sweetness that you notice, sweetness that prevents the wine from tasting good with the kinds of foods you expect a so-called dry wine to taste good with. The perception of sweetness depends on your own tongue and on the particular balance of the wine, so you have to be the judge of what's too sweet and what isn't.

Another issue can be excessive fruitiness—so much fruitiness that you suspect you're drinking fruit juice instead of wine. And some tasters who detect the flavor of candied fruit (as opposed to fresh fruits, dried fruits, or cooked fruits) in a wine could consider that a sign of lower class, if not necessarily lower quality.

SERVING TIP: USE IT OR LOSE IT

*W*ine drinkers who enjoy wine only occasionally can end up accumulating bottles of wine that go unopened for a couple of years. That's a particular pity for soft, fruity reds, because these wines are best young. As they get older, they can lose their exuberant fruitiness and their fresh personality. Aim to drink soft, fruity reds within two to three years of the vintage date.

Many soft, fruity reds—especially inexpensive, mass-market wines—might taste contrived to expert tasters, meaning that the taster can perceive the winemaking in the wine. (The wine doesn't taste as if it could naturally have the flavors and characteristics that it does.) To a regular wine drinker, such a wine can be delicious, because the winemaker did his or her job very well. If you like the wine, don't worry about what another person thought of it; just enjoy. And certainly many wines in this style are truly enjoyable even to connoisseurs.

AT THE TABLE

As the lightest and fruitiest of red wines, wines in this style occupy the middle ground of food compatibility—where you find yourself when you're not sure whether to choose red or white. Meaty fish such as swordfish and salmon, pastas and risottos that are not strong in flavor, vegetarian dishes with delicate or subtle flavors: all these foods are candidates for soft, fruity red wines (or white wine).

A soft, fruity red could also be good with fairly mild meat dishes, such as a simple veal roast or a pork roast. Their fruitiness will bring another dimension to the meal, like another food on the table. They also can contrast nicely with spicy dishes, giving your mouth a welcome, fruity break between tastes of fire.

Unlike red wines in the subtle, mild-mannered style that we

discussed in the previous chapter, fruity reds have enough flavor intensity to stand up to flavorful foods, even if the wines are not full-bodied. We almost always reach for a soft, fruity red on Thanksgiving, because any red wine with a lot of tannin seems to make the white-meat turkey taste dry and metallic. For the same reason, wines in this style are our choice for an easy weeknight meal of roast chicken. They're particularly good with the very flavorful rotisserie chicken that you can buy ready-made.

Sometimes the choice of a soft, fruity red hinges on the season or occasion more than the food. If you love red wine and it's a hot, muggy day, anything heavier will seem more like work than pleasure. Likewise, if you want a red wine to sip at a party, where you'll mostly be drinking it without food, this style is ideal. And if you're serving red wine to guests who aren't really into red wine, these wines give you the best odds of pleasing them.

If you want a red wine to sip at a party, where you'll mostly be drinking it without food, a soft and fruity red is ideal.

Because these wines are low in tannin, they can take a chill better than other styles of red wine. And because they are so intense in fruity aromas and flavors, they can benefit from a wine glass that's no less than 12 ounces in capacity, so that it shows off the aromas when it's filled just halfway. But for informal occasions, you could even drink these wines out of tumblers.

One of the only ways you can go wrong in serving a light, fruity red is to pair it with heavy foods that overwhelm it in terms of weight. A generously sauced spaghetti with meatballs or a rich lasagna, for example, would wipe out all but the richest wines in this style.

PAIRINGS: SOFT AND FRUITY REDS WITH . . .

Salted nuts

Hard salami

Turkey burgers

Fried chicken

Steak with mild barbecue sauce

Mild beef and veggie stir-fry

Ham

Crab cakes

Ratatouille

Monterey Jack cheese

SOFT AND FRUIT REDS: WINES TO TRY

The most typical examples of the soft, fruity red style today come from Australia, especially Australian Shiraz wines. Most Australian Shiraz reds in this style retail for less than $12. (In the chapter on powerful reds, we name some complex, powerful Shiraz wines from down under.) Because Australians are big on naming their wines for two or even three varieties, you'll frequently spot a Shiraz-Cabernet or Cabernet-Shiraz-Merlot (the variety that's named first being the dominant grape in the blend). These can be soft, fruity reds, too, especially if they are inexpensive.

WINE	PRODUCER/BRAND	REGION	COUNTRY
Shiraz	Black Marlin ▪ Black Opal ▪ Brown Brothers ▪ Buckeley's ▪ Grant Burge ▪ Jacob's Creek ▪ Rosemount Estate ▪ Rothbury Estate ▪ Stonehaven Vineyards ▪ Wyndham Estate	Various regions	Australia

California—and Oregon to a lesser extent—also make many wines in the soft, fruity style. The best clue is price: look for inexpensive Pinot Noirs from California and Oregon. The same holds true for other reds from California: even though California produces more than its share of powerful Cabernets, Merlots, and Zinfandels, practically all of those that retail for $15 or less are soft, fruity reds.

WINE	PRODUCER/BRAND	REGION	COUNTRY
Cabernet Sauvignon	Bargetto ▪ Beaulieu Vineyard "Napa" and "Coastal" ▪ Chateau Julien ▪ Corbett Canyon ▪ Estancia Estates ▪ Fetzer "Valley Oaks" ▪ Guenoc "North Coast" ▪ Hahn Estates ▪ Lockwood Vineyards ▪ Mill Creek ▪ Napa Ridge "Lodi" ▪ R. H. Phillips ▪ Ravenswood "Vintners Blend" ▪ Sebastiani ▪ Sutter Home ▪ Trefethen "Eshcol Ranch" ▪ Wente Vineyards	Various regions, CA	USA
Merlot	Beaulieu Vineyard ▪ Chateau Julien ▪ Chateau Souverain ▪ Estancia Estates ▪ Foppiano ▪ Hahn Estates ▪ J. Lohr ▪ Lockwood Vineyards ▪ Mill Creek ▪ Napa Ridge "Lodi" ▪ Poppy Hill ▪ Gallo of Sonoma "Sonoma County" ▪ Taft Street "Coastal"	Various regions, CA	USA
Pinot Noir	Carneros Creek "Côte de Carneros" ▪ Estancia Estates ▪ Carmenet "North Coast" ▪ Gallo of Sonoma ▪ Mont St. John ▪ Napa Ridge "North Coast" ▪ Santa Barbara ▪ Shooting Star (2nd label of Steele)	Various regions, CA	USA
Pinot Noir	Amity Vineyards ▪ Benton Lane ▪ Bethel Heights "Willamette" ▪ Cooper Mountain ▪ Duck Pond ▪ Erath ▪ Firesteed ▪ Hinman Ridge ▪ Montinore ▪ Oak Knoll ▪ Willamette Valley Vineyards	Willamette Valley (OR)	USA
Zinfandel	Bandiera ▪ Beringer ▪ Bogle Vineyards ▪ Chateau Souverain ▪ Cline Cellars ▪ Estancia Estates ▪ Fetzer "Valley Oaks" ▪ Lolonis "Redwood Valley" ▪ Ravenswood "Vintners Blend" ▪ Rosenblum Cellars "Vintner's Cuvée" ▪ Sebasatiani ▪ Seghesio "Sonoma" ▪ Shenandoah Vineyards ▪ Shooting Star (2nd label of Steele) ▪ Wild Horse Vineyards	Various regions, CA	USA

WINE	PRODUCER/BRAND	REGION	COUNTRY
Zinfandel Blends	Laurel Glen "Reds" ▪ Marietta Cellars "Old Vine Red"	Sonoma County (CA)	USA

Soft and fruity French reds come from the Burgundy region—home to Beaujolais, made from Gamay grapes, as well as Burgundy proper, based on Pinot Noir grapes—and from Southern France. Perhaps no European wine is a better example of the soft, fruity red style than Beaujolais Nouveau; other Beaujolais wines can fall into this style, too, depending on the producer. Burgundian Pinot Noir, in its simplest expression, technically named "Bourgogne Rouge," represents a restrained, European rendition of the soft, fruity style. The soft, fruity reds from France's Southern Rhône Valley, such as certain Côtes du Rhône wines, and from the Languedoc region are usually great values.

WINE	PRODUCER/BRAND	REGION	COUNTRY
Beaujolais Nouveau	Any producer	Burgundy	France
Beaujolais; Beaujolais-Villages; Brouilly; Chiroubles; Morgon	Georges Duboeuf	Burgundy	France
Beaujolais; Beaujolais-Villages	Jean-Paul Brun ▪ Michel Tête	Burgundy	France
Bourgogne Rouge	Domaine A. & P. de Villaine ▪ Bouchard Père et Fils ▪ Joseph Drouhin "La Foret" and "Bourgogne Pinot Noir" ▪ Faiveley ▪ Geantet-Pansiot ▪ Louis Jadot ▪ Labouré-Roi ▪ Olivier Leflaive ▪ Maison Leroy ▪ Mongeard-Mugneret ▪ Domaine Pierre Morey ▪ François Parent ▪ Nicolas Potel ▪ Domaine Daniel Rion ▪ M. & P. Rion ▪ Antonin Rodet ▪ Domaine Guy Roulot	Burgundy	France

WINE	PRODUCER/BRAND	REGION	COUNTRY
Côtes du Rhône	Chapoutier "Belleruche" ▪ Delas-Frères ▪ Guigal ▪ Paul Jaboulet Ainé "Parallele 45"	Rhône Valley	France
Merlot; Cabernet Sauvignon	Georges Duboeuf	Languedoc	France

You can find soft, fruity reds throughout the Italian peninsula and islands. The simplest, most inexpensive Bardolinos and Valpolicellas from the Veneto region in the north are slightly less soft than some other wines in this style. The simplest Montepulciano d'Abruzzo wines, from Central Italy, are great values in this style—as are some inexpensive Sangiovese reds from Tuscany, particularly those from the most modern producers. From southern Italy, Puglia's popular Salice Salentino wine, made primarily from the indigenous Negroamaro variety, represents this style, along with some inexpensive varietal Primitivo wines—an Italian version of Zinfandel. Likewise, wines in the $10 to $15 price range from Sicily's native variety, Nero d'Avola, can be soft and fruity.

WINE	PRODUCER/BRAND	REGION	COUNTRY
Montepulciano d'Abruzzo	Casal Thaulero ▪ Citra ▪ Cantina Tollo	Abruzzo	Italy
Primitivo	Apollonio ▪ Botromagno ▪ La Corte ▪ Leone de Castris ▪ Masseria ▪ Pervini ▪ Villa Fanelli ▪ Zonin	Puglia	Italy
Salice Salentino	Apollonio ▪ Cantele ▪ Leone de Castris ▪ Li Veli ▪ Taurino ▪ Agricole Vallone	Puglia	Italy
Nero d'Avola	Fazio ▪ Valle dell'Acate ▪ Zonin Principe di Butera	Sicily	Italy
Sangiovese	Antinori "Santa Cristina" ▪ Banfi "Centine" ▪ Cecchi ▪ Ruffino "Fonte al Sole"	Tuscany	Italy
Bardolino	Bertani ▪ Cavalchina ▪ Guerrieri-Rizzardi ▪ Lamberti ▪ Masi ▪ Santa Sofia ▪ Fratelli Zeni	Veneto	Italy

WINE	PRODUCER/BRAND	REGION	COUNTRY
Valpolicella	Bertani ▪ Brigaldera ▪ Masi ▪ Santa Sofia ▪ Tenuta Sant'Antonio ▪ Santi ▪ Tommasi ▪ Venturini ▪ Zenato ▪ Fratelli Zeni	Veneto	Italy

Here are a few soft, fruity reds from Spain and Chile that we recommend.

WINE	PRODUCER/BRAND	REGION	COUNTRY
Cabernet Sauvignon, Merlot, and blends	Carmen ▪ Concha y Toro's Frontera, Xplorador, and Sunrise lines ▪ Walnut Crest	Maipo and Rapel Valleys	Chile
Rioja	Conde de Valdemar "Crianza" ▪ Marqués de Cáceras "Crianza" ▪ Marqués de Murrieta "Coleccion 2100"	Rioja	Spain

WINES ON THE MOVE: THE TEMPTATION TO OAK

Soft and fruity wines give tens of thousands of wine drinkers exactly what they want—fruity, delicious wines that are easy to enjoy. So why would this style ever change?

In a word: oak. The wine trade generally considers oaky-tasting wines to be important and serious, and some producers might oak their wines in order to earn them respect. Also, the flavor of oak is so easy and so inexpensive for winemakers to add today (see "How Wines Get Their Oaky Character" in the chapter on oaky whites) and so popular that many wines in this style might inevitably gain more than a little smokiness in future vintages, and possibly some oak tannin. Such future wines might still be delicious—or the oak flavor might compete with their fruitiness in an unpleasant way. Time will tell.

Fresh, Spicy Reds

Savory, firm reds with lots of personality, such as

Dolcettos, Barberas, some Zinfandels, cru Beaujolais

wines, Argentine Malbecs, Chilean Carmenères, and

other wines

*Y*ou want a red wine with character. Something more intense than a mild-mannered red, more compelling than a pretty, fruity red but nothing very imposing or powerful. A spicy red is probably just what you'd enjoy.

Spicy reds are what we reach for almost every evening when we want red wine. They're wines that go well with the kinds of foods we like to eat—medium-substantial foods with savory flavor and often a little bit of heat. They're good when they're young and fresh, and they offer us lots of variety. The spicy red category encompasses wines from dozens of grape varieties and just about every wine-producing country on earth.

SUBTLETY, BE GONE!

The fresh, spicy style of red wines combines two main taste characteristics:

- Medium to high intensity of aroma and flavor

- Assertive but not imposing structure

Let's deal with the structural characteristics first. Wines in this style are usually medium-bodied to nearly full-bodied, and they do have perceptible tannin and/or acidity. Their alcohol can be medium or high, but even if it's high, it doesn't define the wines by making them generous or sweet or causing them to give a "hot" sensation in the rear of the mouth. These wines have substantial texture: they're moderately dense, and they can be fleshy, velvety, or grainy in mouth feel. They are not thin, and you wouldn't call them soft, because their tannin is too operative a structural element. When you taste a spicy red, you get a sense of angularity rather than roundness.

Spicy reds can have flavors of pepper, cinnamon, or clove, but also fruit flavors, especially fresh fruits.

The aromatics of fresh, spicy reds are fairly pronounced. As the name of this style implies, spiciness is one of the common types of aromas and flavors present: these wines can have notes of black pepper, cinnamon, clove, or just a more generic spicy flavor. But they also usually have fruity aromas and flavors, especially of fresh fruits (as opposed to baked fruits, stewed fruits, or dried fruits), often berries. Sometimes the fruit flavors are tart, and they're hardly ever what you might call "plump." Many spicy reds also have a minerally component to their taste.

Even though many of these wines have spicy aromas and flavors, not all of them do: The word *spicy* in the name of this style is descriptive partly of the actual aromas and partly of the wines' personality. Just as spices enliven a dish and add a note of complexity (even if you don't always explicitly taste the spice), these wines enliven your palate and bring a new complexity to your meal.

What defines wines of this style is their particular combination of fresh, vibrant aromas and flavors with firm, solid structure.

Of course, like every other stylistic category, this style covers a range of taste profiles, some of them verging toward softness and others toward leanness. But the vibrancy of aromatics is a common chord.

STYLISTIC SIBLINGS

*H*ere's how the other three styles of red wines relate to fresh, spicy reds:

- Mild-mannered reds could be described as firm because they are lean, but they are much less flavorful than these wines, and their aromas and flavors are less vibrant.

- Soft, fruity reds also can have fresh and vibrant aromas, but they have a softer structure and smoother texture.

- Powerful reds, which we discuss in the next chapter, are altogether bigger and bolder than wines of this style.

In a way, fresh and spicy reds occupy a middle ground between the biggest and most flavorful wines and the most subtle, elegant wines.

How Fresh-and-Spicy Happens

Spicy red wines tend to come from grapes grown in moderate climates, rather than the very warmest areas. (Very warm climates would naturally encourage so much ripeness in the grapes that the wines' aromatics would express overripe or baked fruits rather than fresh-fruit character; they would also encourage fuller body, higher alcohol, riper tannins and lower acidity than this style has—a richer, softer style all around.) Wines of this style also come from winemakers more interested in producing moderate wines that work well with food rather than the richest, most extreme wines possible.

The grape varieties for spicy reds tend to be those that are expressive in aroma and flavor, particularly those that have spicy aromatics. The wines might or might not be aged in oak. For those that are, the oak can bring, or supplement, the element of spiciness. The oak's tannin can also contribute to the firm structure of wines in this style.

A quintessential spicy red wine comes from Argentina, where the Malbec grape is practically a national treasure.

More than any other red wine style, the spicy-red category is about individuality. In other words, you will find less sameness from wine to wine in this category. That's because wines of this style come from a wide assortment of grape varieties and places.

THE GRAPES OF SPICY REDS

This taste category is an extremely eclectic one, and it's the home for dozens of unusual grape varieties that are cultivated only here and there around the world. Classic varieties such as Cabernet Sauvignon and Merlot hardly figure in this category, in fact. The only truly major red variety that is significant here is **Syrah**. And even then only some Syrah wines—the leaner, and less powerful of them—fall into this style.

Pinot Noir, another major red variety, can make spicy red wines, but this seems to occur mainly when the grapes are not as ripe as most winemakers and critics feel that they ought to be. Therefore, this style is not the norm for Pinot Noir.

Here are some grape varieties that make wines that fairly consistently fall into the spicy red style. You'll see most of these names on wine labels, because many spicy reds are varietal wines. We list them alphabetically:

- **Barbera** is a high-acid, low-tannin grape from Italy that makes lively, refreshing red wines with vivid fresh-fruit flavors.

- **Blaufrankisch** is a Germanic grape that makes exciting spicy reds in Austria and Hungary; under the name **Lemberger**, it also grows in Germany and in parts of the United States.

- **Cabernet Franc** is frequently used for blending, but by itself, in the Loire Valley, it is a source of well-knit, substantial red wines with earthy and fruity aromatics; it also makes some varietal wines in North and South America.

- **Carignan** brings firm, tannic, spicy character to blended wines in Spain and Southern France.

- **Dolcetto**, from Italy's Piedmont region, produces medium-bodied reds with black-peppery and fruity aromas and flavors.

- **Gamay** is the grape of France's Beaujolais district; depending on winemaking technique, it can produce soft, fruity reds or spicy reds.

- **Kadarka** is a Hungarian grape making red wines with high acidity and cherry fruitiness.

- **Lagrein**, from Northern Italy, makes wines that are fairly firm in tannin, with red berry and plum flavors.

- **Malbec** forms the backbone of Cahors wine in Southwestern France and also makes very fruity, spicy reds in Argentina.

- **Montepulciano**, an Italian grape that grows mainly in coastal Adriatic regions, makes wines with berry fruit aromatics; the wines can be fairly light-bodied wines in the soft, fruity red style, but the more substantial among them are spicy reds.

- **Mourvèdre**, a grape of Spanish origin that's grown in Southern France and also somewhat in California, is a small, thick-skinned grape that makes full-bodied, tannic wines with aromatics that range from fruity to gamy.

- **Pinotage**, a South African grape that's a cross between Pinot Noir and Cinsault, makes fairly tannic but rich reds with berry-fruit aromatics.

- **Sangiovese**, central Italy's ubiquitous grape, makes wines in all four styles, including many spicy reds characterized by tart cherry aromas and flavors and firm but not overpowering tannin.

- **Tempranillo**, Spain's important red grape variety, is grown all across that country and makes dark, fairly tannic wines with aromas that include berries and spice; very long aging, which was once the norm in Rioja, can mellow Tempranillo wines into the mild-mannered style.

- **Xynomavro** is a Greek grape whose wines are marked by firm tannin and acidity.

- **Zweigelt** is an Austrian grape that's a cross between Blaufrankisch and **St. Laurent**, which is a relative of Pinot Noir; Zweigelt wines are gentler and inherently less spicy than Blaufrankisch wines.

AROUND THE WORLD OF SPICY REDS

Italy, France, Austria, South Africa, California, Washington, Chile, and **Argentina** are just some of the places that boast wines in the spicy red style. If part of what you love about wine is adventure and discovery, exploring this style will please you.

The Back Roads of France

Many of France's spicy reds come from some of the country's lesser-known wine regions. That's a bonus, because it means that they're good values. **Southwestern** and **Southern France** make lots of wines in this style, usually under geographical names. **Cahors** comes mainly from the Malbec grape and varies in weight and richness according to the producer; most of the less expensive Cahors wines are in this style, while the most expensive wines tend to be powerful reds (see the next chapter). **Madiran**, made mainly from the Tannat grape, is another spicy red from Southwestern France.

From southern France, **Corbières**, made from Carignan with Syrah and Mourvèdre, is a terrific value wine in this style, as is **Minervois**, a wine blended from the same varieties plus Grenache. **Fitou, Faugères, St.-Chinian, Côtes du Roussillon,** and **Côtes du Roussillon-Villages** are other red wines from the same general area with similar grape blends. Many other wines from southern France, including **Provence**, could be in this style or not, depending on their growing area, grape blend, and winemaking. Cooler zones, such as the hilly **Coteaux Varois** area, are most likely to make this style.

Although not a lesser-known region, the **Rhône Valley** boasts some spicy red wines such as **Gigondas** and some **Côtes du Rhônes**, from the southern part of the region, and some **Crozes-Hermitage** wines, from the north.

The red wines of France's **Loire Valley** are quintessential spicy reds. These wines are made from Cabernet Franc grapes and carry district names such as **Chinon, Bourgueil, St. Nicolas de Bourgueil**, and **Saumur-Champigny**. They tend to be very dry-textured, with vegetal and red-fruit aromatics and sometimes a provocative coffee-grounds character. They are extremely versatile with food.

Finally, the better **Beaujolais** wines are spicy reds. These are the so-called *cru* Beaujolais, which are named for specific towns or districts, such as **Fleurie** or **Brouilly**. These wines tend to have more substance and tannin than basic Beaujolais wines, which are soft, fruity reds. But a basic Beaujolais or **Beaujolais-Villages** from a small, traditional producer could also fall into the spicy red category.

Those Spicy Italians

The better red wines of Southern Italy are robust, rich wines that would fall into the powerful red style. But **Northern** and **Central Italy** have dozens of red wines in the fresh, spicy style.

Two of our favorite wines are Dolcetto and Barbera—varietal wines that come from various districts in the **Piedmont** region. Dolcetto is, literally, the spicier of the two, with aromas and flavors of black pepper as well as ripe berries. For its forthcoming spicy flavor and its firm texture, we'd consider it something of a poster child for the whole spicy red category. Barbera wines can express this style when they are not very ripe and oaky; the less expensive bottlings tend to have little or no oak, and those are the best to look for. Barbera is an unusual wine for this category in that it is hardly tannic at all unless it is oak-aged. But it is high in acidity, and that acidity gives it the zestiness appropriate for this style.

The **Trentino–Alto Adige** region grows Lagrein and makes a delicious varietal wine from it. The lightest versions of Teroldego, another varietal wine from this region, are spicy reds (the richer versions tend to be powerful reds).

Central Italy has tons of wines based on the Sangiovese grape, which can make wines in all four red styles. Your best bet for finding a spicy style is to try a **Chianti Classico**—as opposed to a varietally-labeled Tuscan Sangiovese—that's fairly inexpensive, say $15 or less. Ask your wine merchant for recommendations in this price range.

Among the best-value reds in Italy—if not the world—is Montepulciano d'Abruzzo. Made from the Montepulciano grape, these reds are amazingly consistent in quality, and great food wines. In **Abruzzo**, the home of the Montepulciano grape, the least expensive Montepulciano d'Abruzzo wines tend to be soft, fruity reds, while the better wines are spicy reds. In the nearby **Marche** region, winemakers blend Sangiovese with Montepulciano, and these blends—wines such as **Rosso Cónero** and **Rosso Piceno**—can be spicy reds.

Finally, there are the islands. Cannanou di Sardegna is a **Sardinian** wine that's often spicy in style, and wines from the cool pocket of **Mount Etna** in **Sicily** are far fresher and spicier than is the norm for Sicilian reds. A relatively recent discovery for us came from visits to the cool-climate regions of Sicily, where we found exciting, spicy reds bearing names such as **Etna Rosso, Faro, Cerasuolo di Vittoria**, and Frappato. The last of these comes from a light-colored, indigenous, spicy red variety of the same name, grown in Southeastern Sicily. The Frappato grape adds a distinct, delicious flavor of cherries to its wines, which include Cerasuolo di Vittoria—a wine that's typically a blend of Nero d'Avola and Frappato.

THE STYLE FOR VALUES

*S*picy reds represent some of the wine world's real values, for those who enjoy this style. Many of these wines come from relatively unknown grape varieties and/or regions and therefore can't command the high prices of wines from famous regions and grapes. Also, many wines of this style are not ambitious wines—not a winemaker's attempt to make a special, small-production wine of today's international standards, reflecting very ripe grapes and new-oak aging. (Such efforts would likely tip a wine into the powerful red style.) In many regions of the world that make both powerful reds and spicy reds, such as Tuscany, Piedmont, the Rhône Valley, and parts of Spain and Portugal, it is the less expensive wines that are spicy reds and the pricier wines that are powerful reds.

The Rest of Europe

Spain's spicy reds come from various regions. **Rioja** wines can have this style provided that they are vinified and aged more in a modern rather than a traditional manner, so that they emphasize freshness rather than an aged character. Riojas with some oak aging—Crianza- and Reserva-level wines—are also more likely to be spicy reds, provided again that they are not from very traditional producers. Wines from **Jumilla** and other Spanish wine zones made from the Monastrell grape variety (the grape called Mourvèdre in France) can qualify as spicy reds. So can various Spanish wines blended from Tempranillo and Cabernet, sometimes with other varieties; producers all over Spain are making these wines, which often carry appellations in the "Vino de la Tierra" category rather than the more traditional "Denominación de Origen" category. In the **Penedès** region of **Northeastern Spain**, some producers make wines that derive partially from the Carignan variety, which gives the wines a tannic, spicy edge.

Portugal makes many dozens of types of red wines, mainly from native grape varieties, but many are soft and lack the freshness and edginess of spicy reds. In the **Douro** region in the north, reds that are based on the Touriga Nacional and Touriga Francesa grape varieties can be spicy, provided that they are not so huge that they fall into the powerful red style instead. The **Alentejo**, **Ribatejo**, and **Estremadura** regions also make wines in this style.

Although Austria is white wine territory, the country does make red wines in its warmer regions, such as **Burgenland**. Most of Austria's spicy reds are varietal wines from the Blaufrankisch or Zweigelt grape variety; both types are definitely worth trying. Many other elite Austrian red wines can have a spicy personality due to aging in small barrels of new oak—but some of these elite wines are rich enough to be powerful reds.

In **Greece**, some **Naoussa** wines and other Greek wines made from the Xynomavro grape variety are spicy reds. **Hungary's** contribution to the style includes wines from the Kadarka grape as well as from Blaufrankisch.

The New World Spice Route

A quintessential spicy red wine comes from **Argentina**, where the Malbec grape is practically a national treasure. Argentine Malbecs are generally medium-bodied, with forthcoming aromas and flavors of red and black berries and spice. These delicious wines are so affordable, usually $15 and less, that you really should try them.

Chile has no comparable wine. Some Chilean reds can be classified as spicy, but not categorically. The best likelihood of finding a spicy Chilean red is to try Syrah wines from Chile, or Carmenère wines. For that matter, Argentine Syrahs also fall into this category.

We've already classified inexpensive Australian Shiraz wines (made from the Syrah grape) as soft and fruity reds. But in the mid-price range—between the soft, fruity style and the powerful style of the very top wines—are some spicy versions. These wines tend to have a specific geographic origin, rather than being blended from various parts of Southeastern Australia; the most peppery of them come from Victoria, in our experience.

AT THE WINE SHOP

*Y*ou can find many spicy reds wines at just about any decent wine shop and in better supermarket wine sections. But no one store, no matter how large, can carry every wine. If you want to try a particular wine or a particular type of wine, ask your wine merchant to get it for you.

South Africa's own grape variety, Pinotage, makes wines in this style. Producers make many variations on Pinotage, depending on their vineyard location and personal inclination. Some are meaty and rich, at the richest extreme of the spicy red style, while others fall squarely into the spicy red taste profile.

Not so with Zinfandel in California. Only the leanest, most reserved Zins are spicy reds. In the richer style of Zin, the grape's spicy character is lost in the wine's ripe, jammy fruitiness, creating a powerful red instead. But you can find plenty of spicy Zinfandels, especially among wines with no more than 13.5 percent alcohol. Check our listings at the end of this chapter, or ask your wine merchant.

Some California Pinot Noirs can qualify as spicy reds; these are mainly those in the lighter, leaner style. You can find an occasional spicy California Syrah (when they're not busy being powerful or very fruity). Some California wines from Italian grape varieties, such as Sangiovese or Barbera, can also be spicy. But generally the ripe, rich fruitiness of California's wines mitigates against the spicy style. Washington reds are more frequently spicy, especially Syrahs, but even some Merlots and Cabs. And a few wineries in Washington make Lemberger, which is a wine from the same grape as Austria's Blaufrankisch. The **Finger Lakes** region of **New York** also grows Lemberger.

The **United States** has plenty of other spicy reds—Cabernet Franc wines from the **North Fork of Long Island**, Chambourcin from **Pennsylvania**, and so forth—and we heartily recommend that you seek them out if you enjoy this style.

RECOGNIZING QUALITY IN SPICY REDS

While other red wine styles have inherent risk factors that could compromise quality—mild-mannered reds can be too light, powerful reds can be too huge, and fruity reds can be sweet, for example—the spicy red style has no such built-in risks. Perhaps that's because it's a moderate style, in the middle of the range of red wine tastes rather than at the lightest or richest end of the range.

Or maybe it's because the definition of the style encompasses balance between aromatics and structure, and if a wine transgresses that balance, then it no longer represents the style. If too much tannin overpowers the flavors of a particular wine, for example, it's no longer flavorful enough to be a spicy red. (Or maybe we just like this style so much that we're blind to possible flaws!)

The very best wines in this style will be truly dry and attractively flavorful, with a presence of structure in your mouth that complements the wine's aromatics. They will taste neither too structured (too tannic, too full-bodied) nor too aromatic (just flavorful, without any character contributed by tannin or acid to capture your interest beyond sheer flavor). They will strike a balance that tastes just right.

If you want to critique a spicy red wine—for example, if you're evaluating the comparative quality of several wines in this style—here are some issues you can consider:

- Some wines can give a slightly sweet impression from oak or high alcohol; does this apparent sweetness detract from the lively freshness of the wine's flavors?

- Some wines can have a slight bitterness of tannin.

- Many wines in this style can be short; their flavor, delicious as it is, is a front-of-the mouth impression that does not carry across the whole experience of the wine in your mouth.

- Some wines can be too dense in texture, which can detract from their vividness of expression.

TANNIN IS NOT (NECESSARILY) A DIRTY WORD

*T*oo much tannin in a wine—whether from oak barrels or from the grapes themselves—can render a wine tough, at least when the wine is young. But a moderate amount of tannin can energize a red wine and give it substance without making it harsh. Tannin can enhance a wine's weight and make its texture richer or denser than it would otherwise be. Most spicy reds have a moderate amount of tannin.

- Some wines can be too watery in texture and lack concentration of flavor (even if they have intensity of flavor).

- With age, a wine's flavors could fade.

Somehow, though, wines of this style tend to defy close critical analysis. They are, above all, wines for drinking.

MAKING THEMSELVES HEARD AT THE TABLE

A week seldom goes by without our consuming at least one bottle of Piedmont's Barbera or Dolcetto, often with pizza or a tomato-rich pasta dish. We find that spicy reds such as these are great with a wide range of foods. Wines in the fresh, spicy red style are also so delicious that they're good for drinking even without food—for example, at a party. For that matter, they're good with party foods, such as spicy cheese sticks, nachos, and nuts.

Because spicy red wines have plenty of flavor, they can accompany flavorful meals.

Because spicy red wines have plenty of flavor, they can accompany flavorful meals. Nothing (not even beer) is better with a sausage-and-pepper pizza. They also are delicious with spicy Mexican foods, grilled meats (even if you add a spicy barbecue sauce), chili, and pasta with an *arrabbiata* sauce (tomatoes, pancetta, and hot red pepper).

What you should avoid pairing with these wines are very mild dishes, of the sort that you wouldn't normally consider having a red wine with in the first place, such as shellfish, delicate white fish, or dishes with lemony flavor. Not only are the wines too flavorful, but also their tannin will do nothing for the dish, and the wine will probably taste bitter.

Another combination that's less than ideal is fresh, spicy reds with stews and similar long-cooked dishes. These dishes have lots of flavor but not of a fresh sort, and the wines' vivid, fresh flavors are likely to taste out of place as a result. But plain dishes with earthy flavors, such as grilled portobello mushrooms or green, leafy vegetables, make a nice contrast with these fruity-spicy wines.

PAIRINGS: FRESH, SPICY REDS WITH . . .

Monterey Jack cheese with jalapeños

Pizza with everything

Cheesy tacos with jalapeños

Gazpacho

Spaghetti with a spicy arrabbiata sauce

Grilled Italian sausages

Meatloaf

Chicken cacciatore

Grilled swordfish with a soy-ginger marinade

Blackened fish

Paella

FRESH, SPICY REDS: WINES TO TRY

We drink more fresh, spicy red wines than any other type because they go with so many foods. Also, almost every red-wine-producing region in the world makes them. They're our in-between wines: more assertive than mild-mannered reds, but not as big and forceful as the powerful reds in the next chapter. We love them all.

If there is a spiritual home for spicy reds, it might be Southern France. Provence, the dual region of Languedoc-Roussillon, and the various districts of Southwestern France, such as Cahors and Madiran, are hallowed vineyard ground for classic spicy red wines.

WINE	PRODUCER/BRAND	REGION	COUNTRY
Pic St.-Loup	Ermitage ▪ Château Lancyre ▪ Mas de Mortiès	Coteaux du Languedoc	France
Corbières	Château La Baronne ▪ Les Deux Rives ▪ Domaine de Fontsainte ▪ Château Grand Moulin ▪ Château Meunier St.-Louis ▪ Château Les Ollieux Romanis ▪ Roquefort St.-Martin ▪ Château St.-James ▪ Château Tersac	Languedoc	France
Coteaux du Languedoc	Domaine d'Aupilhac ▪ Domaine Le Conte de Floris ▪ Château de Lascaux ▪ Domaine Mas Champart ▪ Mas de Chimères ▪ Domaine de Nizas ▪ Château de Pech Redon ▪ Château La Roque ▪ Domaine des Tourelles	Languedoc	France
Faugères	Abbaye de Sylva Plana ▪ Château Anglade ▪ Domaine Leon Barral ▪ Château Haut Fabregues	Languedoc	France
Fitou	Domaine Gauthier ▪ Domaine Lerys ▪ Champs des Soeurs	Languedoc	France
Minervois	Bonhomme ▪ Borie de Maurel ▪ Domaine des Combes Hautes ▪ Château Coupe Roses ▪ Château La Croix Martelle ▪ Château Maris ▪ Château Oupia ▪ Château Paraza	Languedoc	France
St.-Chinian	Château de Combebelle ▪ Château Miquel ▪ Cave de Roquebrun ▪ Domaine Trianon	Languedoc	France
Bandol	Domaine du Gros'Noré ▪ Domaine de Pibarnon ▪ Mas de la Rivière ▪ Sainte Anne ▪ Domaine Tempier ▪ Château Vannières	Provence	France

WINE	PRODUCER/BRAND	REGION	COUNTRY
Coteaux d'Aix-en-Provence	Château Calissane ▪ Château Janet ▪ Château Revelette ▪ Château Vignelaure	Provence	France
Coteaux Varois	Château Routas ▪ Domaine de Triennes	Provence	France
Côtes de Provence	Les Domanièrs ▪ Château du Galoupet ▪ Domaine Houchart ▪ Domaine Richeaume	Provence	France
Les Baux-de-Provence	Mas de la Dame ▪ Mas de Gourgonnier ▪ Mas Ste.-Berthe ▪ Domaine des Terres Blanches ▪ Domaine de Trévallon	Provence	France
Côtes du Rhône	Jean-Luc Colombo "Les Abeilles," Réserve Perrin	Rhône Valley	France
Crozes Hermitage	Domaine Albert Belle ▪ Bernard Chave ▪ Domaine Alain Graillot ▪ Domaine du Pavillon	Rhône Valley	France
Gigondas	Domaine du Cayron ▪ Domaine Roger Combe ▪ Domaine de Font-Sane ▪ Domaine Les Goubert ▪ Domaine Raspail-Ay ▪ Domaine St.-Gayan ▪ Domaine de Santa Duc	Rhône Valley	France
Côtes du Roussillon	Domaine du Mas Cremant ▪ Primo Palatum ▪ Domaine St.-Luc ▪ Calvet Thunevin	Roussillon	France
Côtes du Roussillon-Villages	Domaine Bila-Haut ▪ Château de Jau ▪ Château De Pena	Roussillon	France
Cahors	Château La Caminade ▪ Domaine de Lagrezette	Southwest France	France
Côtes du Frontonnais	Château Bellevue La Forêt ▪ Château Le Roc	Southwest France	France
Irouleguy	Domaine Brana (Rouge)	Southwest France	France
Madiran	Château Bouscassé ▪ Château Laffitte-Teston ▪ Domaine Laffont ▪ Château Montus ▪ Domaine Moureou	Southwest France	France
Marcillac	Domaine du Cros	Southwest France	France

France's central Loire Valley boasts a different version of spicy red wines—medium-bodied, cool-climate, spicy red wines based on the Cabernet Franc grape. We must confess that we have a weakness for well-made Cabernet Franc wines, and the Loire Valley is the place we find them.

WINE	PRODUCER/BRAND	REGION	COUNTRY
Anjou; Anjou-Villages	Château de Fesles ▪ Domaine de la Genaiserie ▪ Domaine de Montgilet ▪ Domaine Ogereau ▪ Château Perray ▪ Château Pierre-Bise ▪ Domaine Richou ▪ Domaine des Rochelles	Loire Valley	France
Bourgueil	Pierre Breton ▪ Domaine de la Chanteleuserie ▪ Pierre-Jacques Druet ▪ Domaine de la Lande ▪ Domaine des Ouches	Loire Valley	France
Chinon	Philippe Alliet ▪ Domaine Bernard Baudry ▪ Marc Brédif ▪ Château de Coulaine ▪ Couly-Dutheil ▪ Domaine Dozon ▪ Château de la Grille ▪ Domaine Jacques Grosbois ▪ Charles Joguet ▪ Domaine Olga Raffault ▪ Domaine Roncée	Loire Valley	France
Saumur-Champigny	Domaine Filliatreau ▪ Domaine des Roches Neuves ▪ Clos Rougéard ▪ Domaine Saint-Vincent ▪ Château de Targé ▪ Château de Villenueve	Loire Valley	France
St.-Nicolas-de-Bourgueil	Cognard-Taluau ▪ Domaine Joël Taluau	Loire Valley	France

Italy is teeming with spicy red wines, and most of them are widely available in wine shops and, of course, in Italian restaurants.

WINE	PRODUCER/BRAND	REGION	COUNTRY
Montepulciano d'Abruzzo	Capestrano ▪ Cataldi Madonna ▪ Barone Cornacchia ▪ Guelfi ▪ Illuminati ▪ Marramiero ▪ Masciarelli ▪ Monti ▪ Camillo Montori ▪ La Valentina ▪ Valentini ▪ Valle Reale ▪ Zaccagnini	Abruzzo	Italy

WINE	PRODUCER/BRAND	REGION	COUNTRY
Rosso Cònero	Garofoli ▪ Lanari ▪ Moroder ▪ Le Terrazze ▪ Umani Ronchi	Marche	Italy
Rosso Piceno	Le Caniette ▪ Cocci Grifoni ▪ Monte Schiavo ▪ Saladini Pilastri	Marche	Italy
Barbera d'Alba	Poderi Colla ▪ Giacomo Conterno ▪ Elio Grasso ▪ Marcarini ▪ Renato Ratti ▪ Vietti	Piedmont	Italy
Barbera d'Asti	Michele Chiarlo ▪ Coppo ▪ Prunotto ▪ Vietti	Piedmont	Italy
Dolcetto d'Alba	Tenuta Carretta ▪ Elvio Cogno ▪ Poderi Colla ▪ Marchesi di Gresy ▪ Marcarini ▪ Renato Ratti ▪ Vietti	Piedmont	Italy
Dolcetto di Dogliani	Chionetti ▪ Luigi Einaudi	Piedmont	Italy
Cannonau di Sardegna	Argiolas "Costera" ▪ Contini ▪ Dettori ▪ Gabbas ▪ Sella & Mosca	Sardinia	Italy
Cerasuolo di Vittoria; Frappato	COS ▪ Planeta ▪ Valle dell'Acate	Sicily	Italy
Etna Rosso	Benanti ▪ Calabretta ▪ Cottanera ▪ Murgo ▪ Spadafora ▪ Val Cerasa	Sicily	Italy
Faro	Palari	Sicily	Italy
Lagrein	Abbazia di Novacella ▪ Alois Lageder ▪ Bottega Vinaia ▪ Colterenzo ▪ Franz Haas ▪ Hofstätter ▪ Tiefenbrunner ▪ Elena Walch	Trentino–Alto Adige	Italy
Teroldego	La Vis ▪ Cantina Rotaliana di Mezzolombardo ▪ Roberto Zeni	Trentino–Alto Adige	Italy
Chianti Classico (non-Riserva)	Isole e Elena ▪ Melini "Isassi" ▪ Riseccoli ▪ San Giusto a Rentennano ▪ Tenuta di Lilliano ▪ Villa Cafaggio	Tuscany	Italy
Chianti Rufina	Frescobaldi "Nippozzano" ▪ Renzo Masi ▪ Selvapiana	Tuscany	Italy

The remainder of our spicy red recommendations take you to Austria, Hungary, Greece, Portugal, and Spain, then to the Southern Hemisphere—Argentina, Chile, Australia, South Africa—and back to California, Oregon, Washington, and New York. Some of the wines below are varietal wines, while others go by regional names; we indicate the regional names with an asterisk.

WINE	PRODUCER/BRAND	REGION	COUNTRY
Malbec	Bodega Norton ▪ Bodegas Salentein ▪ Catena ▪ Santa Julia ▪ Terrazzas ▪ Trapiche	Mendoza	Argentina
Shiraz	Brown Brothers ▪ Green Point ▪ Petaluma	Victoria; South Australia	Australia
Blaufran-kisch	Heinrich ▪ Krutzler	Burgenland	Austria
Zweigelt	Heidi Schrock ▪ Heinrich ▪ Höpler ▪ Pockl ▪ Umathum	Burgenland	Austria
Syrah	Errazuriz	Aconcagua	Chile
Carmenère	Caliterra ▪ Carmen ▪ Concha y Toro ▪ Santa Rita	Maipo, Rapel	Chile
Syrah	Casa Lapostolle ▪ Montes	Rapel	Chile
Xynomavro	Boutari	Naoussa	Greece
Kadarka	Takler Estate	Szekszârd	Hungary
Alentejo*	Joao Portugal Ramos Marqués de Borba Reserva ▪ Quinta do Carmo "Don Martinho"	Alentejo	Portugal
Douro*	Bago de Tourigo Gouvyas ▪ Manuel Pinto Hepañol Calços do Tanha Touriga Francesca ▪ Quinta de Couvelhas ▪ Quinta de Santa Julia de Loureiro ▪ Quinta do Cotto ▪ Quinta Seara d'Ordens ▪ Quintodo Vale da Raposa	Douro	Portugal
Estremadura*	Campania das Quintas "Prova Regia" ▪ Quinta de Cidro ▪ Quinta de Pancas	Estremadura	Portugal
Ribatejo*	Falua Duas Castas	Ribatejo	Portugal
Pinotage	Backsberg Estate	Paarl	South Africa
Pinotage	Kanonkop Estate ▪ Middelvlei Estate ▪ Simonsig Estate ▪ Warwick Estate	Stellenbosch	South Africa

WINE	PRODUCER/BRAND	REGION	COUNTRY
Jumilla*	Carchelo ▪ Olivares	Jumilla	Spain
Rioja*	Bodegas Muga ▪ Marqués de Riscal ▪ La Rioja Alta	Rioja	Spain
Toro*	Dehesa La Granja "Bodegas Alejandro Fernandez"	Toro	Spain
Monastrell	Tierra Salvaje	Penedès	Spain
Zinfandel	Burgess ▪ Elyse Vineyards ▪ Fife ▪ Franus ▪ Grgich Hills ▪ Green and Red ▪ Niebaum-Coppola "Edizione Pennino" ▪ Sky Vineyard	Napa Valley (CA)	USA
Cabernet Franc	Castello di Borghese ▪ Corey Creek ▪ Gristina ▪ Palmer Vineyards ▪ Pellegrini Vineyards	North Fork of Long Island (NY)	USA
Pinot Noir	Davis Bynum ▪ J Wine Company	Sonoma (CA)	USA
Pinot Noir	Saintsbury "Garnet"	Carneros (CA)	USA
Pinot Noir	Wild Horse Vineyards	Central Coast (CA)	USA
Cabernet Franc	W. B. Bridgman ▪ Columbia Winery	Columbia Valley (WA)	USA
Syrah	Barnard Griffin ▪ Columbia Winery ▪ Gordon Brothers ▪ Hogue Cellars ▪ McCrae Cellars ▪ Owen-Sullivan ▪ Snoqualmie ▪ Thurston Wolfe	Columbia Valley/ Yakima Valley (WA)	USA
Lemberger	Covey Run ▪ Hogue Cellars "Blue Franc" ▪ Hoodsport ▪ Kiona	Columbia, Yakima Valleys, WA	USA
Lemberger	Fox Run Vineyards	Finger Lakes (NY)	USA
Zinfandel	Cline Cellars ▪ Marietta Cellars ▪ Preston ▪ Quivera ▪ Rabbit Ridge ▪ A. Rafanelli ▪ Sausal ▪ Seghesio ▪ Trentadue	Sonoma (CA)	USA
Pinot Noir	Amity ▪ Anne Amie ▪ Elk Cove ▪ Eyrie Vineyards ▪ Sokol Blosser "Meditrina"	Willamette Valley (OR)	USA

WINES ON THE MOVE: THE THREAT OF INTERNATIONALIZATION

Part of what makes this taste category so appealing is its inherent diversity, born of the fact that so many unusual grape varieties make wines in this style. These wines really are all about their individual grape varieties and less about their winemaking techniques.

But winemakers today face tremendous pressure to make wines that are international rather than ethnic in style—to make rich, soft, dense wines with ripe, fruity flavors and a polish that comes from oak aging. Such wines receive high scores from wine critics, command international respect, and garner high prices. When winemakers attempt to mold their Malbecs, Cabernet Francs, or Zweigelts into the international style, the wines can lose their innate beauty. Like so many long-haired, lip-glossed, bleached-smile contestants in a Miss Universe competition, spicy red wines can normalize to boring sameness.

Powerful Reds

Full-bodied, intense red wines, such as elite California

Cabernets and Merlots, elite red Bordeaux wines,

Barolos, Brunello di Montalcinos, most Northern

Rhône reds, and similar wines

*J*n wine as in life, power often fascinates. Powerful red wines seem more important than other wines; they can amaze and impress you with their richness, intensity, weight, or majesty. In the sense that they are just interesting beverages, like any other wines, powerful reds don't hold any special status in the wine realm. But because wine drinkers and critics often consider them a thing apart from "regular" wines, and because many of the world's most collectible wines fall into this taste category, they enjoy cultural acclaim. Lighter, more subdued red wines find it hard to compete with powerful reds by today's standards of judging wine quality.

In a sense, therefore, this style of red wine represents more than just a taste profile. Some wine drinkers choose a powerful red for dinner not so much because they want to accompany their meal with a huge, intensely flavored wine as because they believe that such a wine represents the correct choice. Along the same lines, people who collect wine often own lots of powerful reds because these wines can be good investments. If any style of wine could confer instant status on those who drink it, it is powerful reds.

In this chapter, we deal with the other face of powerful reds—not their importance, quality ratings, or collectibility, but how they taste. "Important" or not, all wines exist to be consumed and enjoyed!

MIGHT AND MAJESTY IN A GLASS

Powerful red wines almost always have big structure—full body, lots of tannin, high alcohol—and they often have intense aromatics. Their precise aromas and flavors vary according to their grape variety and origin. In New World wines, for example, ripe fruit usually dominates. Many Old World wines (and Old World–inspired wines) combine fruity characteristics with herbal, animal, vegetative, and/or spicy notes. As another example, Cabernet-based wines—of which this style has plenty—tend to have less complex aromatics than wines derived from Syrah or Nebbiolo, at least when they are young. And the fruit flavors of many powerful reds sometimes hover on the brink of over-ripeness, suggesting jamminess or cooked-fruit character, such as baked fruit or stewed fruit. But whatever aromatics the grapes and the winemaking philosophy bring to a powerful red, the wine usually also has the aroma and flavor of oak barrels, especially when the wine is young. Oak also leaves a strong tannin marker in most of these wines.

In some wines, the whole package is powerful.... In other wines, a particular aspect of the wine's taste can suggest power, such as a rich, chewy texture or explosive fruitiness on the nose and palate.

Many aspects of a wine can be responsible for the sense of power that this style conveys. In some wines, the whole package is powerful—intense aromas and flavors, massive structure, substantial texture. In other wines, a particular aspect of the wine's taste can suggest power, such as a rich, chewy texture;

huge body; or explosive fruitiness on the nose and palate. Of course, a good wine must be balanced, and when a single characteristic stands out as powerful, the wine's other elements can't be wimpy.

Some powerful reds "hit you over the head," as some wine tasters like to describe them. They are "in-your-face" aggressive—maybe aggressively hard and tannic, maybe aggressively opulent, or maybe boldly, hugely delicious. But some other powerful reds are less obvious. They are assertive rather than aggressive. Their power lies under the surface and to some extent in the future, because they need a few years of age to express themselves fully.

The wines that fall into the powerful red style thus form a progression: from strong, solid, well-built wines, to wines with particular elements of power, to wines that are all-around massive.

As the endpoint style for bigness and richness on the red wine spectrum, this taste category picks up where the other styles leave off, incorporating wines that are too firm for the soft, fruity red style; too intense and with too much presence of aroma and structure for the mild-mannered red style; and too plump for the spicy red style.

Powerful reds can be round or smooth, while spicy reds have an angularity (they enliven your mouth).

The boundary between fresh, spicy reds and powerful reds is particularly populous territory, because the richest of the spicy reds verge on powerful. Many times we have tasted a Vacqueyras or Gigondas (from the Southern Rhône Valley) or an Australian Shiraz, for example, and found it to be right on the cusp of the two styles, with elements of both. One of the differences between the two styles, besides a higher degree of intensity in powerful reds, is that powerful reds can be round and ample in your mouth, while spicy reds have an angularity and edginess to them that's the opposite of roundness.

If you decide to explore the powerful red style, bear in mind the range of intensity that this style covers: it is vast enough that you might very well enjoy some wines but not others. Of course, every other style encompasses a range of expressions, too; the dif-

STYLISTIC SIBLINGS

*H*ere's how the other three styles of red wine compare to powerful reds:

- Mild-mannered reds are at the opposite extreme from these wines, lighter in body, far less tannic, and much more subdued in aroma and flavor.

- Soft, fruity reds can have a similar intensity of aroma and flavor as powerful reds, but they are lighter in body and do not pack the tannic wallop that the powerful reds do.

- Spicy reds are diminutives of powerful reds—slightly lighter-bodied, slightly less tannic—with a generally similar aromatic intensity; the fruity character of a spicy red doesn't overpower its structure, however, as can happen in some powerful reds.

ference here is that the most extreme expressions of the powerful red style are truly extreme.

RIPE GRAPES, GUTSY WINEMAKING

Probably the single factor most responsible for the style of powerful red wines is a high level of ripeness in grapes. Warm climates, where grapes ripen completely, make powerful red wines. So do winemakers who take the risk to delay their harvest so that their grapes have extra time to ripen.

The single factor most responsible for the style of powerful red wines is a high level of ripeness in grapes.

Remember the equation: ripeness = lots of sugar in the grapes = lots of alcohol in the wine. And high alcohol is a key component of the powerful style. Wines with high alcohol give the impression of filling your mouth more than lower-alcohol wines, and they also have a certain viscosity of texture. Sometimes when a wine's alcohol is very high, it can give a hard edge to the wine in the back of your mouth (often referred to as a "burn"), and that characteristic is not uncommon in powerful reds. High alcohol can also bring an impression of sweetness to a wine—another frequent attribute of wines in this style; the apparent sweetness often balances the high tannin, for a pleasant effect.

Most wines in this style have rich aromas and flavors of fully ripe fruits, and sometimes even a jammy fruit character.

Intense ripe aromatics in the grapes and the wine (as opposed to "green," unripe aromas and flavors) go hand in hand with the grapes' ripeness. That's why most wines in this style have rich aromas and flavors of fully ripe fruits, and sometimes even a jammy fruit character. Along with high alcohol, ripeness can also create ripe, soft tannins in the wine. But the amount of tannin in most powerful reds is not necessarily a function of ripeness. Winemaking issues such as the length of time that the grape skins remain in the juice (see "Soaking up Sturdiness," in this chapter) and the use of new oak barrels can also affect the wine's tannin content.

Grapes need sunshine and heat to ripen fully, but winemakers can also help push the ripening along. Growing small crops, for example, or cutting off some of the grape bunches so that others will ripen more can bring grapes to a higher level of ripeness than they would otherwise attain. Postponing the harvest date can do the same. And very old grapevines, which don't produce much fruit, produce riper fruit.

Some parts of the wine world are naturally disposed to making powerful reds, either because their climate is warm, because the vines are old, or because the grapevines traditionally are pruned for small crops. Other vineyards and regions make powerful reds because the winemakers make it their goal.

SOAKING UP STURDINESS

*L*ogic would have it that the more tannin in the grapes, the more tannin in the wine. But winemakers have several clever ways to control the tannin content in their red wines. The label of a wine won't tell you what sort of "tannin management" they used to diminish or accentuate the extraction of tannin from the grapes, but the taste of the wine will reflect the method.

The phase of winemaking when the wine absorbs tannin from the grape skins is called *maceration*. Generally speaking, the shorter the maceration—or soaking—of the skins in the grape juice, the less tannin that transfers into the wine; the longer the maceration, the more tannin that leaches into the wine. Winemakers can give the juice a maceration as short as a couple of days or as long as a month. That's why tannin levels can vary dramatically in wines from the same grape variety.

In powerful reds, though, the tannin you perceive in the wine probably derives not just from the skins of the grapes but also from aging in fairly fresh oak barrels. Ironically, after giving the juice a very short maceration, to avoid absorbing the grapes' tannin, many winemakers then use 100 percent new oak barrels to contribute tannin to the wine!

THE GRAPES OF POWERFUL REDS

Grape varieties that are inherently tannic are the most common in this style. These varieties tend to make substantial wines, particularly when they are grown at moderate to low crop levels, with the intention of producing top-quality wines. Even a tannic grape such as **Cabernet Sauvignon** won't make a powerful wine when it grows at very high yields in industrial-scale vineyards.

Cabernet Sauvignon is one of the most common grape varieties for powerful reds. (But you can also find mild-mannered Cabernet wines and soft, fruity Cabernet wines. Cabernet grows in so many different places, under so many different conditions, that it can make multiple styles of wine.) Cabernets from specific origins within California, such as Napa Valley, Sonoma County, Alexander Valley, and so on—as opposed to those labeled broadly as being from "California"—are usually powerful. Some of them are extremely so, while others fall into the more gentle end of this style. Other powerful Cabernet-based wines include:

- The top Super-Tuscan wines that are entirely Cabernet, or have a significant (about 40 percent or more) Cabernet component to their blend
- Elite red Bordeaux wines
- Top-of-the-line Washington Cabs
- Australia's better Cabernets—although their power varies
- Chile's top Cabernet wines

Merlot, often blended with Cabernet to soften that wine's tannin, makes powerful reds despite the fact that it is a less tannic grape. Examples include California's and Washington's top Merlot wines, some Merlots from Italy (the pricey, ambitious wines, not the value brands), and the most elite of the "Right Bank" Bordeaux wines, which are based mainly on Merlot.

Syrah makes many gutsy reds, especially in the Northern Rhône Valley of France and in Australia (but again, not the inexpensive wines). Powerful Syrahs also come from Washington, California, Italy, Argentina, Chile, and South Africa. Not only are the wines tannic, but also they tend to be intense in aroma and flavor.

Zinfandel is less tannic than some other grapes, but it can definitely make powerful reds, with very high alcohol and huge fruit intensity. The richest Zins are among California's most powerful wines, in fact. Primitivo, in Southern Italy, has similar power potential.

Two native Italian varieties—**Nebbiolo** from the northwest and **Aglianico** from the south—also make wines in this category. Aglianico's power is all about its tannin, while **Nebbiolo's** has to do with a fierce combination of tannin, acidity, and alcohol, at least in the top-tier wines. Sangiovese also has enough tannin to produce powerful red wines, but we find that many more Sangiovese-based wines fall into the other red styles; Super-Tuscan Sangioveses that are aged in new oak barrels are those most likely to be powerful.

Spain's **Tempranillo** has thick skins, which give its wines color and tannin. In regions where the crop levels are kept low to produce top-quality wines, such as Ribera del Duero, Tempranillo makes some powerful reds.

Finally, there is the question of **Pinot Noir**. This variety is not particularly tannic, and many of its wines are spicy or soft and fruity in style. But grown at very low crop levels, in just the right location, it can have a certain power from its concentration; certain winemaking techniques, including aging in new oak, can then give the wines tannin. But the power of a great Pinot Noir wine is much less straightforward than just tannin: it has the power to seduce you with its complex aromatics and silky texture. It's a different kind of power, but power nonetheless.

Keeping these grape varieties in mind can help you find a powerful red, when that's the kind of wine you want to drink. Powerful reds come at all price levels, but the surest way to find one is probably to buy by price—high price. The more expensive the wine, the greater the chances are that it will be full-bodied, rich, intense, and gutsy. The high prices of some wines in this style might suggest that this style is inherently higher in quality than other styles; in fact, many of these wines earn critical acclaim (or hope to), and that affects their prices. But high prices and scores don't mean that these are the best wines for you if, or when, you prefer lighter-bodied, less tannic, and milder wines.

AROUND THE WORLD OF POWERFUL REDS

Two parts of the wine world that lead the pack in making powerful reds are **California** and **Australia**. Various wine regions in both places have plenty of heat and sunshine for ripeness, and plenty of winemakers who favor this style of wine. Shirazes from Australia's **Barossa Valley**, Cabernets from **Napa** and **Sonoma**, Zins from **Alexander Valley**—these wines reach the apex of richness and intensity.

But frankly, powerful red wines exist in almost every red wine region of the world. Even when an area specializes in lighter reds— such as fresh, fruity Bardolino and Valpolicella, from the vineyards around Verona, Italy—powerful red can also be made. Sometimes it's a traditional wine, such as **Amarone** in the Verona area, and sometimes it's a newfangled type of wine, such as the Super-Tuscan wines that have emerged from **Central Italy** since the 1980s, or the "Pannobile" wines from **Austria's Burgenland**, an area that otherwise makes spicy reds. Sometimes producers who regularly produce wines in other styles will make just one wine in the powerful style—but almost everywhere, where there's red wine, there's a powerful red.

One of the reasons that rich, powerful reds are ubiquitous is that they are considered elite wines.

One of the reasons that rich, powerful reds are ubiquitous is that they are considered elite wines, and winemakers naturally want to try their hand at them. In regions where this style is not the norm, winemakers use non-traditional techniques such as severely restricting the size of their crop in a particular vineyard, or aging a wine in new French oak barrels, that will take their wine in the direction of power. These wines are often referred to (sometimes disparagingly) as "international" wines, because they reflect a New World ethic of winemaking, usually at the expense of traditional regional character.

But some European wine regions have always made powerful reds:

- In the **Piedmont** region of Italy, **Barolo** and **Barbaresco** fall into this style.

- **Northern Rhône** reds such as **Hermitage** and **Cornas** are nothing if not powerful.

- Some **Burgundies** are powerful, although in a distinctly less austere way than wines such as Hermitage, and in a more delicate way than many an elite Californian or Australian red.

- Many **Southern Italian** reds are traditionally powerful, thanks to the warm climate.

- The very top wines of **Bordeaux**—the expensive, collectible ones—are powerful reds, but they tend to be among the most finessed of that style.

- **Spain's** relatively newly elite wines from **Ribera del Duero** and **Priorat** are concentrated, intense and age-worthy. **Rioja** wines at the Reserva and Gran Reserva level can also fall into the powerful style thanks to their rich aromatics and firm structural backbone, although they are at the more restrained end of this style in terms of their weight.

- Many **Portuguese** wines, based on native grape varieties, are powerful; some of them are fresh, modern, and oaky, while others offer a more rustic expression of power.

WHEN POWER EQUALS QUALITY

In reading this chapter, you might very well have come to the conclusion that powerful wines are by definition high-quality wines. After all, we say that these wines get high grades from critics, that they are usually expensive, and that for many types of wines, the priciest examples are likely to represent this style.

In fact, this style does encompass many truly great red wines.

But just because a wine is powerful doesn't necessarily make it great, or even good. Take a look back at the chapter "Tasting Wine for Quality and Style," where we discuss the criteria for quality in wines: intensity, hugeness, and boldness are not among the traditional quality markers. These traits are just characteristics of some wines, and they are good or bad only according to whether they are well executed and whether you like that style or not.

The only characteristic of powerful reds that might give them an edge in quality over red wines of other styles is their concentration. Concentration of aromatics and a well-knit texture are typical for wines of this style, possibly because so many of them come from carefully tended vineyards with low crop yields. Concentration derived by natural means such as these is a mark of high quality. (Some wines are unnaturally concentrated; see "Power on Demand" in this chapter.)

But apart from having concentration, a truly great wine must have balance, length, and age-worthiness, and it must have a distinctive expression (it should taste, to experienced tasters, not quite like any other wine). It is in these aspects that some powerful reds fall short of quality.

For example, some powerful wines are top-heavy: their ripe, slightly sweet fruitiness and high alcohol are not sufficiently balanced by firm tannin, and rich as they are, they seem to have no grounding in your mouth. Other wines are front-heavy: they are explosive in the front of your mouth, but their high alcohol and tannin cut them short, depriving you of a full-mouth experience. Wines like this can still be pleasing, but their quality falls short of greatness. In some cases, however, they can improve with age as their tannin softens.

Wines don't have to be age-worthy any more than they have to be red, or dry. But when a winery expects you to pay big bucks for its important and presumably great wine, you can reasonably expect that this wine has the ability to develop and age for many years. For some powerful reds from the New World, the jury is still out on age-worthiness, because the wines have not existed for very

GETTING WHAT YOU WANT

*I*f you like powerful reds but find some of them extreme for your taste, consider qualifying your request when you're asking for advice in a wine shop or restaurant. Ask for "a powerful red, but not one that's over the top," or something to that effect. In wine shops, check the alcohol level that's stated on the bottle, and avoid wines that have more than 14 percent alcohol.

long. But some powerful reds are clearly made to be pleasurable now and for the next few years, not longer; they can be extremely good wines, but not great in the classic model.

Distinctiveness of expression is an increasingly common quality issue in powerful reds, for several reasons:

- Just as underripe grapes can make a wine taste generically lean, meager, and undeveloped in flavor, overripe grapes can make a wine taste generically rich, powerful, and jammy or baked. Some winemakers believe that extreme ripeness obliterates the expression of *terroir* in a wine, rendering the wine geographically anonymous. Because a high level of ripeness is a cornerstone of this style, some powerful reds fail to be distinctive, which limits their quality in the eyes of some experts. Other experts believe that intensity itself is a quality marker, and to them, such wines are indeed great.

- Techniques that manipulate juice or wine (such as removing water or alcohol; see "Power on Demand" in this chapter) can also obscure distinctiveness, and these practices are growing in popularity among winemakers.

- Winemakers all over the world are aspiring to this internationally popular style for some of their red wines because some critics and moneyed wine buyers love it. But when this style is not traditional in their wine region, these "international" wines lose regional distinction.

When you want to evaluate the quality of a powerful red, look beyond its power, to its balance, length, and distinctiveness of expression. To judge its age-worthiness, look for concentration of aromatics on the finish, just as you swallow the wine; sometimes a great wine can be too young to be appreciated, but that concentration on the finish tells you that the wine has what it takes to develop.

Our final word on quality for this style is to urge you to remember that style is more meaningful than quality in choosing a wine. Powerful reds earn impressive grades from critics who admire this style, but that does not mean that you should drink such a wine if you don't enjoy the style. Very good wines exist in all four red wine styles, and you don't have to spring for a powerful red on a special occasion just because it's some people's idea of the best wine.

FOODS THAT WON'T WIMP OUT

Powerful reds are not necessarily food-friendly. Certain segments of the style are, such as many of the traditional European wines and any of the Pinot Noir–based wines, which generally are not among the biggest of the big. Powerful wines that are very ripe and very high in alcohol can actually be difficult to drink after the first glass, and they can overpower most foods. (One winemaking consultant in California, in fact, has proposed that such wines be officially reclassified as "social wines" instead of "table wines.")

Some powerful reds develop extraordinary finesse with age.

Some powerful reds develop extraordinary finesse with age. Top Bordeaux reds, for example, become silky and perfumed after fifteen or more years, depending on the wine and the vintage. Old Barolos can develop almost a fragile character after fifteen or twenty years, despite their full body. Rioja's Gran

POWER ON DEMAND

*O*nce upon a time (and not so long ago), the richness and weight of a powerful red was directly attributable to the nature of the grapes. But today, many powerful reds are the product of winemaking manipulations that enable a wine to taste as if it were made from characterful, ripe, first-rate grapes, when in fact its origin is far more ordinary. One of the most common manipulations is *concentration* of the wine. This process involves either removing some of a wine's alcohol (if the wine comes from extremely ripe or overripe grapes that were high in sugar) or removing water from the grape juice (if the grapes were insufficiently ripe or insufficiently concentrated due to rain or high crop levels). In either case, the effect is that all of the wine's other components become concentrated in what is now a smaller quantity of liquid. Winemakers can also add color, flavor, and oakiness (both the flavor and the tannin of oak) to give a wine a more powerful taste profile.

These techniques mean that wine drinkers who like powerful reds can find more wines they'll like at more affordable prices. (It costs a lot less to manipulate a common wine than to grow a great wine.) But natural-born powerful reds are ultimately wines of a higher pedigree.

When you buy a wine, you can't know whether it has been manipulated or not, and to what degree. If a wine seems too good at its price to be true, it probably is. But the bottom line, as always, is your taste: if you like it, just enjoy it.

Reservas can become almost sweet as they age. Wines such as these, the aged subset of this style, can be easy to drink with or without food, and memorable experiences.

But the overwhelming majority of powerful reds that you'll encounter are young and bold. When you want to pair food with these young reds, think big and flavorful. Think fruity if the wine

SERVING TIP:
COMPENSATING FOR ALCOHOL AND TANNIN

*W*hen you are planning to serve a powerful red, open it at least half an hour in advance and take a sip to determine how high in alcohol (as in burning sensation) or tannin (as in mouth-puckering) it is.

- High-alcohol wines will benefit from being chilled down a bit, about fifteen minutes in the fridge, until the bottle feels cool to your hand. The cool temperature tames the wine's alcohol and makes it less noticeable. A relatively slim-shaped glass can also help.

- If the wine is very tannic, avoid serving it cool, because cold will accentuate the tannin. Choose a large, wide glass, which will amplify your impression of the wine's alcohol and body and thus diminish the tannin impression a bit. And consider pouring a tannic wine into a carafe or pitcher to aerate it.

is very fruity, and opt for fatty protein, such as a hard cheese or a marbled steak, if the wine is extremely tannic. Choose spicy-hot foods only if the wine is fairly soft. The more complex the wine's aromas and flavors, the simpler you should go in the food you pair with that wine.

Beef, lamb, game, and game birds are good choices, as are ribs, rich pasta dishes such as lasagna, and extra-cheese pizza. Given the price and social status of most of these wines, however, it's unlikely that you'd opt to serve them at a pizza and pasta party!

Considering the expense and the richness of the wine, you might want to serve your powerful red wine with the cheese course, by which time your guests will already have enjoyed other wines and might not expect as big a pour. These wines can go great with all sorts of cheeses except fresh goat's-milk cheeses and soft ripened cheeses such as Brie or triple crèmes. Exactly which cheese to serve depends on the wine. Amarone can handle Gorgonzola, but Bordeaux is better with aged Gouda or Comté. We like ripe California Cabs with farmhouse cheddar, but not blue-veined cheeses. And our favorite cheese, Parmigiano Reggiano, seems to work with everything!

Remember that these wines will steal the show. If you have slaved in the kitchen to produce a masterful, multiple-course meal, they might not be your psyche's best ally on the table.

PAIRINGS: POWERFUL REDS WITH . . .

Extra-aged Gouda cheese

Lasagna

Beef braised in red wine

Steak with onions and rich steak sauce

Leg of lamb

Grilled sausages and other meats

Barbecue

Ribs

Venison

POWERFUL REDS: WINES TO TRY

Perhaps the paragon of the powerful red style is California Cabernet Sauvignon and its cousins, California red blends made from the same grapes as you find in Bordeaux red wines—often called Meritage red wines. The home of most of these powerful red wines is California's Napa Valley, but they also come from Sonoma and other California wine regions, plus Washington. You'll find an especially prodigious number of outstanding powerful reds from Napa Valley on our recommended list.

WINE	PRODUCER/BRAND	REGION	COUNTRY
Cabernet Sauvignon	Anderson's Conn Valley Reserve ▪ Araujo Estate "Eisele Vineyard" ▪ Beaulieu Vineyard "Georges de Latour Private Reserve" ▪ Beringer "Private Reserve" ▪ Cakebread Reserve ▪ Chateau Montelena (especially "Estate") ▪ Clos du Val ▪ Corison ▪ Dalla Valle Estate ▪ Dunn "Howell Mountain" ▪ Far Niente ▪ Flora Springs Reserve ▪ Forman Vineyard ▪ Freemark Abbey, "Bosché" and "Sycamore Vineyards" ▪ Grgich Hills ▪ Groth Reserve ▪ Harlan Estate ▪ Heitz "Martha's Vineyard" and "Bella Oaks" ▪ Hess Collection Estate (Mount Veeder) ▪ Mayacamas ▪ Robert Mondavi Reserve ▪ Nickel & Nickel Single-Vineyard Cabernet Sauvignons ▪ Shafer "Hillside Select" (Stags Leap District) ▪ Silver Oak ▪ Silverado Vineyards "Reserve" and "Stags Leap" ▪ Spottswoode ▪ Staglin Family Vineyard ▪ Stag's Leap Wine Cellars "Fay Vineyard" and "SLV" ▪ Swanson ▪ Trefethen ▪ Turnbull Cellars	Napa Valley (CA)	USA
Cabernet blends	Anderson's Conn Valley "Eloge" ▪ Cain Cellars "Cain Five" ▪ Cardinale ▪ Dalla Valle "Maya" ▪ Dominus ▪ Flora Springs "Trilogy" ▪ Niebaum-Coppola "Rubicon" ▪ Opus One ▪ Pahlmeyer ▪ Joseph Phelps "Insignia" ▪ Quintessa Estate ▪ Stag's Leap Wine Cellars "Cask 23" ▪ Swanson "Alexis"	Napa Valley (CA)	USA

WINE	PRODUCER/BRAND	REGION	COUNTRY
Cabernet blends	Bernardus "Marinus" ▪ Justin "Isosceles"	Monterey, San Luis Obispo (CA)	USA
Cabernet Sauvignon	Fisher Vineyards "Coach Insignia" and "Lamb Vineyard" ▪ Laurel Glen "Estate" and "Reserve" ▪ Ravenswood "Pickberry Vineyard" ▪ Stonestreet (Alexander Valley)	Sonoma County (CA)	USA
Cabernet Sauvignon	Kendall-Jackson "Grand Reserve"	California	USA
Cabernet Sauvignon	Andrew Will Cellars ▪ Chateau Ste. Michelle "Cold Creek Vineyard" ▪ Columbia Winery "Red Willow," "Sagemoor," and "Otis" ▪ Columbia Crest "Cabernet Reserve" ▪ Quilceda Creek	Columbia and Yakima Valleys (WA)	USA
Cabernet Sauvignon	Leonetti Cellar ▪ Waterbrook ▪ Woodward Canyon "Artist Series"	Walla Walla (WA)	USA
Cabernet blends	Andrew Will "Ciel du Cheval" ▪ Col Solare "Meritage" ▪ DeLille Cellars "Chaleur Estate" ▪ Hedges Cellars "Red Mountain Reserve" and "Three Vineyard Red" ▪ L'Ecole No. 41 "Apogée" ▪ Columbia Crest "Walter Clore Red Reserve"	Columbia, Walla Walla, and Yakima Valleys (WA)	USA

Merlot is really at home in Washington, and its more expensive versions are powerful reds; we also name several fine examples from California. Zinfandels fall into several red wine styles; among the powerful wines, we prefer those that have some finesse and balance, rather than the tannic, over-ripe, high-alcohol monsters. We hope that you'll enjoy our powerful Zin recommendations and find them relatively food-friendly.

WINE	PRODUCER/BRAND	REGION	COUNTRY
Merlot	Beringer "Howell Mountain" ▪ Duckhorn ▪ Fisher "RCF Vineyard" ▪ Newton Vineyard ▪ Selene ▪ Shafer ▪ Swanson	Napa Valley (CA)	USA
Merlot	Matanzas Creek ▪ Ravenswood "Sangiacomo Vineyard" (Carneros)	Sonoma County (CA)	USA
Merlot	Canoe Ridge Vineyard "Reserve" ▪ Chateau Ste. Michelle "Cold Creek Vineyard" and "Canoe Ridge" ▪ Columbia Crest "Reserve" ▪ Columbia Winery "Red Willow Milestone" ▪ L'Ecole No. 41 "Seven Hills Vineyard" ▪ Hogue Cellars Merlot "Reserve" ▪ Leonetti Cellar ▪ Northstar	Columbia, Walla Walla, Yakima Valleys (WA)	USA
Zinfandel	Château Montelena ▪ Dry Creek Reserve ▪ Hendry "Hendry Ranch" ▪ Martinelli "Jackass Hill" ▪ Ravenswood (all single-vineyard Zinfandels) ▪ Ridge (all single-vineyard Zinfandels) ▪ Rosenblum (all single-vineyard Zinfandels) ▪ Storybook Mountain (all single-vineyard Zinfandels) ▪ Williams & Selyem	Sonoma and Napa (CA)	USA
Zinfandel blend	Ridge "Geyserville"	Alexander Valley (CA)	USA

Shiraz, the red wine that has popularized Australian wines throughout the world, also comes in several styles, just like Zinfandel. The difference is that Shiraz, also known as Syrah, is regarded as a "noble" red variety, and so you might have to pay a bit more for the best examples of powerful Shiraz wines than you would Zinfandels. We offer you a noble selection of powerful Australian Shirazes here, plus some wonderful, powerful Australian Cabernet Sauvignons.

WINE	PRODUCER/BRAND	REGION	COUNTRY
Shiraz	Brown Brothers "Patricia" Reserve ▪ Grant Burge ▪ Henschke "Hill of Grace" and "Mount Edelstone" ▪ Penfolds "Grange," "Coonawarra," and "Kalimna" ▪ Tim Adams ▪ Wolf Blass Gold Label ▪ Wynns "Michael"	South Australia; Victoria	Australia
Shiraz	Cape Mentelle ▪ Leeuwin Estate	Margaret River	Australia
Syrah	Rosemount "Balmoral Show Reserve"	Hunter Valley	Australia
Cabernet Sauvignon	Cape Mentelle ▪ Leeuwin Estate	Margaret River	Australia
Cabernet Sauvignon	Petaluma ▪ Rosemount "Show Reserve" and "Coonawarra" ▪ Wynns "John Riddoch" ▪ Wolf Blass Yellow Label	Coonawarra; Hunter Valley; South Australia	Australia

Many of Italy's powerful reds are among our very favorite red wines. From Piedmont, we recommend many fine Barolos and Barbarescos; from Veneto, the awesome Amarone; from Tuscany, that wonderful collection of reds known as Super-Tuscans (usually blends of Sangiovese, Cabernet Sauvignon, and/or Merlot); plus monumental Brunello di Montalcino wines—one of Italy's great treasures. In addition, we recommend some powerful southern Italian reds, including Taurasi, based on one of Italy's most noble red varieties, Aglianico.

WINE	PRODUCER/BRAND	REGION	COUNTRY
Aglianico del Vulture	Basilisco ▪ D'Angelo ▪ Paternoster ▪ Tenuta Le Querce ▪ Venosa	Basilicata	Italy
Taurasi	Feudi di San Gregorio ▪ Mastroberardino "Radici" ▪ Terredora	Campania	Italy
Barolo	Carretta ▪ Ceretto ▪ Podere Colla ▪ Aldo Conterno ▪ Giacomo Conterno ▪ Bruno Giacosa ▪ Manzone ▪ Marcarini ▪ Bartolo Mascarello ▪ Giuseppe Mascarello "Monprivato" ▪ Pio Cesare ▪ E. Pira ▪ Prunotto ▪ Renato Ratti ▪ Giuseppe Rinaldi ▪ Sandrone ▪ Paolo Scavino ▪ Vietti "Rocche" and "Villero" ▪ Gianni Voerzio ▪ Roberto Voerzio	Piedmont	Italy
Barbaresco	Ceretto ▪ Angelo Gaja ▪ Bruno Giacosa ▪ Marchesi di Gresy ▪ Produttori del Barbaresco ▪ Albino Rocca ▪ Bruno Rocca	Piedmont	Italy
Langhe	Gaja "Sori San Lorenzo," "Sori Tildin," "Costa Russi" ▪ Gaja "Sperss," and "Conteisa"	Piedmont	Italy
Teroldego	Foradori	Trentino	Italy
Brunello di Montalcino	Altesino (especially Montosoli Vineyard) ▪ Biondi-Santi ▪ Camigliano ▪ Campogiovanni ▪ Canalicchio di Sopra ▪ Tenuta Caparzo (especially "La Casa" Vineyard) ▪ Case Basse (Soldera) ▪ Castello Banfi (especially "Poggio all'Oro" and "Poggio alle Mura") ▪ Castelgiocondo ▪ Casanova di Neri ▪ Cerbaiona ▪ Ciacci Piccolomini ▪ Col d'Orcia ▪ Costanti ▪ Fattoria dei Barbi ▪ Tenuta	Tuscany	Italy

WINE	PRODUCER/BRAND	REGION	COUNTRY
	Friggiali ▪ Fuligni ▪ Il Greppone Mazzi ▪ Il Poggiolo ▪ Il Poggione ▪ La Pieve di Santa Restituta ▪ La Poderina ▪ Lisini ▪ Mastrojanni ▪ Tenute Silvio Nardi ▪ Pertimali (Angelo Sassetti) ▪ Pertimali (Livio Sassetti) ▪ Poggio Antico ▪ Poggio Salvi ▪ Salvioni-La Cerbaiola ▪ Siro Pacenti ▪ Talenti-Pian di Conte ▪ La Torre ▪ Uccelliera ▪ Valdicava		
Super-Tuscans	Antinori "Solaia" and "Tignanello" ▪ Castello di Rampolla "Sammarco" ▪ Castellare "I Sodi di San Niccolò ▪ Felsina "Fontalloro" ▪ Fontodi "Flaccianello" ▪ Grattamacco ▪ Isole E Olena "Cepparello" ▪ Luce; Montevertine "Le Pergole Torte" ▪ Tenuta dell'Ornellaia "Ornellaia" and "Masseto" ▪ Ruffino Cabreo "Il Borgo" ▪ Tenuta San Guido "Sassicaia" ▪ San Giusto a Rentennano "Percarlo"	Tuscany	Italy
Amarone della Valpolicella	Allegrini ▪ Bertani ▪ Brigaldera ▪ Dal Forno ▪ Le Ragose ▪ Masi ▪ Quintarelli ▪ Tommasi	Veneto	Italy

Many of France's powerful reds come from the Rhône Valley, especially the Northern Rhône, home of Hermitage, Côte Rôtie, and Cornas wines—all based on Syrah. Many critics regard these wines as the greatest expression of the Syrah variety. Of the three, Côte Rôtie is perhaps the most difficult to categorize, because many Côte Rôtie wines of today are more soft, fruity, and even elegant than powerful; we do offer one recommendation that fits the powerful red style. From the Southern Rhône Valley, we recommend some great Châteauneuf-du-Pape reds; these wines are usually blends of Syrah, Grenache, Mourvèdre, and other varieties.

WINE	PRODUCER/BRAND	REGION	COUNTRY
Château-neuf-du-Pape	Château de Beaucastel ▪ Château de la Nerthe ▪ Château Fortia ▪ Château Rayas ▪ Clos des Papes ▪ Domaine de la Janasse ▪ Domaine de Mont Redon ▪ Domaine du Vieux-Télégraphe	Rhône Valley	France
Cornas	Domaine Guy de Barjac ▪ Auguste Clape ▪ Jean-Luc Colombo ▪ Paul Jaboulet Aîné ▪ Domaine Marcel Juge ▪ Domaine Robert Michel ▪ Domaine Noël Verset ▪ Domaine Alain Voge	Rhône Valley	France
Côte Rôtie	Guigal "La Landonne"	Rhône Valley	France
Hermitage	Chapoutier ▪ Jean-Louis Chave ▪ Jean-Luc Colombo ▪ Delas Frères ▪ Domaine Bernard Faurie ▪ Paul Jaboulet Aîné ▪ Domaine Marc Sorrel	Rhône Valley	France

Those two classic French red wines, Bordeaux and Burgundy, offer some of the greatest examples of the powerful red style—but at a price. Most of the wines we recommend here, mainly classified-growth Bordeaux and *grand* or *premier cru* Burgundies, are some of the best red wines in the world.

WINE	PRODUCER/BRAND	REGION	COUNTRY
Bordeaux	Château Angélus ▪ Château Canon-La-Gaffelière ▪ Château Chasse-Spleen ▪ Château Clerc-Milon ▪ Château de Pez ▪ Château Figeac ▪ Château Gruaud-Larose ▪ Château Haut-Beauséjour ▪ Château Haut-Brion ▪ Château Lafite-Rothschild ▪ Château Lafleur ▪ Château La Mission-Haut-Brion ▪ Château Latour ▪ Château Latour de By ▪ Château Léoville-Las Cases ▪ Château L'Evangile ▪ Château Lynch-Bages ▪ Château Meyney ▪ Château Montrose; ▪ Château Mouton-Rothschild ▪ Château Pétrus ▪ Château Pichon-Lalande ▪ Château Pichon-Longueville-Baron ▪ Château Poujeaux ▪ Château Sociando-Mallet ▪ Château Troplong-Mondot ▪ Château Trotanoy	Bordeaux	France
Cahors	Château Lagrezette "Cuvée Dame Honneur" and "Cuvée Le Pigeonnier"	Southwest France	France
Various Burgundy appellations	Bouchard Père & Fils "La Romanée," "Bonnes Mares," "Le Corton," and "Beaune L'Enfant Jesus" ▪ Domaine Comte de Vogüé "Musigny" ▪ Domaine de La Romanée-Conti "La Tâche," "Richebourg," and "Grands Echézeaux" ▪ Anne Gros "Richebourg" ▪ Louis Jadot "Romanée-St.-Vivant" and "Chambertin Clos de Bèze" ▪ Hubert Lignier "Clos de la Roche" ▪ Domaine de Montille "Pommard Rugiens" and "Volnay Les Champans" ▪ Domaine Jacques-Fréderick Mugnier "Musigny" and "Bonnes Mares" ▪ Georges et Christophe Roumier "Musigny" ▪ Ponsot "Clos de la Roche" ▪ Armand Rousseau "Chambertin"	Burgundy	France

Spain weighs in with some superb powerful reds from two of its hot, newly rediscovered regions, Ribera del Duero and Priorat. (Actually, one of the Ribera del Duero wines, Vega Sicilia, has been one of the world's great wines for decades.) The new category of elite wines from Chile, which we call "Super-Chileans," for lack of a more specific term, are on the expensive side ($40 to $80) compared to simpler Chilean reds. They're mainly blends of Cabernet Sauvignon, Merlot, and/or Carmenère.

WINE	PRODUCER/BRAND	REGION	COUNTRY
Priorat	Alvaro Palacios ▪ Clos Erasmus ▪ Clos Martinet ▪ Clos Mogador ▪ l'Hermita ▪ Mas d'En Gil ▪ Morlanda ▪ Pasanau	Priorat	Spain
Ribera del Duero	Bodegas Mauro ▪ Bodegas Téofilo Reyes ▪ Condado de Haza (Bodegas Alejandro Fernández) ▪ Pesquera ▪ Valdubuena ▪ Valdubon ▪ Vega Sicilia "Unico" ▪ Viña Pedrosa	Ribera del Duero	Spain
Super-Chileans	Carmen "Gold Reserve" Cabernet Sauvignon ▪ Casa Lapostolle "Clos Apalta" ▪ Concha y Toro "Don Melchor" Cabernet Sauvignon ▪ Cousiño Macul "Finis Terrae" ▪ Errázuriz "Don Maximiano Founder's Reserve" ▪ Montes "Alpha M" ▪ Seña	Maipo, Rapel, Aconcagua	Chile

WINES ON THE MOVE: THE RICH GET RICHER

If you favor rich, powerful red wines, you're probably set for life, because more and more wines seem to be gravitating toward this style. And within this style, wines seem to be inching inevitably toward the richer end of it. Global warming, high-tech winemaking, critical acclaim, and the importance of the U.S. wine market, which appreciates this style, are all factors conspiring to make the powerful ever more powerful.

In the spirit of "what goes around comes around," we suppose that eventually the market will favor more moderate wines, and the extreme powerful reds will become less common. But we don't foresee that happening in the near future.

Rosé Wines in Two Styles

Blush wines such as those from Zinfandel, Merlot, or

Grenache grapes in California and dry rosés such

as those from Tempranillo in Rioja, Spain, and

blends from Provence

*W*hen we say "pink wine," what image comes to mind for you? You might remember the first wines you ever drank, before you discovered reds and whites. You might imagine sitting on the patio with a refreshing glass of chilled Spanish rosé on a day way too hot for your favorite reds. Or you might think, "What I drink!" because pink wines are what you prefer all year long.

Rosé wines, as people in the wine business tend to call pink wines, mean different things to different people. In the United States, White Zinfandel, a pink wine, is one of the most popular types of wine. In some parts of Europe, dry rosé wines are the local specialty. But some wine drinkers think that rosés are sissy wines, too sweet and not serious enough for their consideration. Every summer, like many other wine writers, we write about rosé wines in the hope of converting hard-core wine lovers to the charms of these wines.

Truth be told, rosé wines are a much smaller category than whites or reds, but they definitely have their place with certain wine drinkers and in certain seasons. And, with apologies to Gertrude Stein, a rosé is not a rosé is not a rosé. Two distinct styles of rosé wines exist.

VARIATIONS ON A THEME

Pink wines come from red grapes. They end up as pink wines instead of red wines because the dark grape skins don't bathe in the grape juice long enough to give the wine a normal, deeper red color.

The brief skin contact period means not only that the juice doesn't have the chance to pick up much color but also that the juice doesn't have the chance to absorb much tannin from the grape skins. Generally speaking, the paler the wine, the less tannin it has.

Pink wines range in color intensity from hues so pale that you're almost tempted to call them white to tones so dark that you think the wine might actually be red. In terms of their actual color, they can be orangey, copper-hued, true pink, or near-red. The color depends, among other factors, on the grape variety or varieties that made the wine. For example, Grenache-based rosés tend to be somewhat orange, while Cabernet-based wines tend to be pink.

But the meaningful differences among rosé wines are in their taste. Some wines have more intense aromas and flavors than others, and some are fuller-bodied than others (within the light- to medium-bodied range). Some have fruity aromatics and some are minerally. More importantly, some pink wines are distinctly sweet while others are bone dry.

We believe that sweetness is the key characteristic that delineates pink wines into two styles:

- **Blush wines,** pink wines that are soft, flavorful, and fairly sweet, ranging from medium-dry at their dryest to medium-sweet

- **Dry rosés**, pink wines that range from very dry to off-dry and have fairly firm structure

But sweetness isn't the only dividing line. The softness of blush wines—which derives from low acidity relative to the residual sugar—sets those wines apart from dry rosés that are structured by crisp acidity or sometimes a wee bit of tannin. Although the dry end of the sweeter blush wine style can overlap in sweetness with the sweetest of the dry rosés, each of these styles is unique, and each appeals to different tastes.

BLUSH WINES HAVE MORE FUN

The term *blush wine* came into existence a couple of decades ago with the birth of White Zinfandel. As we remember it, rosé wines weren't very popular then. (They're still less popular than we wish they would be, but in those days, they were even less so.) Wine drinkers wanted to drink what they believed to be dry wines, and rosés had a reputation of being sweet and not of very high quality. When producers began making a sweetish pink wine from Zinfandel grapes, they named it White Zinfandel rather than call it a rosé. Because of the name, and because of everyone's desire to disassociate these wines from the poor image of rosés in general, wine marketers and analysts began referring to these wines as blush wines.

Blush is not an official category of wine; in sales statistics, for example, these wines are simply grouped with other pink wines. But we like the term as a moniker for the sweeter style of rosé, because it's one that's immediately understood by people in the trade (and therefore if you use it, they'll know what you mean).

This style includes all the pink wines that are called "white," such as White Merlot and White Grenache. Using the word *white* on the label of a wine that's obviously pink is the winery's way of saying, "If you like the taste of White Zinfandel, you'll also like this wine."

Blush wines tend to have at least some sweetness. For the past few years, some wineries have been making them dryer than previously, but even the dryest of them fall into the medium-dry bracket of sweetness (see "Off-dry Versus Sweet" in the "Aromatic Whites" chapter for sweetness descriptors), and most of them are medium-sweet. They tend to have aroma and flavor intensity typical of New World wines—in other words, fairly intense—and their acidity is generally not high. They are lower in alcohol than you'd expect from wines grown in warm climates; alcohol levels are about 9.5 to 11.5 percent. The combination of sweetness, low acid, and alcohol low enough to not bite results in a soft, supple mouth feel.

We know lots of people who love blush wines and drink them almost exclusively. If you have a taste for these wines, other wines can seem too dry or austere.

The Grapes and Regions of Blush Wines

Blush wines are a New World invention, developed specifically to appeal to a certain market segment. Almost all of them come from **California**.

The red grapes that wineries use to make blush wines grow mainly in the vineyards of **Central California**, where warm temperatures enable grapes to get good and ripe. (The scale of production in these vineyards also ensures that the wines can be priced affordably.) The grapes generally have enough sugar to make a high-alcohol wine, but the wines are made in such a way that they are not as high in alcohol as they could be. The grapes also have relatively low acidity levels and aromatics that suggest very ripe fruits—depending, of course, on the variety of grape.

To make these grapes into a blush wine, with at most a moderate amount of color, the winemaker minimizes contact between the grape skins and the juice, as we mentioned earlier in this chapter. The wines' low alcohol and sweetness derive from winemaking techniques that either leave sugar unfermented in the wine or add it back into a dry wine in the form of unfermented juice. (Refer to

"Off-Dry Styling" in the chapter on aromatic whites for an explanation of these techniques.) The ripe flavors of the grapes remain in the wine, sometimes supplemented by fruity flavors that occur during the winemaking, such as candied fruit or tutti-frutti notes. The winemaker might bolster the soft acidity of the grapes with an addition of acid, but the final acidity will be low enough that the wine has a soft, generous structure.

Like most other wines named after a dominant grape variety, of course, these wines do not have to derive entirely from the named grape. Some blush wines certainly taste to us as if they come partially from white grapes, because of their floral aromatics, which are not typical for red grapes. Blending grapes or mixing white juice with red is, of course, perfectly legal.

The grapes that make blush wines are an open-ended group because blush wines don't have a long tradition behind them. **Zinfandel** is the major grape, but **Merlot** and **Grenache** also make blush wines. **Cabernet Sauvignon** blush wine exists, but so do many dryer rosés from Cabernet.

Because the taste of blush wines is very much winemaking-driven—in the sense that the grapes themselves would never produce this style without sophisticated winemaking intervention—just about any red grape variety could become the starting point for a blush wine. But because the marketers want the names of these wines to be recognizable to wine drinkers, the field of grape varieties is limited to the best-known types, such as those already being used for this style. One variety that does have some market recognition, Pinot Noir, does not grow in enough quantity in California to permit the volume of wine that a successful blush wine requires. Neither does Syrah at present, but we wouldn't be at all surprised to see a White Syrah or White Shiraz some day.

Judging Quality in Blush Wines

Blush wines can be delicious, easy to like, and quaffable, but most wine professionals don't consider them serious wines. (Some are

SERVING TIP: CHILL THE WINE, THEN CHILL

*Y*ou should always chill rosé wines at least a little. The sweeter they are, the more we like to chill them, because the cold temperature enhances whatever acidity the wine has and makes the wine more refreshing. The dryer and more delicate in flavor the wine is, the less we chill it; when delicate rosés are just slightly cool, rather than cold, their flavors are more forthcoming.

The most important rule of all for enjoying rosé wines, though, is to just enjoy them. Obsessing over temperature, food pairings, glassware, or any other service detail just defeats the whole spirit of these wines.

seriously successful, though!) Judging the quality of blush wines therefore might seem pretentious. In fact, most blush wines are well-made wines of good quality, because they are produced by large companies that care about their brand image and have enough money to employ skilled winemakers. And anyway, most people who drink blush wines drink them for the pleasure, not for the quality ratings. More than for any other type of wine, the measure of a blush wine's quality is how much you like it. Because the whole point of these wines is to be enjoyable.

From a technical point of view, the best blush wines would be those that have an appropriate balance of acidity and sweetness. What's "appropriate"? We like these wines on the dry side, so we'd say that less sweetness and/or higher acidity that minimizes the impression of sweetness make the ideal balance. But if you enjoy the sweetness, then you'll prefer a wine whose balance is skewed toward sweetness rather than acidity. In any case, the wine should have enough acidity that it refreshes your mouth rather than leaving a cloying, sugary impression.

Blush wines should be young and fresh. If their flavors taste slightly cooked or flat, that's a sign of bad storage or old age. Flavors of fresh fruit rather than candied fruit can be an indication of quality, as can a bit of complexity—for example, delicate herbal notes along with fruity aromas and flavors.

Some blush wines can give you a prickly sensation when you first put them in your mouth; that's caused by a bit of carbon dioxide in the wine and is a sign of freshness. But the lack of it is not a flaw.

If you want to determine the quality of your favorite blush wine, just taste it thoughtfully, noticing the same aspects that you would in any wine, such as balance, depth, and length, as well as flavor intensity. The best wines of this style can survive this scrutiny, while others will reveal their shortcomings. But remember: the first responsibility of the wine is to please you, and if you enjoy the wine, you might decide that a lack of length or a slightly exaggerated sweetness is no shortcoming at all.

Foods to Enjoy with Blush Wines

Just as it seems somewhat pretentious to evaluate the quality of a blush wine, it seems a bit ridiculous to discuss appropriate and inappropriate foods for these wines. Most people we know who drink blush wines drink them with everything, from chef's salad to lasagna, because these wines have the taste that they prefer, period. But in case you're someone who drinks blush wine only occasionally, or you're a regular blush drinker who wants to try other styles of wine when the food warrants, here are the foods and occasions that we believe are best for blush wines.

Blush wines are ideal for picnics, outdoor summer parties, and other casual occasions when you want an easy-to-drink, cold glass of flavor. They're also good for parties year-round, provided that your guest list isn't peopled with wine sophisticates who would prefer something dryer.

The sweetness of blush wines can balance nicely with salty foods such as salted nuts, party mix munchies, or popcorn. It can also be refreshing with slightly spicy foods such as spicy taco chips or cheese sticks that have a slight bite of red pepper.

These wines are best with medium-weight dishes. They can be too flavorful for a delicate fish filet, for example, and too light for a beef stew. Dishes that have elements of fruitiness to them, as some fusion cuisine dishes do, can accompany blush wines nicely because the wines themselves are fruity. For that matter, they can work with dishes that include ketchup, such as burgers and fries.

In general, we suggest serving blush wines when the occasion, the food, and the setting are informal. Serve them in tumblers if you like. Pour them when the playoffs are on and you're eating in front of the TV set. Serve them when you just want to enjoy.

PAIRINGS: BLUSH WINES WITH . . .

Cold cuts

Cobb salad

Chicken salad or tuna salad

Potato salad

Stuffed potato skins

Hot dogs with relish

Turkey burgers with ketchup

Spicy chicken wings

Sweet-and-sour chicken

Barbecue that's slightly sweet

Ham with pineapple

BLUSH ROSE: WINES TO TRY

Most rosé wines from California have some sweetness, ranging from fairly sweet White Zinfandel, in the blush wine style, to off-dry rosé wines that have firmer structure and contain more acidity, which we recommend in the section on dryer rosés. Here are our White Zinfandel/blush recommendations.

WINE	PRODUCER/BRAND	REGION	COUNTRY
White Zinfandel/ Blush	Bel Arbors ▪ Beringer ▪ Buehler Vineyards ▪ De Loach Vineyards ▪ Glen Ellen ▪ Gossamer Bay ▪ Hacienda White Merlot and White Zinfandel ▪ Kenwood ▪ Sutter Home White Cabernet and White Zinfandel ▪ C. K. Mondavi (Charles Krug) ▪ Monteviña Nebbiolo Rosato and White Zinfandel ▪ Parducci ▪ R. H. Phillips ▪ Round Hill ▪ Rutherford Vintners White Merlot and White Zinfandel ▪ Talus ▪ Turning Leaf ▪ Woodbridge (Robert Mondavi)	Various regions (CA)	USA

THE SERIOUS FACE OF ROSÉ

Okay, it's true: no pink wine will ever be a truly serious wine because it has no potential to age. The fresh-and-young spirit of rosés puts these wines in a different class than reds or whites, and it's a class that precludes true greatness. Nevertheless, some rosé wines can be serious wines in the sense of being well-made expressions of grape variety and *terroir*, without the contrivance of sweetness designed to attract the mass market. These wines are in the taste category of dry rosés.

Some wines in the dry rosé style are bone-dry wines and others have some sweetness, up to what might be considered an off-dry level, in the total impression of the wine. But regardless of their sweetness or dryness, wines in this style are fairly firm in structure compared to the easy generosity of structure that blush wines have. These wines often have a strong backbone of acidity, or they have a slight amount of tannin that gives them firmness. The best of them also have a good concentration of aromatics.

So much for similarities. Apart from these general shared traits, the dry rosé style encompasses a varied group of wines of different color, weight, intensity, and flavor. The diversity of dry rosés is one of the reasons that we and many other wine writers love them.

Here are a few examples of individual taste characteristics you can find in dry rosés:

- Pale salmon color, earthy/mineral aromatics, and crisp acidity in a Côtes de Provence rosé blended from Cabernet, Cinsault, and Grenache

- Deeper salmon color, ripe melon and strawberry flavors, crisp acidity, and mouth-filling weight in a Cabernet Franc rosé from the Loire Valley district of Saumur

- Light ruby color, carbon dioxide spritziness, grapey flavor, and a dry, bracingly crisp structure in an Italian Brachetto d'Acqui

- Orangey pink color, spicy and herbal aromatics, and crisp acidity with a touch of sweetness in a Rioja rosé blended from Grenache and Tempranillo

- Rosy color, intense fruity flavors, and some sweetness in a relatively full-bodied rosé of Pinot Noir from California

At the lightest end of their spectrum, dry rosés can resemble white wines—particularly fresh, unoaked whites—but with some of the aromatics of red wines, such as berry notes. At the richest end of their spectrum, dry rosés resemble the lightest of the soft and fruity reds. As a taste category, these wines bridge the gap between white wines and red wines.

Vin Gris

*S*ome of the most interesting rosés are those that come about as a by-product of red wine making—as sacrificial juice, you might say, whose absence makes the red wine better. When winemakers want to intensify the color, structure, and flavor of their red wines, they sometimes "bleed" some juice from their tanks in the early stages of fermentation. Removing some juice from the tank creates a higher skin-to-juice ratio in the juice that's left, enabling the wine-maker to make a more intense red wine. Meanwhile, the pink juice that's bled off ferments into a rosé wine.

The French term for this process is *saignée*, meaning "bled." Some rosé wines made in this way are called *vin gris*—gray wine—as in Vin Gris de Pinot Noir. Often these wines come from serious winemakers, in the New World as well as in Europe.

The Grapes and Regions of Dry Rosé

Apart from the general restriction that dry rosés, like other pink wines, must come from red grape varieties, the grape varieties that make dry rosé include just about everything. We've tasted dry rosés made from **Cabernet Sauvignon, Cabernet Franc, Syrah, Pinot Noir, Merlot, Grenache, Gamay, Sangiovese, Nebbiolo, Montepulciano, Tempranillo,** and many other varieties. We have also enjoyed rosé wines made from **Pinot Gris**, which is normally considered a white variety; Pinot Gris grapes in fact can be pinkish or slightly blue in color. This range of grape varieties speaks to the diversity of wines in this style, which is one of this style's attractions.

Many rosés are blends of several varieties. For example, a classic blend is **Grenache, Cinsault**, and **Mourvèdre** in rosés from Southern France.

Dry rosés populate the whole world of wine, especially many of

Europe's classic wine regions. They're usually a sideline production to red wines, rather than the main focus of a region's winemaking. About the only wine region we can think of where rosés are more important than reds is **Provence**, and that could very well be because of something as pragmatic as summer tourist season demand for pink wine.

Key European wine countries for dry rosé production include the following:

- **France**: the regions of **Provence, Loire Valley, Southern Rhône Valley (Lirac** and **Tavel), Burgundy (Marsannay)**

- **Italy: Abruzzo** (where the wine is called Cerasuolo), **Bardolino** (where it goes by the name Chiaretto), the **Salento** area of **Puglia**

- **Spain: Navarra, Rioja**, and **Catalonia** in general

- **Portugal**: various regions throughout the country

California also boasts several good dry rosés. Several come from **Sonoma County** or **Santa Barbara**, and others carry a general "California" appellation. But you can find a dry rosé from just about anywhere; **South Africa, Australia, Austria, Chile, Argentina, Oregon,** and **New York,** for example, all boast at least a few dry rosés.

Judging Quality in Dry Rosés

Like blush wines, dry rosés are about enjoyment, not analysis. Nevertheless, here's how to tell a good rosé from a better one.

Color is not a quality consideration, unless it's somewhat brown or very orangey—which indicates old age—or it's inconsistent with the taste of the wine. For example, if a rosé is very pale and yet its taste is rich and characterful, the color could be inappropriate. Conversely, a deep-toned rosé that tastes light and simple would be illogical.

AFAP: As Fresh as Possible

*I*n general, pink wines of both styles are best when they are very young. How young is that? If a wine is vintage-dated, we like to see that the vintage date represents the most recent harvest in that wine region. For Northern Hemisphere rosés, that means by summer we prefer to drink a wine from the previous fall, and for Southern Hemisphere rosés, from earlier that same year, if possible. In no case would we buy a rosé that's three full vintages old—for example, a 2003 rosé in 2006. If your wine shop has older rosés on the shelves and won't buy the new vintage until the older wines sell, consider looking for a wine shop with more turnover.

In terms of their aromas and flavors, dry rosés can be herbal, fruity, floral, earthy, and so forth; no particular aromatic profile is more valid than the next, as long as the aromas and flavors are fresh and clean. They can also be intense in aroma and flavor, or subtle; aromatic intensity is a stylistic issue but not a quality criterion.

The two most important quality markers for dry rosés are balance and concentration. If the wine has any sweetness, it must have enough acidity to distract you from the sweetness when you taste the wine, so that the wine is refreshing. Sometimes a bit of tannin supplements the acidity to balance any sweetness that might exist. If the wine is from a warm wine region and is high in alcohol but dry, the acidity needs to be crisp enough that the alcohol does not taste excessive to you.

The very finest dry rosés are marked by concentration of flavor. When you get the impression that a wine's flavors are well knit rather than loosely knit within the wine's structure—whether that structure is full for a rosé or fairly light—then you probably are tasting a superior rosé.

Just as in blush wines, any suggestion of oxidation or tired aromas and flavors indicates a wine that's past its best drinking.

Foods to Enjoy with Dry Rosés

The most common image of rosé wines with food is the restaurant situation when he's eating fish and she's eating roast beef: rosé is neither red nor white, so it's thought to be the ideal solution. Frankly, so many restaurants offer several good red and white wines by the glass these days that we're more inclined to buy a glass of white and a glass of red instead of the compromise bottle of rosé. But we truly love rosé wines and find no shortage of foods or occasions to suit them.

Dry rosés represent a range of flavors and weights and therefore can be suitable with a wide variety of foods. The more delicate and the dryer the wine, the more it needs a simple, delicately flavored dish, and the sweeter and richer the wine, the more it can stand up to somewhat richer or more flavorful foods.

As a rule of thumb, think of the foods that you would enjoy eating in very warm weather. Salads, simple grilled meats and fish, sandwiches, and cold soups are all good with pink wines, generally speaking. We particularly like these combinations:

- Fairly light-bodied dry rosés with cold seafood salad, grilled trout, Niçoise salad, frittatas, chicken stir-fry, egg salad

- Fruitier, off-dry rosés with chef's salad, Cobb salad, chicken salad or tuna salad, potato salad, ham, nachos, ribs, cold cuts

- Fuller-bodied, more characterful dry rosés with grilled sausage, turkey burgers, grilled portobellos, mozzarella with tomatoes, grilled squid, vitello tonnato (veal with tuna sauce), baked clams

PAIRINGS: DRY ROSÉS WITH . . .

Fresh tomatoes with basil and mozzarella

A delicately flavored omelet and Canadian bacon at brunch

Tortilla española (Spanish potato omelet)

Quiche

Turkey hash

Pork chops

Grilled veal paillard topped with arugula and fresh tomatoes

Rare tuna burgers or tuna tartare

DRY ROSÉS: WINES TO TRY

For truly dry rosés, European wines are your best bet. The following California rosé wines are in the off-dry range. Although they all have some degree of sweetness, their acidity and their overall structure place them into the dry rosé style.

WINE	PRODUCER/BRAND	REGION	COUNTRY
Syrah Rosé	Renwood	Amador County (CA)	USA
Pinot Noir Rosé	Handley Cellars	Mendocino (CA)	USA
Cabernet Franc Rosé	Chimney Rock	Napa Valley (CA)	USA
Merlot Rosé	Rutherford Hill	Napa Valley (CA)	USA
Other California rosés	Cakebread Cellars Rosé (Zinfandel/Pinot Noir) ▪ Iron Horse Rosato di Sangiovese ▪ Iron Horse Rosé de Pinot Noir ▪ SoloRosa ▪ Swanson Vineyards Rosato (Sangiovese)	Various regions, CA	USA

Rosé wines from France are quite dry, especially those from Provence and the Rhône Valley. Rosé wines from the Loire Valley usually have some sweetness, falling toward the off-dry end of this style.

WINE	PRODUCER/BRAND	REGION	COUNTRY
Loire rosés	Château de Fesles Rosé d'Anjou ▪ Château de la Genaiserie Rosé d'Anjou ▪ Château Pierre-Bise Rosé d'Anjou ▪ Domaine de Montgilet Rosé d'Anjou ▪ Domaine des Rochelles Rosé d'Anjou	Loire Valley, various appellations	France
Provence rosés	Château Routas "Rouvière Rosé" ▪ Clos Ste.-Magdelene "Cassis Rosé" ▪ Domaine Houchart ▪ Domaine La Courtade "L'Alycastre Rosé" ▪ Domaines Ott Château de Selle and Les Domanièrs-Domaine Richeaume ▪ Domaine Tempier "Bandol Rosé" ▪ La Côte Bleue (Jean-Luc Colombo) "Pioche & Cabanon Rosé" ▪ Mas de la Dame "Cuvée Gourmande Rosé" ▪ Mas Ste.-Berthe "Les Baux Rosé"	Côtes de Provence; other Provence regions	France
Rhône rosés	Caves des Papes Côtes du Rhône Heritage Rosé ▪ Château d'Aquéria Tavel ▪ Château Saint-Roch Lirac ▪ Château Trinquevedel Tavel ▪ Domaine Méjan-Taulier Tavel and Lirac	Rhône Valley, various appellations	France

Just about every region in Italy makes rosé wines, most of which are dry and very food-friendly. The most full-bodied rosé in Italy, Cerasuolo, is made from the Montepulciano variety in Abruzzo and is more like a light red wine than a typical rosé.

WINE	PRODUCER/BRAND	REGION	COUNTRY
Cerasuolo	Cataldi-Madonna ▪ Illuminati "Campirosa" ▪ Valentini	Abruzzo	Italy
Ciró Rosato	Fattoria San Francesco ▪ Librandi	Calabria	Italy
Brachetto d'Acqui	Banfi Vintners ▪ Giacomo Bologna	Piedmont	Italy
Nebbiolo Rosé	Tenuta Carretta	Piedmont	Italy
Rosa del Golfo	Alezio Rosato del Salento ▪ Vigna Mazzi Rosato	Puglia	Italy
Sicilian Rosé	Tasca d'Almerita Rose di Regaleali	Sicily (Contea di Sclafani)	Italy
Pinot Grigio Rosé	Roberto Zeni	Trentino	Italy
Chiaretto (Bardolino)	Guerrieri-Rizzardi ▪ Fratelli Zeni	Veneto	Italy

The two regions in Spain that specialize in rosé wines are Navarra and Rioja. They are invariably on the dry side, and Tempranillo is typically the main grape variety.

WINE	PRODUCER/BRAND	REGION	COUNTRY
Navarra Rosé	Bodegas Julian Chivite "Gran Feudo Rosato" ▪ Bodegas Guelbenzu Rosato ▪ Bodegas Magana Rosato ▪ Bodegas Nekeas "Vega Sindoa Rosé"	Navarra	Spain
Rioja Rosé	Bodegas Montecillo Rosado ▪ Bodegas Muga ▪ Conde de Valdemar Rosado ▪ El Coto ▪ Marqués de Cacéres	Rioja	Spain

WINES ON THE MOVE:
LESS SWEET, FRESHER, MORE POPULAR

Every year when the warm weather rolls in, we hear more and more talk in the wine trade about rosé wines. The rosé bandwagon exists, and more people jump onto it every time it passes through. More sommeliers urge their customers to try a rosé, and more wine critics espouse the charms of rosés to their readers. Just as importantly, more wineries focus serious efforts on making a rosé wine. For example, one new winery in California, SoloRosa, has committed itself to making only rosé wines.

This growing enthusiasm for rosé wines among wine professionals could result in a better turnover of these wines, and fresher bottles on store shelves. That could lead to more enthusiasm for these wines among wine drinkers.

Along the way, it's likely that both styles of rosé wine will get dryer. We've already tasted several blush wines that were much less sweet than they were a few years ago. But if you enjoy the sweeter brands of blush wines, don't worry: as long as there are wine drinkers who like the wine, the wineries will continue to make it.

Sparkling Wines in Two Styles

Fruity bubbly wines such as Prosecco,

and serious, complex sparklers such

as Champagne

We have nothing but good memories involving Champagne and sparkling wines. It was, in fact, an Italian sparkling wine, Prosecco, that brought us together many years ago. Mary was selling a particular Prosecco, and Ed—still a teacher but also a serious wine collector, impassioned with wine—worked in a wine store part time. A mutual friend had the idea of pairing Chinese cuisine with Italian white wines, and invited a group of ten wine enthusiasts, including Mary and Ed, to a restaurant in New York City's Chinatown for a tasting and dinner. Mary, of course, brought along her Prosecco. The tasting part of the dinner was a disaster; the spicy, savory, or slightly sweet dishes wiped out the dry, neutral-tasting Italian white wines. Only Mary's Prosecco paired well. But more importantly, Mary and Ed paired well—and we still do.

The second wonderful memory involves Champagne. In France, on our honeymoon, we came across 1975 Krug Champagne on the wine list of an inn near Périgord. We were excited to discover it, because the '75 Krug was not available in the United States at that time, and we were both big fans of this Champagne house. We ordered it, but the captain didn't want to give it to us! He exclaimed, "It's too green, monsieur!" meaning that it was too young. (What we thought he really meant was that these young American tourists were incapable of appreciating such a serious Champagne.) But we insisted. The wine was so good that we later ordered a second bottle—to the captain's dismay. We've had many excellent bottles of Champagne since then, but we'll never forget the magic of the '75 Krug that night.

Sparkling wines are a rich and magical category, and not all of them are expensive. Sometimes an $8 bottle of Ballatore Gran Spumante from California can be just right, or a $10 bottle of Freixenet Cordon Negro Brut from Spain. Your choice in sparkling wine really depends on the setting. Picnic? Ballatore. Party? Cordon Negro. Engagement dinner? Bring out the Champagne!

THE RANGE OF BUBBLY TASTES

Just about every wine region in the world includes sparkling wines as part of its repertoire. In some places, such as the Champagne region in France and the Penedès region in Spain, sparkling wines are the region's raison d'être.

Because sparkling wines are a diverse group, we could categorize them in all sorts of ways: dryness versus sweetness, vintage versus non-vintage, countries of origin, grape varieties, and so forth. But in terms of the wines' overall taste, we divide sparkling wines into two general styles: fruity sparklers and complex sparkling wines.

The first category is the larger of the two. It includes all sparkling wines made in a fairly simple, quick manner with the aim of expressing the primary fruitiness of the grapes. Fruity sparkling wines are just that—fruity and uncomplicated, without layers of complexity, comparable to biting into a juicy apple, pear, or grape.

The mass-produced bubblies of California and New York (such

as André, a best-selling sparkling wine made by Gallo of California), most German *sekt*, Italy's Prosecco, and Asti are all examples of the fruity style of bubbly. Price is a fairly reliable identifying criterion for this style of sparklers: most bubbly wines that cost under $15 are in the fruity style—and in the case of the volume-production sparkling wines from California and New York, the wines cost less than $10, with some even less than $5 a bottle.

Most bubbly wines that cost under $15 are in the fruity style.

An exception to this rule is Cava, Spain's national sparkling wine, which can cost as little as $10 but has enough complexity that all Cavas belong in the second style. We highly recommend Cavas; they are great values for the money.

Champagne, from the Champagne region of France, is the paragon of our second style. These are the sparkling wines that express subtlety, complexity, and secondary flavors other than fruitiness, derived from long aging—aromas and flavors such as biscuit, caramel, mushroom, and/or honey. Champagne itself is not the only wine in this category. Sparkling wines from various other regions that are made in the same method as Champagne also fit into the complex style. With the exception of the least expensive Cavas, most sparkling wines in this style retail for $15 or more—in the case of Champagne, usually $25 or more per bottle.

Fruity Sparkling Wines

Some fruity sparkling wines are unmistakably fruity and others are less so, but they all share a personality of freshness and straightforward enjoyability. You don't have to think about them; just drink them. The first rule for these wines is to express the fruitiness of the grapes, in all its exuberance. These wines are typically frothy as well as effervescent, and many of them also tend to be fairly sweet, especially the inexpensive, mass-produced sparklers.

Producers making fruity sparkling wines usually employ the Charmat, or closed-tank, method to make their bubblies. The

WHERE DO THOSE BUBBLES COME FROM?

A sparkling wine by definition is a wine with bubbles that derive naturally from the fermentation process. Wines that owe their bubbles to a tank of carbon dioxide are known as carbonated wines.

To make a sparkling wine, the winemaker traps carbon dioxide gas that forms during fermentation, so that it remains in the wine as bubbles. (CO_2 is a by-product of the conversion of sugar into alcohol.) But dozens of variations exist regarding how and when the bubbles are trapped—and the different techniques result in different personalities in the wines.

Most of the time, the winemaker produces a regular, still (non-sparkling) white wine and then induces a second fermentation by adding yeast and sugar to that wine. The second fermentation produces the bubbles. This second fermentation can happen in a large tank (more economical) or in individual bottles. If it occurs in a tank, the sparkling wine usually goes to market within a year of the second fermentation; if it occurs in bottles, the wine generally ages for several years before the wine is considered ready for sale.

Bubbly wines also vary according to the grape varieties that make them, and of course the climate and soil where the grapes grow.

winemaker induces a second fermentation of the base wine in large, closed, pressurized tanks, where carbon dioxide can be trapped and dissolved into the wine. This is the quickest, most economical way to make sparkling wines.

Sparkling wines made by the Charmat method—named after the Frenchman Eugène Charmat, who championed this process a century or so ago—are less expensive than those that have their second fermentation in individual bottles, for the following reasons:

- This method is very quick and efficient.

- Sparkling wines made by this process do not require prolonged aging.

- The grapes used in this process, such as Chenin Blanc,
  Colombard, Muscat, and so on, are generally much less
  expensive than the varieties used to make complex
  sparkling wines.

- Vineyard sites for grapes that make fruity-style sparkling
  wines are plentiful, and thus grapes are readily available.

Some tank-fermented sparkling wine producers use this
method because they want to make a wine that they can sell at a
low price. Others use it specifically to preserve the freshness and
aromatic fruitiness of the grapes. Even though this method is the
most economical, for certain bubbly wines it is also the best in
terms of the quality of the wine.

The Grapes and Regions of Fruity-style Bubblies

Fruity sparkling wines are produced in almost every wine region in
the world. Although all sparkling wines benefit from cool climates—which foster the acidity that's mandatory in anything bubbly—generally speaking, the climate for grapes that make fruity
sparklers doesn't have to reach the outer limits of coolness that you
find in the Champagne region. Even many of the world's warmer
regions invariably have some districts cool enough for sparkling
wine grapes to grow.

The grape varieties that make fruity sparkling wines vary with
the region; for example, in **Italy's Piedmont** region, aromatic
Muscat is the variety of sparkling Asti, while in the **Veneto**,
Prosecco is the grape variety for many sparklers. In **California**,
Colombard and **Chenin Blanc** are frequently used for fruity-style
bubblies.

Quality Markers for Fruity Sparkling Wines

If you want to evaluate the quality of a particular wine in this style, first of all decide whether it tastes good to you, because taste appeal is the whole point of these wines. Then consider whether the wine has freshness and exuberance—a liveliness of flavor as well as the structural liveliness that bubbles bring. If the aromas and flavors are dull, or if the bubbles are somewhat flat, the wine could be too old. Many bubblies in this category bear no vintage date, and you can't tell how old the wine is before you buy it. You can improve your odds of getting a fresh bottle by purchasing these inexpensive sparklers in shops and supermarkets that have a fairly rapid turnover in their wines.

The very best fruity sparklers have a delicacy of aromas and flavors, and they feel light and fresh in your mouth.

Another important quality marker in this category is balance—especially because many of these wines are sweet. A sparkling wine that's simply sweet without having counterbalancing acidity can taste insipid. Of course, a wine in this style shouldn't be harshly acidic, either.

The very best wines in this category have a delicacy of aromas and flavors rather than overly rich, heavy aromatics, and they feel light and fresh in your mouth.

Foods to Enjoy with Fruity Sparkling Wines

Italy's Asti and the *spumante*-type bubblies made in California have a simple, overt fruitiness that's perfect when you drink the wine alone, without food. But they can also be delicious with cakes; Asti and wedding cake, for example, is a great match—a much better one than a dry Champagne would make. Asti is also good with creamy cakes, cannoli, and cream puffs. We don't like Asti with chocolate cake or chocolaty desserts, though, because we find the flavor of chocolate a bit too strong for the wine; with chocolate desserts, we love Port, a sweet, fortified red wine (see "Three Faces of Dessert and Fortified Wines" in the chapter on aromatic whites).

Prosecco, the inexpensive sparkling wine from the northeastern part of Italy, is dryer than Asti and less fruity but still has a fresh, uncomplicated style and is surprisingly versatile with food. Who could imagine that any wine in the universe could possibly taste good with pickled vegetables such as you sometimes find on an Italian antipasto tray? Prosecco does! It's also great with salami, prosciutto, calamari, anchovies, and olives, and it works well with light chicken and fish dishes.

PAIRINGS:
FRUITY-STYLE SPARKLING WINES WITH . . .

Seasoned nuts and similar party nibbles

Cooked seafood dishes

Fried fish

Mild-flavored sandwiches such as ham and cheese

Fried chicken

Barbecued meats

Spicy Chinese dishes

Most Asian cuisines, such as Japanese, Thai, and Indian

Mildly sweet desserts

Fruity desserts

All tank-fermented sparkling wines are made to be consumed when they are young and fresh. None of them are renowned for their aging capacity. Serve them very cold, to reinforce their fresh flavor and effervescence, and to minimize their sweetness.

FRUITY-STYLE BUBBLY: WINES TO TRY

Many sparkling wines in the fruity style are a bit too sweet for our taste, and as a result, we don't mention them among our recommendations. The following sparkling wines are all under $10 a bottle, not too sweet, and would be great choices for picnics and large gatherings.

WINE	PRODUCER/BRAND	REGION	COUNTRY
Brut NV	Veuve du Vernay	France	France
Spumante	Riunite Spumante	Emilia	Italy
Brut NV	Le Domaine	California	USA
Gran Spumante	Ballatore	California	USA
Brut NV	Taylor	Finger Lakes (NY)	USA

Prosecco, from Italy's Veneto region, has become quite popular in the United States because it's the sparkling wine of choice in the country's many Italian restaurants, and because the price is right; it retails for $10 to $18. Most Prosecco wines come in the *frizzante* (slightly sparkling) style, but they're also available in the *spumante* (fully sparkling) style. Asti, from the Asti district in Piedmont, Italy, can be a wonderfully aromatic, delicious wine when it's fresh.

WINE	PRODUCER/BRAND	REGION	COUNTRY
Asti	Cinzano ▪ Fontanafredda ▪ Gancia ▪ Martini & Rossi	Piedmont	Italy
Prosecco	Astoria ▪ Bisson ▪ Canevel ▪ Carpenè Malvolti ▪ Mionetto ▪ Nino Franco ▪ Valdo ▪ Zardetto ▪ Zonin	Veneto	Italy

COMPLEX SPARKLING WINES

Complex sparkling wines are more subtle and less fruity, and they have a greater range of aromas and flavors than fruity-style sparkling wines do. Rather than being wines whose sole purpose is

Champagne's Special Assets

*C*hampagne is the main example of the complex style of sparkling wine. It's also the wine that pioneered this style, and it happens to be one of the greatest types of wine there is, of any color or style.

What makes Champagne so great? The cool climate of the Champagne region in France dictates that the grapes will always be high enough in acidity (even in relatively warm years) to make complex sparkling wines. Champagne's chalky, limestone soil is another major factor: the soil's drainage is outstanding, and the vine roots grow deep in their search for nutrients. The region has the added bonus of cold, deep, chalky cellars—some dating back 2,000 years to the Gallo-Roman era—where the wine's second fermentation takes place, naturally, in the very bottle that you buy.

to be enjoyable, they are serious wines that can warrant aging and/or critical analysis. They're also more expensive, with just a couple of exceptions. Everything from their grapes to their production process is costlier for the producer—and also, many of these wines are considered luxury products and are priced accordingly.

Complex sparkling wines owe their style to the particular places where their grapes grow (like all great wines, these are wines that express place, or *terroir*) as well as to an elaborate production process that involves conducting the second fermentation in bottles, and the aging of those bottles for many years.

This is the so-called *méthode champenoise*, or champagne method, of producing bubbly wines—also known as the classical or traditional method in many wine regions. Almost all complex sparkling wines are born of this method. It involves a long, slow second fermentation that produces the wine's bubbles within individual bottles. Second fermentation in the bottle is clearly more labor-intensive and more costly than tank fermentation. The very slow fermentation, combined with years of aging, produces an elegant sparkling wine that retains millions of tiny bubbles and develops complex flavors and a lengthy finish. In fact, the changes that take place to create complex, sparkling wines are almost magical.

During prolonged aging on the fermentation lees, profound chemical changes occur in the finished product. The wine's youthful fruity aromas subside, and the wine takes on secondary aromas and flavors such as toastiness, nuttiness, yeastiness, sometimes a biscuity character, and often caramel-like or honeyed flavors. The longer the aging at the winery, the more complex these characteristics become.

Champagne-method sparklers undergo structural changes as well. The long aging on the lees makes the wine's texture creamier and smoother; the carbon dioxide bubbles become tinier, so that they are far less aggressive in your mouth than the bubbles of tank-fermented wines. Champagne and sparkling wines made in this method can take on a complexity of taste, character, and flavor that can never be achieved in tank-fermented sparkling wines.

Complex sparkling wines run the gamut from *extra brut* (bone dry) to *demi-sec* (relatively sweet). The largest production is *brut* (dry), followed—at least in popularity within the United States—by *extra dry* (in reality, only fairly dry). Most wines in this style are white, although rosé Champagnes and other pink complex sparklers do exist. The pink versions are invariably just as dry as complex-style white bubblies, but they are usually fuller-bodied and more suitable with entrées at dinner.

In Champagne and other cool regions, grapes don't ripen sufficiently in some years. To even out the ups and downs in ripeness from one year to another, producers make non-vintage bubbly—wines that are blends of several years' harvests. In fact, about 85 percent of Champagne is non-vintage. Champagne producers and other winemakers who produce complex-style sparkling wines must be master blenders, combining wines from many different vineyards, each having its own character, with wines from different vintage years. In top years, Champagne houses do produce vintage-dated wine, as do wineries in other sparkling wine regions. (For more information on Champagne, see Ed McCarthy's *Champagne For Dummies*.)

The Grapes and Regions of Complex-style Bubblies

Two noble grape varieties have proven over time to be the most suitable for complex sparkling wines and have come to dominate production in most wine regions that make this style: *Pinot Noir* and *Chardonnay*. Although Pinot Noir is a dark-skinned grape, it's usually vinified without its skins, to make a white sparkling wine.

In the **Champagne** region and in parts of **California** and **Oregon**, another black grape plays a role: **Pinot Meunier**, a relative of Pinot Noir. Pinot Meunier is especially useful in Champagne because it buds later than Pinot Noir and Chardonnay, making it less vulnerable to spring frosts, and it ripens earlier, which makes it invaluable in the frequent early autumn rainy seasons..

Pinot Blanc and **Chenin Blanc** also go into some complex sparkling wines in various wine regions, such as California, **Alsace**, the **Loire Valley**, and **South Africa**. Complex sparkling wines from **Spain** use mainly local white grape varieties—**Parellada**, **Macabeo**, and **Xarel-lo**—sometimes along with Chardonnay.

When a complex bubbly comes only from white grapes, usually Chardonnay, it's often called a *blanc de blancs*—a particularly elegant type. When the wine comes only from black grapes, which is more unusual, the resulting bubbly is a *blanc de noirs*; these wines are usually more powerful in structure than other sparkling wines.

Besides Champagne itself, complex sparkling wines include just about all bubblies from California, **New York**, and other states that retail for $15 or more; almost all sparkling wines from France; Spain's Cava; many **Australian**, **New Zealand**, and South African sparkling wines; and most Italian sparklers other than Prosecco and Asti. Cava, from Northeastern Spain, is a huge exception to

ONE OF THE WORLD'S GREAT WINE VALUES

*A*n inexpensive Cava that sells for $7 to $10, when well made, represents a tremendous value—perhaps the best value in the entire wine world. Considering the expense involved in producing a sparkling wine with two fermentations—the second of which occurs in individual bottles—as well as the storage space needed to house those bottles for several years and the capital costs involved, we find it nearly incomprehensible that a complex-style bubbly could cost so little.

the $15 retail price we use as a general guide to distinguish our two styles: most Cavas retail between $7 and $14. You can find some classic-method French sparklers from outside of the Champagne region that sell for under $15 as well.

Quality Markers for Complex Sparkling Wines

This style encompasses a wide quality range, from the inexpensive Spanish Cavas made from local grapes and given a minimum of aging to the hand-crafted prestige cuvées of Champagne made of the finest grapes from the best vineyards and given years of aging before they are released, such as Krug, Salon, Dom Pérignon, and Roederer Cristal.

While the criteria of quality are the same for all complex-style bubblies, obviously your expectations will vary according to which end of the quality spectrum a particular wine falls into. For Cavas, as well as any other complex sparkling wines that retail for about $20 or less, key quality considerations are freshness, balance of sweetness and acidity, liveliness, a lack of coarseness, and proper expression of the grape varieties. For example, an overly fruity wine, a sparkler lacking elegance, or one with too-large bubbles or a harsh mouth feel would be less than perfect.

For Champagne and for complex sparkling wines that are pricier—especially those from California, Italy, and Australia—your expectations should be higher. First of all, these wines should always be perfectly balanced—neither too sweet, too acidic, nor too high in alcohol. A perfect balance makes such wines taste round and harmonious. Depending on the wine, a complex sparkling wine can taste light, medium-bodied, or full-bodied; crisp or soft; delicate or relatively powerful; dry or slightly sweet. It should have good length across the palate. Its texture should be creamy and smooth—never harsh or coarse. And a complex-style sparkler that's good should have a pleasant, lingering aftertaste or finish; any impression of bitterness is a sign of poor quality.

The aromas of complex sparkling wines can be flowery, fruity, toasty, smoky, caramelly, honeyed, mushroomy, and/or biscuity.

The finest of complex sparkling wines feature the widest range of flavors, along with an endless stream of tiny bubbles that tickle your mouth. The aromas can be flowery, fruity, toasty, smoky, caramelly, honeyed, mushroomy, and/or biscuity—often depending on the age of the wine. Some of the better *blanc de blancs* wines offer zesty, lemony aromas and flavors. The very best Champagnes—usually prestige cuvées (a producer's top-of-the line wine, such as Dom Pérignon or Cristal) or older vintage-dated Champagnes—often exhibit a pronounced biscuity and mushroomy bouquet.

Foods to Enjoy with Complex Sparkling Wines

The major complaint we hear from Champagne producers goes like this: "Why don't Americans enjoy Champagne with food? They open it only for celebrations!"

We can sympathize. Even though Champagne and other complex sparkling wines do go extremely well with most foods—except, perhaps, red meat, tomato-based dishes, and hearty entrées—many wine drinkers never get past birthdays, anniversaries, New

SERVING TIP:
WHEN TO DRINK THE REALLY GOOD STUFF

*D*on't expect the finest complex sparkling wines to be at their best when they're first released; in our experience, Champagnes such as Dom Pérignon, Roederer Cristal, Krug, Salon, Taittinger Comtes de Champagne, and others need a minimum of ten years in most vintages to really show their stuff, and in many cases may well be at their best with fifteen to twenty years of aging. But cool, dark storage is a must if you plan to age sparkling wines.

Always use fine crystal glasses with fine Champagnes; large tulip-shaped glasses are particularly good choices. Serve fine, mature Champagne very cool (about 50°F), but not ice cold! You can't appreciate all the wonderful aromas and flavors if it's too cold.

Year's Eve, and other celebrations for drinking them. That's probably why the United States ranks a distant third, behind the French and the British, in Champagne sales—although this country does buy the most prestige cuvée Champagne.

We've found that Champagne and other complex-style sparkling wines go extremely well with egg dishes and all sorts of mushrooms. The earthiness of mushrooms blends especially well with earthy, aged complex sparklers.

Fish and shellfish are natural, slam-dunk matchups with this style of sparkling wine, either as appetizers or as first courses. Caviar, of course, is a traditional partner with Champagne, but choose the Champagne carefully; one that's too flavorful or too full-bodied can overwhelm the delicate flavors of caviar.

Hard or aged cheeses such as Parmesan, aged Gouda, aged Cheddar, Comté, and Gruyère go extremely well with mature, complexly flavored vintage Champagnes, such Bollinger Grand Année or Vintage Krug; Krug and Bollinger Rosé also work extremely well with these cheeses.

We like complex, sparkling wines with pasta, except for tomato-based pastas; the acidity of tomatoes clashes with the acidity in the sparkling wines. But any other pasta is terrific with these bubblies. Also, vegetables such as asparagus and artichokes that are difficult companions for red or white wine typically pair very well with complex sparklers.

All sorts of main courses match up well with complex sparkling wines. With spicy, Asian cuisine, no other style of wine works as well. We would only avoid pairing very flavorful meat entrées, such as beef, lamb, or venison, with complex, sparkling wines; certain foods just need red wine.

Don't drink a dry, complex sparkling wine with sweet desserts.

Don't open a dry, complex sparkling wine with sweet desserts; it just doesn't work. Your wine will taste too bitter. Demi-sec (fairly sweet) Champagnes might work if the dessert is not too sweet, such as a bowl of berries. If you're set on having a sweet dessert and want to serve a bubbly with it, open a bottle of cold Asti; that will work!

PAIRINGS:
COMPLEX SPARKLING WINES WITH . . .

Assorted raw or dry-roasted nuts, especially almonds

Parmesan, aged Gouda, Comté, Gruyère, aged Cheddar,
Manchego cheeses

Stuffed mushrooms

Caviar—especially with blanc de blancs and
light-bodied Champagnes

Scrambled eggs (particularly with truffles, white or black)

Mushroom omelet

Quiche

Pasta with vegetables, seafood, or cream sauce; pasta with
broccoli rabe and sausage

Mushroom risotto

Shellfish appetizers, such as smoked oysters or mussels

Poached salmon

Grilled fresh trout

Broiled or poached filet of sole, flounder, turbot, or whitefish
(with a light-bodied or blanc de blancs *Champagne)*

Salmon, mackerel, swordfish, tuna
(with a medium- or full-bodied Champagne)

Simple preparations of poultry and game birds

Vegetables such as eggplant or zucchini, ratatouille, asparagus
(with a blanc de blancs*), and any mushroom dish*

Spicy Asian cuisine and sushi
(with dry or blanc de blancs *sparklers)*

COMPLEX SPARKLERS: WINES TO TRY

Champagne is perhaps our favorite beverage in the world, and so it's difficult for us to limit our selections here! We divide our Champagne recommendations according to the type of Champagne—non-vintage bruts (which generally cost $25 to $45), vintage bruts ($35 to $125), blanc de blancs ($30 to $300), rosé Champagnes ($35 to $300), and prestige cuvées ($70 to $400).

WINE	PRODUCER/BRAND	REGION	COUNTRY
Brut Non-Vintage Champagne	Bollinger Special Cuvée ▪ Deutz Classic ▪ Egly-Ouriet ▪ Gosset Grande Réserve ▪ Alfred Gratien Classique ▪ Charles Heidsieck Brut Réserve ▪ Moët & Chandon Brut Impérial ▪ Bruno Paillard Première Cuvée ▪ Paul Bara ▪ Philipponnat Royale Réserve Brut ▪ Pommery Royal Apanage ▪ Louis Roederer Premier ▪ Taittinger La Française ▪ Veuve Clicquot	Champagne	France
Vintage Champagne (other than Prestige Cuvées)	Bollinger Grande Année ▪ Gosset Grand Millésime ▪ Charles Heidsieck Millésime ▪ Krug ▪ Perrier-Jouët ▪ Pol Roger ▪ Taittinger ▪ Veuve Clicquot Vintage Réserve	Champagne	France
Blanc de Blancs Champagne	Billecart-Salmon ▪ Guy Charlemagne ▪ Delamotte ▪ Diebolt-Vallois ▪ Deutz ▪ Dom Ruinart ▪ Charles Heidsieck Blanc de Millénaires ▪ Jacquesson ▪ Krug Clos des Mesnil ▪ Guy Larmandier ▪ Larmandier-Bernier ▪ J. Lassalle ▪ Mumm de Cramant ▪ Nicolas Feuillate ▪ Bruno Paillard Chardonnay Réserve Privée ▪ Perrier-Jouët Fleur de Champagne Blanc de Blancs ▪ Pierre Peters ▪ Philipponnat Grand Blanc ▪ Salon ▪ Taittinger Comtes de Champagne	Champagne	France

WINE	PRODUCER/BRAND	REGION	COUNTRY
Rosé Champagne	Billecart-Salmon ▪ Bollinger ▪ Cuvée William Deutz Rosé ▪ Dom Pérignon Rosé ▪ Dom Ruinart Rosé ▪ Gosset ▪ Charles Heidsieck ▪ Jacquesson Signature Rosé ▪ Krug ▪ Laurent-Perrier Cuvée Alexandra ▪ Nicolas Feuillate Palmes D'Or Rosé; ▪ Perrier-Jouët (Fleur de Champagne Rosé and Blason de France Rosé) ▪ Pommery Louise Rosé ▪ Louis Roederer (Brut Rosé and Cristal Rosé) ▪ Taittinger Comtes de Champagne Rosé ▪ Veuve Clicquot (La Grande Dame Rosé and Rosé Réserve)	Champagne	France
Prestige Cuvée Champagne (other than Blanc de Blancs or Rosé)	Bollinger (R.D. and Vieilles Vignes Françaises Blanc de Noirs) ▪ de Castellane Cuvée Commodore ▪ Cattier Clos du Moulin ▪ Cuvée William Deutz ▪ Dom Pérignon ▪ Gosset Célébris ▪ Alfred Gratien Cuvée Paradis ▪ Jacquesson Signature ▪ Krug Grande Cuvée ▪ Lanson Noble Cuvée ▪ J. Lassalle Special Club ▪ Laurent-Perrier Cuvée Grand Siècle ▪ Nicolas Feuillate Palmes d'Or ▪ Perrier-Jouët Fleur de Champagne ▪ Philipponnat Clos des Goisses ▪ Piper-Heidsieck Champagne Rare ▪ Pol Roger Cuvée Sir Winston Churchill ▪ Pommery Louise ▪ Louis Roederer Cristal ▪ Veuve Clicquot La Grande Dame ▪ Vilmart Coeur de Cuvée	Champagne	France

California produces some excellent complex-style sparkling bruts today; prices start at about $15 and go up to about $60 for the prestige-level wines. We also include a few of our other favorite complex sparkling bruts from elsewhere in the United States.

WINE	PRODUCER/BRAND	REGION	COUNTRY
Sparkling Brut	S. Anderson ▪ Domaine Carneros ▪ Domaine Chandon ▪ Gloria Ferrer ▪ Handley Cellars ▪ Iron Horse ▪ "J" ▪ Mumm Cuvée Napa ▪ Roederer Estate ▪ Scharffenberger	Various Regions, CA	USA
Sparkling Brut and Blanc de Blancs	Chateau Frank ▪ Fox Run	Finger Lakes (NY)	USA
Sparkling Brut	Argyle	Willamette Valley (OR)	USA
Sparkling Brut	Gruet	New Mexico	USA

In addition to its wonderful Asti and the fairly simple, straightforward Prosecco—both of which fall into the fruity style of sparkling wines—Italy produces some serious brut *spumante* wines, which are invariably very dry. Here are some of the best.

WINE	PRODUCER/BRAND	REGION	COUNTRY
Brut Spumante	Bellavista ▪ Ca' del Bosco ▪ Cavalleri	Franciacorta	Italy
Brut Spumante	Bruno Giacosa ▪ Gancia	Piedmont	Italy
Brut Spumante	Ferrari	Trentino	Italy

France's best sparkling wines outside of Champagne probably are those of the Loire Valley, around the town of Saumur, where Chenin Blanc is the main grape variety; prices are in the $12 to $16 range. Other good-value French complex-style sparkling wines include Crémant d'Alsace, made primarily from Pinot Blanc; and perhaps the world's oldest sparkling wine, Blanquette de Limoux ($10–$12), first made by Benedictine monks in 1531 at Limoux's Abbaye de St.-Hilaire.

WINE	PRODUCER/BRAND	REGION	COUNTRY
Crémant d'Alsace	Lucien Albrecht ■ René Muré ■ Pierre Sparr	Alsace	France
Brut	Brut d'Argent	Jura	France
Blanquette de Limoux	St.-Hilaire	Languedoc	France
Saumur Brut	Ackerman-Laurance ■ Bouvet-Ladubay ■ Gratien & Meyer ■ Langlois-Château	Loire Valley	France

Here are a few fine complex-style sparklers from South Africa and Austria.

WINE	PRODUCER/BRAND	REGION	COUNTRY
NV Brut	Schlumberger	Wien	Austria
NV Brut	Boschendal Le Grand Pavillon ■ Pierre Jourdan Brut and Rosé (Cabrière Estate)	Franschhoek	South Africa
NV Brut	Simonsig Estate	Stellenbosch	South Africa

Spain's Cava, the world's best-value sparkling wine, generally costs about $7 to $12.			
WINE	**PRODUCER/BRAND**	**REGION**	**COUNTRY**
Cava	Codorníu ▪ Cristalino ▪ Freixenet ▪ Juve y Camps ▪ Marqués de Monistrol ▪ Mont Marçal ▪ Paul Cheneau ▪ Segura Viudas	Penedès	Spain

Australia makes an array of interesting bubblies, ranging from the great-value Seaview Brut ($10) to the more serious, age-worthy Mountadam ($40+).			
WINE	**PRODUCER/BRAND**	**REGION**	**COUNTRY**
Brut	Greg Norman Estates ▪ Mountadam ▪ Seaview ▪ Taltarni ▪ Wolf Blass	Various Regions	Australia

WINES ON THE MOVE: DRYER AND BETTER

We perceive that sparkling wines are being made dryer, in both the fruity and complex styles. Producers who specialized in sweet, inexpensive bubblies have been achieving a bit more subtlety in their wines, as this is what the market seems to be demanding.

Along with the movement toward dryer sparkling wines, there has been a definite movement toward higher-quality bubblies. Almost all producers of complex sparklers have introduced special prestige cuvées, from the best grapes of their best vineyards. Single-vineyard sparkling wines are also making an appearance.

The move away from overt sweetness threatens classic sweet sparklers such as Asti, whose popularity seems to be dwindling. This is a pity, because Asti fills a specific niche with sweet foods and is delicious.

WHAT COMMONLY USED WINE-TASTING TERMS REALLY MEAN

Acid—One of the basic structural components of a wine. Acidity forms the backbone of a wine's structure in the mouth, contributing to an impression of depth as well as length across the palate. A wine's acid derives from its grapes, but a winemaker can decrease a wine's acidity, change the nature of the acidity (through malolactic fermentation; see page 98), or increase a wine's acidity by adding acid.

Alcohol—One of the basic structural components of a wine. Alcohol contributes weight, substance, and viscosity to a wine, and can also give an impression of sweetness. A level of alcohol that is too high relative to a wine's acid and tannin can create a hard, burning sensation, sometimes described as "heat," and can shorten the wine's length on the palate.

Ample—Describes a wine that gives the impression of being expansive in the mouth.

Angularity—A tactile sensation in the mouth suggesting that a wine has edges and points rather than being soft or round.

Animal aromas/flavors—Aromas and flavors that suggest leather, meat, lanolin, sweat, and similar substances of animal origin.

Aroma—The smell of a wine. Tasters formerly used this term to refer only to the fresh, primary scents of a wine that derive from its grapes, and used *bouquet* to refer to scents that derive from aging, but today most people use *aroma* regardless of the nature of the scent.

Aromatic compounds—Those substances in wine, derived from the grapes, from winemaking, or from aging, that are responsible for a wine's aromas and flavors.

Aromatics—The characteristics of a wine that are attributable to volatile, aromatic molecules. These include the smell of a wine as well as the flavors it expresses in the mouth.

Astringent—Describes a wine whose acid and/or tannin constricts the pores of the mouth, creating a drying sensation.

Attack—The first impression a wine gives in the mouth. Usually related to sensations gathered in the front of the mouth, especially the tip of the tongue.

Austere—Describes a wine whose overall characteristics give the impression of extreme restraint.

Balance—The interrelationship of a wine's alcohol, residual sugar, acid, and tannin. When no one of these components stands out obtrusively in a wine's mouth impression, the wine is said to be well balanced.

Big—A general, vague descriptor for wines that are either very full or very intense.

Black fruits—Wine aromas and flavors that suggest blackberries, blueberries, black cherries, black currants, and so forth.

Brambly—Describes aromas and flavors that suggest brambly or thorny bush fruits such as raspberries or blackberries. Used particularly to describe the fruit character of Zinfandel.

Body—The weight of a wine in the mouth, generally described as light, medium, or full. Alcohol and extract are the two main components that contribute to a wine's body.

Bold—Describes aromas and flavors that are conspicuous and unabashed, such as bold fruitiness.

Breadth—A characteristic of wines that seem wide from one side of the mouth to the other, as opposed to seeming compact or vertical. A wine's structural components determine the sensation of shape that wines give in the mouth.

Bright fruit—A popular term for fruity aromas and flavors that are fresh and vibrant rather than heavy.

Candied fruit—Aromas and flavors that suggest an artificial, candied version of fruit, as opposed to fresh fruit, dried fruit, or cooked fruit.

Chemical aromas/flavors—Scents and flavors in a wine that suggest chemical substances, such as alcohol, sulfur, nail polish remover, and so forth.

Complex—Describes the aromatics of a wine that expresses a multiplicity of aromas and flavors. When applied to a wine's overall personality, the term has no concrete meaning.

Concentrated—Aromas and flavors that give the impression of being compact and condensed.

Concentration—A trait of high-quality wines. Any particular characteristic of a wine can give the impression of being condensed or tightly knit within the wine's total expression, such as concentrated tannin or color, but when used more generally the term usually applies to an impression of compact aromas and flavors.

Corky—Describes a wine with a chemical taint caused by a faulty cork. In lesser degrees, corkiness manifests itself as a suppressed fruitiness in the wine, and in severe cases it gives a wine a dank, moldy aroma and flavor.

Crisp—Characterizes a wine that feels clean and slightly brittle in the mouth, as opposed to soft. Crispness is usually a function of high acidity and is most often used to describe white wines.

Definition—A trait of wines that have precise, clear characteristics. A wine that's lacking in definition presents a taster with characteristics that are collectively vague or muddled.

Delicate—Describes aromas and flavors that are fine rather than gross. When used to describe a wine in its totality, it suggests finesse rather than power, but is an imprecise description.

Dense—A textural term for wines that seem to have a thick, somewhat inpenetrable mouth feel.

Depth—An impression that a wine has a strong vertical structure in the mouth, usually in the mid-palate and resulting from high acidity.

Dilute—Describes aromas and flavors that give the impression of being loosely knit, watery, and lacking concentration. The term is also often used to describe wines that taste thin and seem to lack sufficient flavor and extract for their weight.

Dry—Describes a wine that is not sweet. The term can also be used to describe the texture of a wine that feels rough in the mouth, as in "dry texture" or "dry mouth feel," but when used alone, it refers specifically to lack of sweetness.

Earthy—Aromas and flavors suggestive of earth, both inorganic substances such as minerals and organic substances such as humus or decaying leaves. As an overall description of a wine, the term indicates a wine that is understated yet substantial, and possibly slightly rustic.

Elegant—A vague, non-specific description that some tasters use for wines whose composite characteristics are refined and have finesse, rather than being forceful.

Extract—The non-volatile components in a wine, such as acids, tannins, coloring matter, mineral salts, and so forth. A wine's extract contributes to its body.

Extracted—Literally, describes a wine that has undergone a thorough transfer of polyphenols and other substances from its grapes during winemaking. The term also describes red wines whose concentrated color, tannin, and flavor give the impression that the wine has undergone this process.

Finish—The final impressions a wine gives after it has left the mouth. A long finish is a virtue. The impression of concentrated fruit character on the finish often indicates a wine that can improve with age.

Firm—A textural term for wines that give an impression of being not soft in the mouth and yet not harsh. The term is also used particularly to describe the feel of tannins that are substantial but not aggressive.

Flabby—Describes a wine that gives the impression of being soft to a fault.

Flavor—The mouth expression of a wine's aromatic compounds. A wine's flavor can be light, medium, or pronounced in intensity; a flavorful wine has a high intensity of flavor expression.

Fleshy—Describes wines that give the impression of having a rich, fairly substantial texture.

Fresh—Can describe a wine whose composite traits—usually relatively light body, high acidity, and vibrant aromatics—make it refreshing to drink. The term can also describe aromas and flavors that are clean and penetrating. As a description of fruitiness, it refers to aromas and flavors of healthy, ripe, uncooked fruits, as opposed to those suggesting overripe, baked, or jammy fruit.

Fruity—Having aromas and flavors that suggest fruit. This is a broad description; in some cases a wine's fruity aromas or flavors can be described more precisely as suggesting fresh fruit, dried fruit, or cooked fruit, or even more precisely as a specific fresh, dried, or cooked fruit, such as fresh apples, dried figs, or strawberry jam.

Generous—Describes a wine whose aromatics and structure are ample and opulent.

Gentle—Indicates mild, unobtrusive aromas and flavors.

Grape tannin—Tannins that derive from a wine's grapes rather than from oak or other secondary sources. Some tasters claim to perceive these throughout the mouth rather than just in the rear of the mouth.

Grip—A characteristic of wines whose tannins seem to exert a strong tactile presence on the tongue.

Harmonious—Describes wines that not only are well balanced but also express their structure in a particularly graceful manner.

Herbal—Having aromas and flavors that suggest herbs, such as fresh herbs, dried herbs, or specific herbs (rosemary, thyme, tarragon, and so forth).

Intensity—The apparent magnitude of aromas and flavors in a wine.

Wines with high aromatic intensity have a strong scent and are very flavorful, regardless of what the specific aromas and flavors are.

Jammy—Aromas or flavors in a wine that suggest fruit preserves or jam.

Lean—A term for a wine with texture that seems somewhat thin and lacking fleshiness.

Leesy—Describes a wine with characteristics that result from lees contact, the extended use of fermentation deposits in aging a white wine. These characteristics include slightly nutty aromatics, a subdued fruitiness, and a somewhat richer texture (see page 57).

Length—The evolution of a wine's taste across the tongue. Wines that are long give a sustained sensory impression across the tongue, expressing themselves in the rear of the mouth as well as at the middle and front of the mouth.

Medium dry—Describes a wine that gives the impression of being slightly sweet; specifically, sweeter than a dry wine, but less sweet than a medium-sweet or sweet wine.

Medium sweet—Describes a wine that gives the impression of being fairly sweet, but less sweet than a sweet wine.

Minerality—Aromas and flavors that suggest inorganic, mineral substances, such as chalk, slate, iron ore, and so forth.

Mouth feel—An imprecise term that could describe the total tactile impression of a wine in the mouth, including texture and body, but usually refers just to a wine's texture.

Neutral—Describes aromas and flavors that do not suggest specific characteristics such as fruity, floral, vegetal, herbal, earthy, animal, or chemical.

Nose—A wine's scent.

Oaky—Having characteristics that derive from the use of oak in winemaking, such as toasty, charry, and vanilla-like aromas and flavors, and tannin that does not come from the grapes themselves.

Off-dry—Having a degree of sweetness that is slightly greater than that of a dry wine but less than that of a medium dry wine. Some tasters use the term less specifically to indicate a wine that is not dry but also not decidedly sweet.

One-dimensional—A wine whose overall expression is simple or artless.

Oxidized—Describes a wine with aromas and flavors that seem cooked or tired and with a general flatness of expression due to damage from exposure to air.

Plump—Describes a soft, full-bodied red wine with fleshy texture.

Polyphenols—A family of substances in wine that includes coloring matter and tannin.

Primary aromas/flavors—Youthful characteristics that derive from the grapes themselves, rather than from winemaking or aging.

Red fruits—Wine aromas and flavors that suggest raspberries, strawberries, red cherries, red currants, and so forth.

Refreshing—Enlivening, stimulating aromas and flavors; can also apply to a wine's structure, specifically high acidity.

Residual sugar—Sugar that remains in a wine after fermentation rather than being converted by yeasts into alcohol.

Rich—Describes aromas/flavors or texture that are agreeably strong.

Round—Describes the structural expression of a wine that seems full, smooth, and not angular.

Secondary—A category of aromas and flavors in wines that derive from aging rather than from the wines' grapes or winemaking processes. Some wine professionals describe these as *tertiary* and use the term *secondary* to apply to aromas that derive from winemaking.

Short—Describes a wine that registers very little impression in a taster's rear palate.

Silky—Having a supple, smooth texture that suggests silk.

Smooth—Describes a wine whose texture is not rough.

Soft—A textural term for wines that do not feel firm in the mouth.

Spicy—Describes aromas and flavors that suggest spices. The term also describes a style of red wines with a lively, fresh personality and a substantial structure.

Structural components—The four major consituents of wine (alcohol, acid, tannin, and sugar) that dictate a wine's apparent size, weight, and texture in the mouth, as well as its sweetness or dryness.

Structure—Those aspects of a wine's taste, such as body, texture, depth, and length, that are formed by the wine's structural components.

Sturdy—Can apply to texture or structure that seems substantial rather than meager.

Style—The set of characteristics through which a wine manifests itself. This includes a wine's visual, aroma, flavor, and structural characteristics.

Substantial—Applies to texture or structure that seems solidly built and strong.

Subtle—Aromas and flavors that are understated.

Sugar—One of the basic structural components of a wine. Some wines have no perceptible unfermented sugar.

Supple—Describes a wine that seems fluid in texture in the mouth, without roughness, sharpness, or grip. The term applies particularly to red wines.

Tannin—One of the basic structural components of a wine, particularly red wine. Tannin derives from grapes themselves as well as from oak treatment, and contributes to an impression of weight and substance in the wine. Tannin varies in quantity from one wine to the next, and also varies in nature. Some wines have relatively soft tannin, and others have firm, grainy, harsh, or astringent tannin—as defined by the feel of the wine in the mouth.

Tart—Describes aromas or flavors of underripe fruit.

Taste—The total impression a wine gives in the mouth, encompassing its flavors as well as its texture, weight, and other structural characteristics.

Texture—The feel of a wine in the mouth. Common textural descriptors include *silky, soft, creamy, crisp, velvety,* and *supple.*

Thin—Describes the weight and texture of a wine that lacks richness and substance.

Tight—Describes a wine, or certain aspects of a wine, that seems inexpressive. This term can apply to a wine's aromas and flavors or to its structure.

Tired—Describes a wine that lacks freshness, or seems to be past its prime.

Up-front—Describes a wine that registers a stronger impression in the front of a taster's mouth than in the rear.

Varietal character—Aromas, flavors, or structural chartacteristics that are typical of the particular grapes that constitute a wine.

Vegetal—Aromas and flavors that suggest vegetables, such as bell peppers or asparagus.

Velvety—Having a rich, substantial texture that suggests velvet.

Vibrant—Aromas and flavors that seem lively rather than dull.

Weight—How light or heavy a wine feels in the mouth. The impression of weight derives from a wine's structural components.

Wood tannin—Tannin in a wine that derives from oak barrels or other forms of wood used in winemaking, rather than from the grapes themselves. Some tasters claim to perceive wood tannin particularly in the rear of their mouths.

Woodsy—Aromas and flavors that suggest forest scents, such as dead leaves, pine, damp or dry earth, underbrush, and so forth.

Woody—Characteristics in a wine that suggest wood. These could be aromatic traits such as the scent of sawdust or structural traits such as particularly harsh tannin.

Index